Noemi Pfister
Heart on Sleeve

Bündner Kunstmuseum Chur   Mousse Publishing

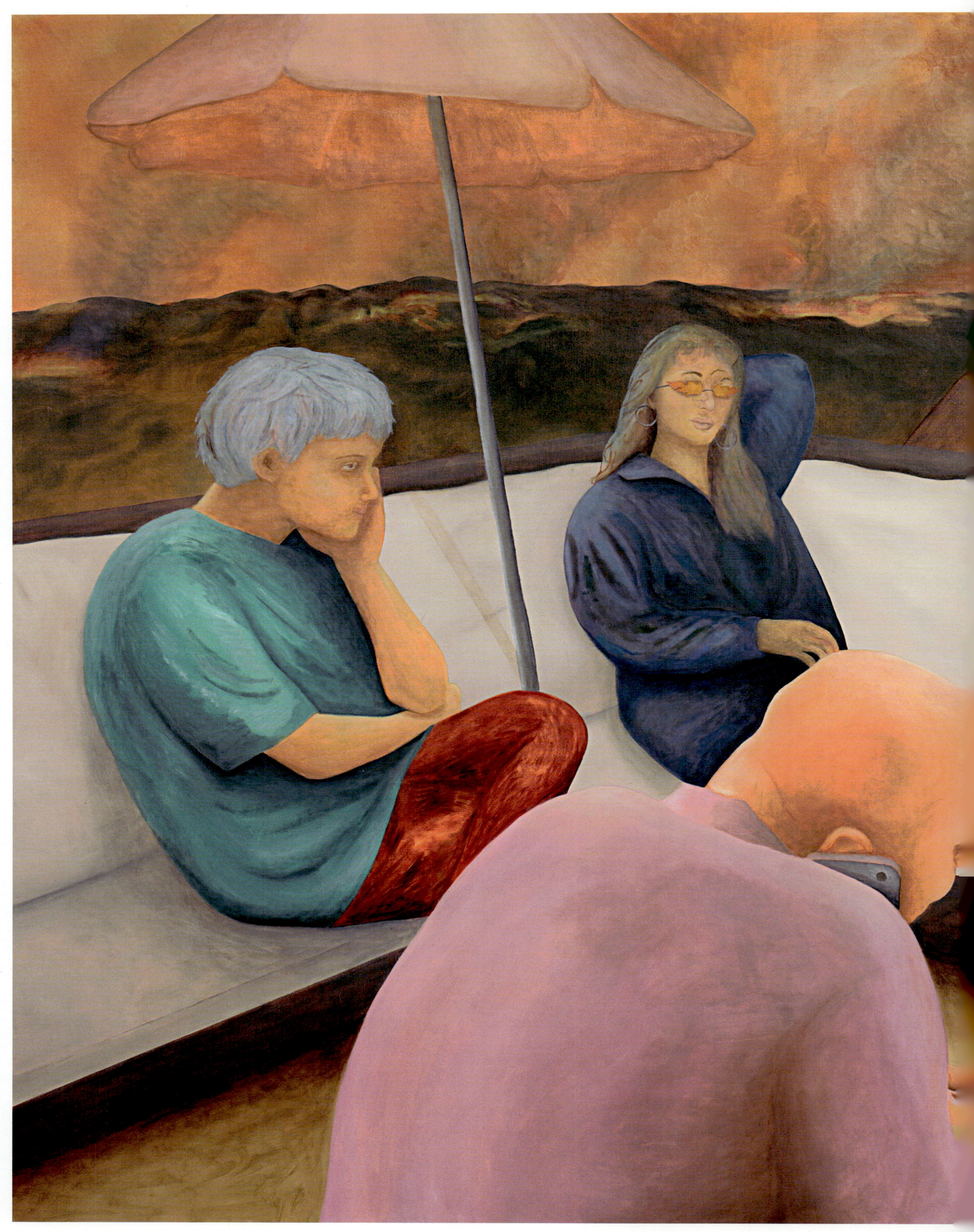

The Long Sit, 2025   190×300 cm

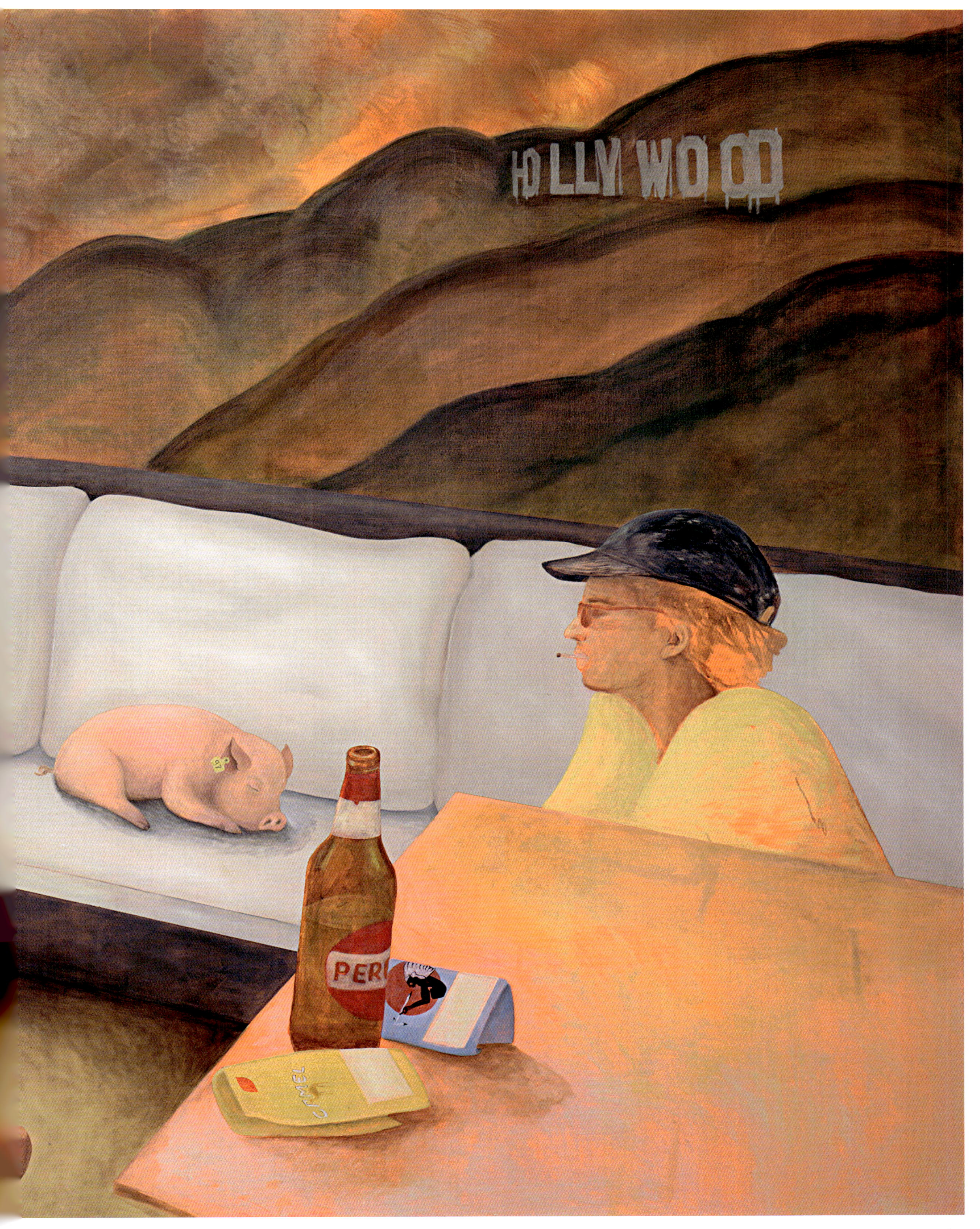

HOLLYWOOD
PER
CAMEL

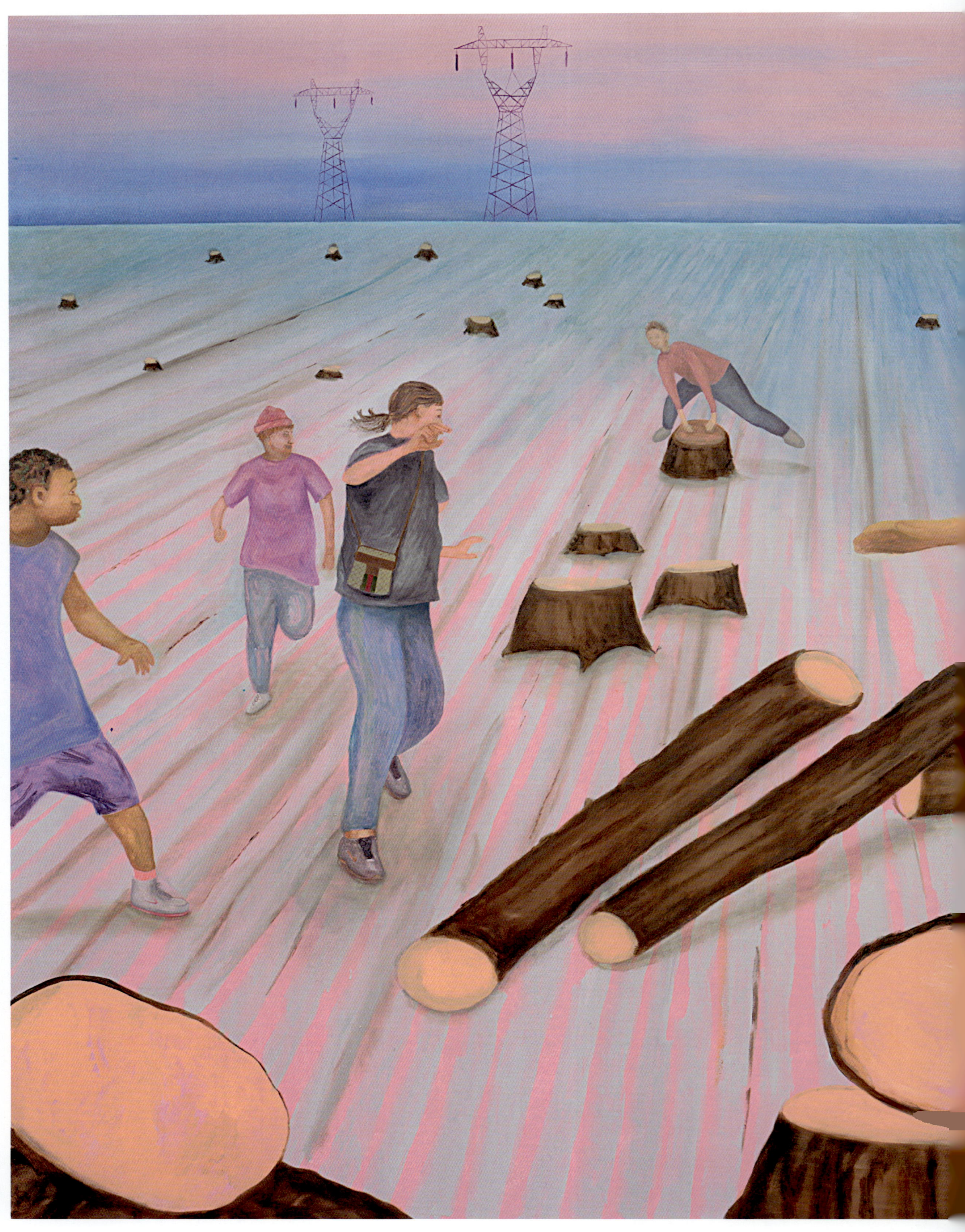

Harvest Time, 2025   190×300 cm

4

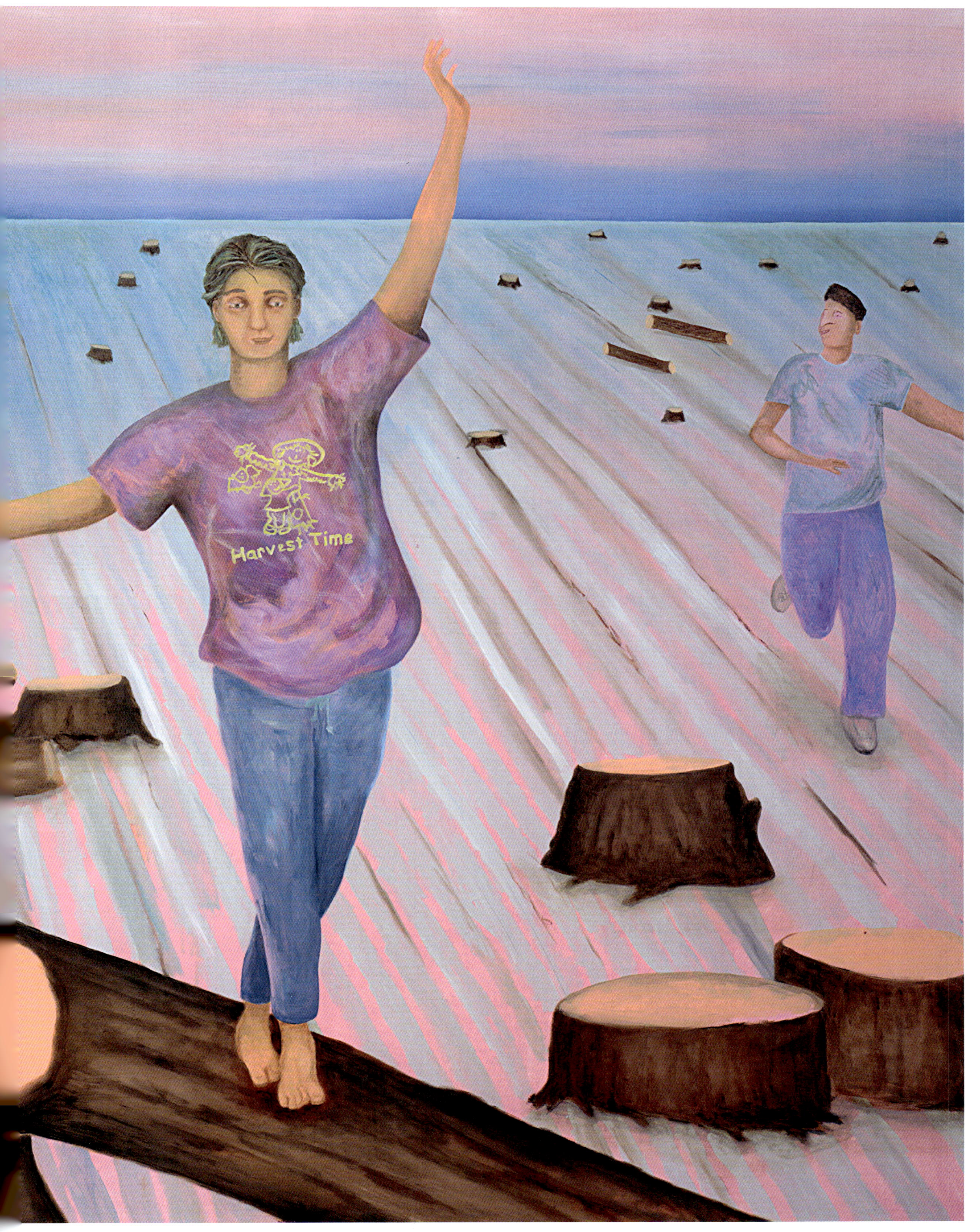
Harvest Time

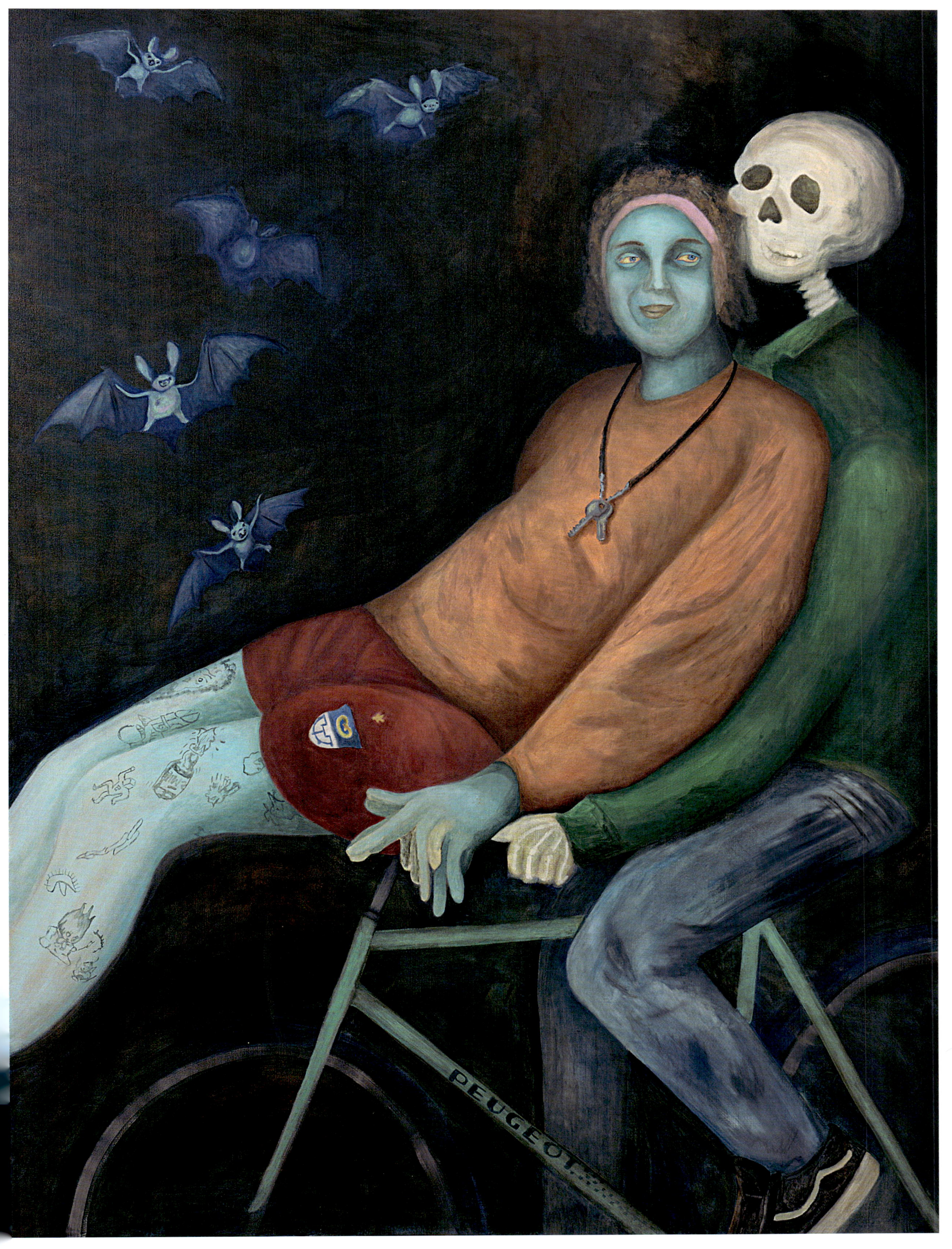

In Your Arms, 2025   190 × 140 cm

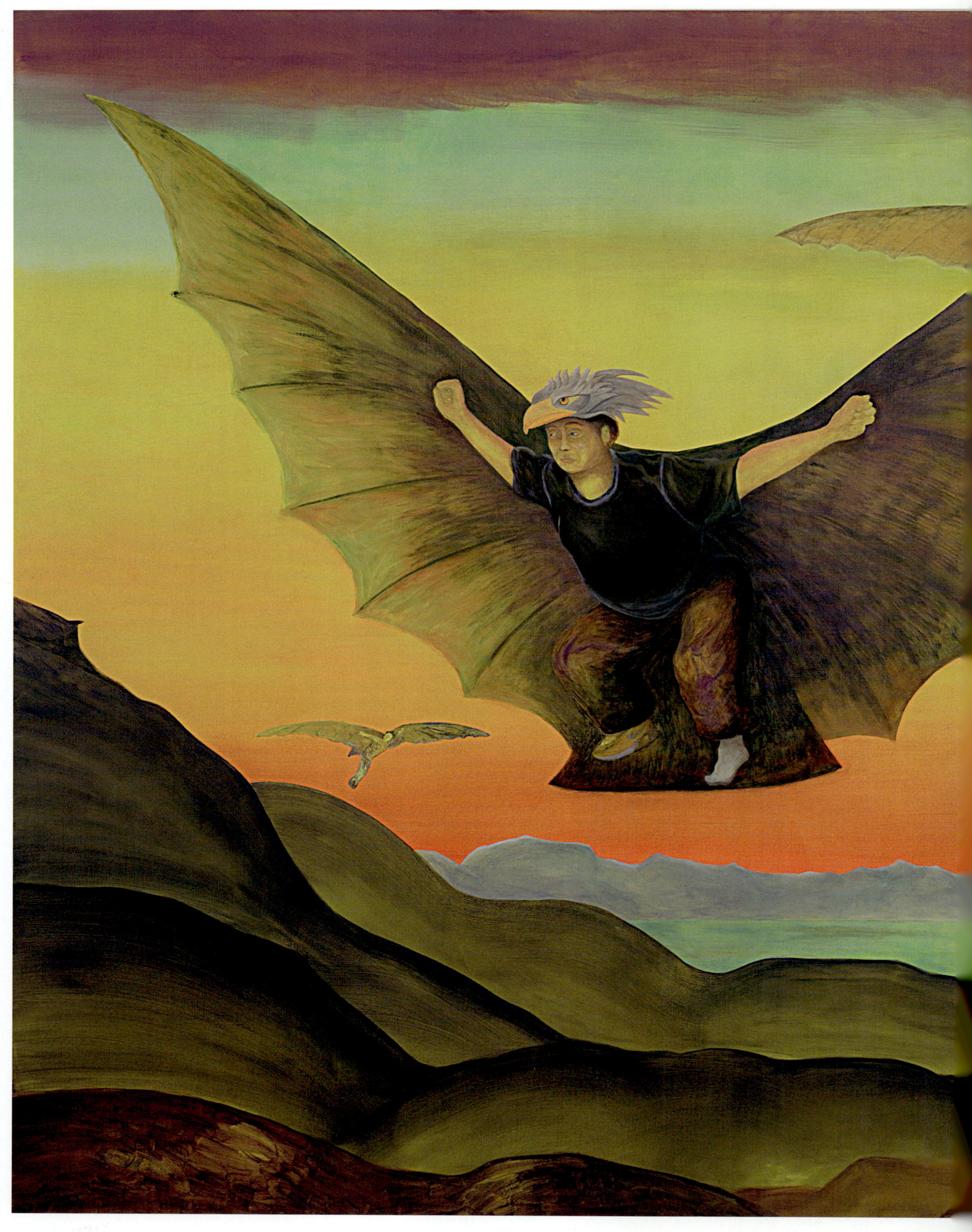

Untitled, 2025   190×300 cm

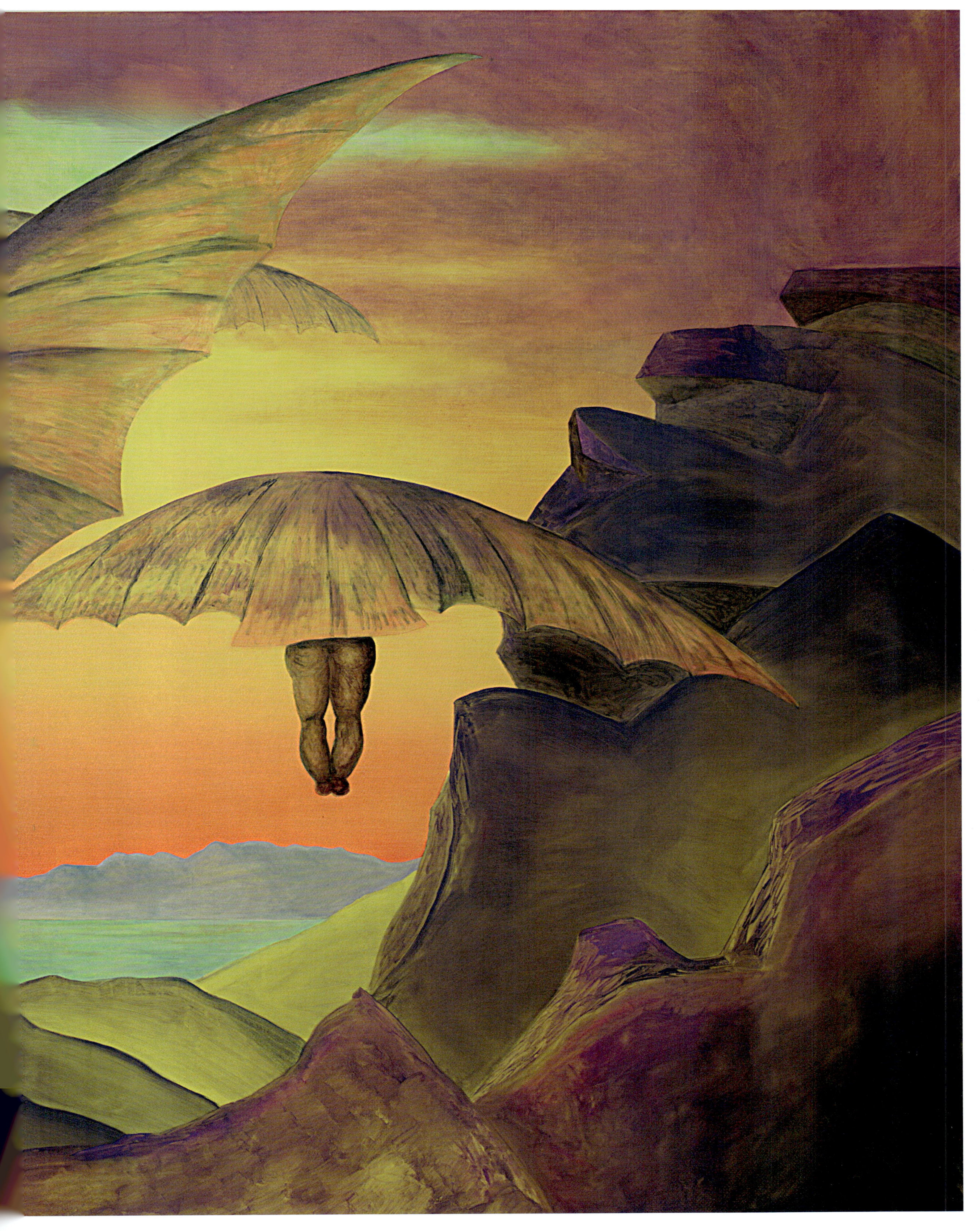

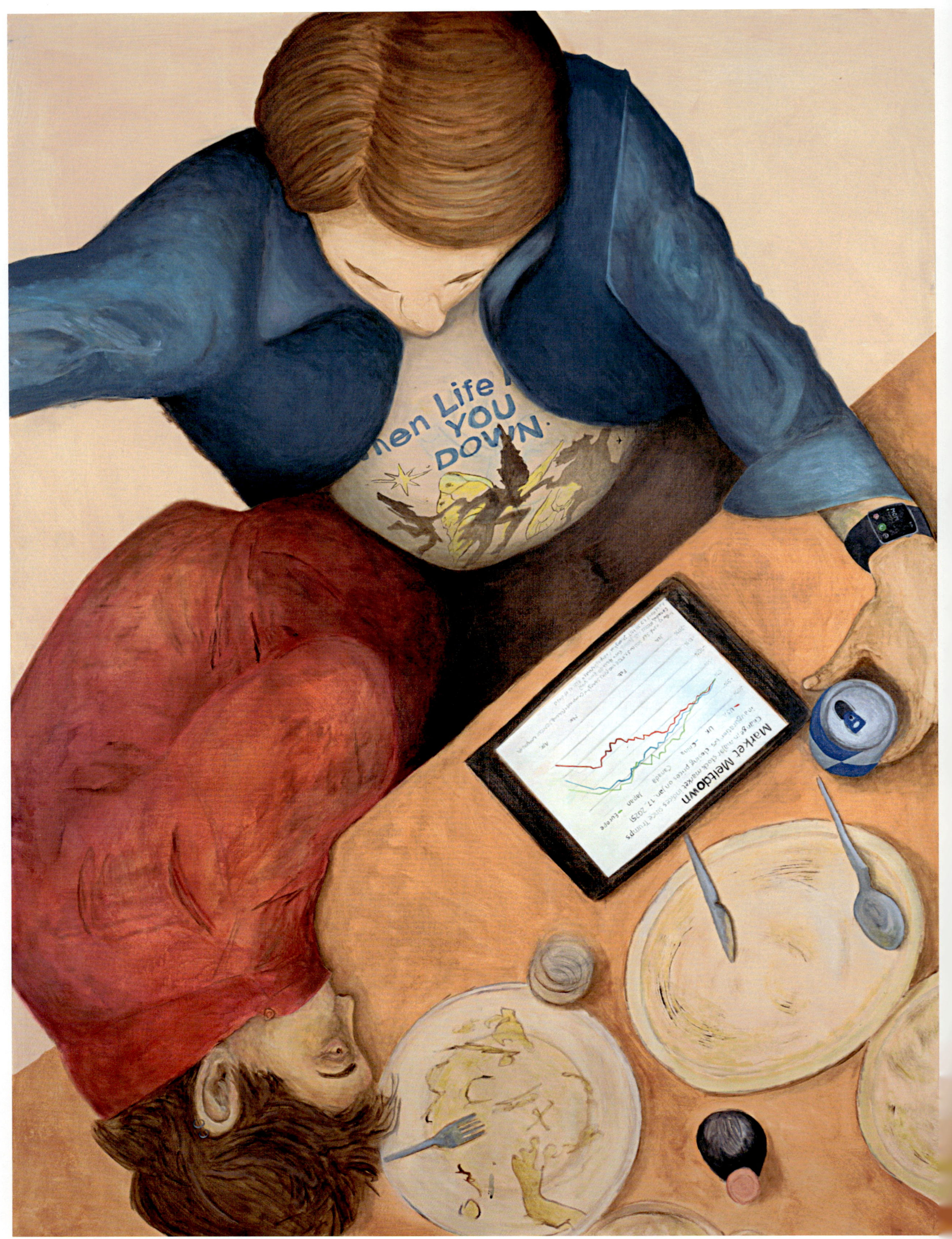

Meltdown, 2025   190×140 cm

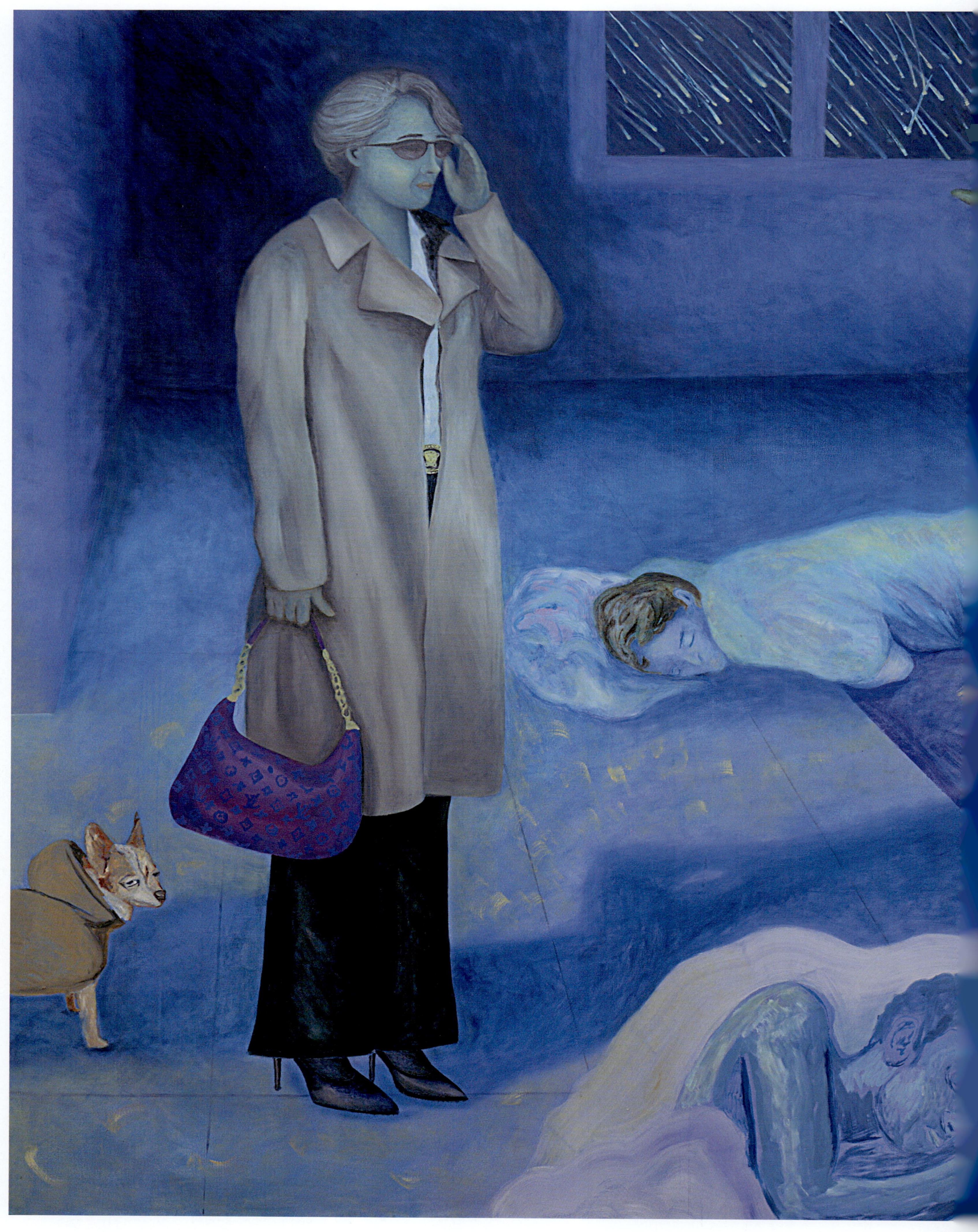

Sleepover (Tinfoil Dreams), 2025   190×300 cm   12

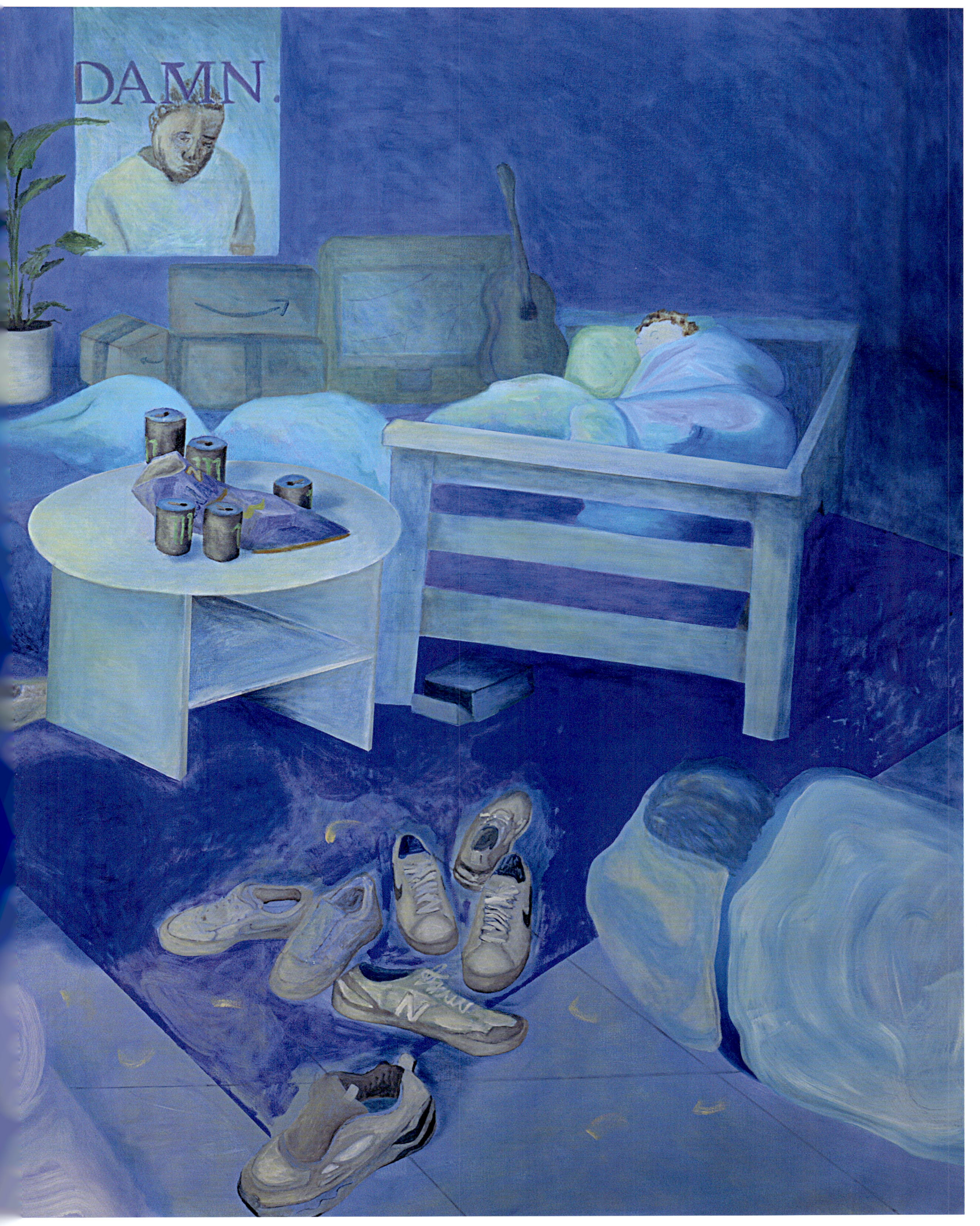

DAMN.

Night after night, a sorcerer conjures up a man in his dreams. In each dream, he completes another aspect of the image: assembling the skeleton, shaping organs, and allowing his hair to grow. Then he teaches him to be a human being and endows him with confidence, until he is able to release him to the world. As the magician seemingly approaches death, he realizes with distressing clarity that he too is a dream: "He walked toward the sheets of flame. They did not bite his flesh, they caressed him and flooded him without heat or combustion. With relief, with humiliation, with terror, he understood that he also was an illusion, that someone else was dreaming him."[1]

Jorge Luis Borges's 1944 short story "The Circular Ruins" reflects reality as an inescapable dream. Waking up only leads to another layer of the dream, and the actual insight consists of understanding that waking up is nothing more than an illusion. Borges's text can serve as a concept for the present, in which every awakening marks a transition to a new uncertainty, to an unstable reality: if we examine our world in which climate change, geopolitical instability, and technological transformation are so all-embracing and pervasive that the external perspective slips away, making an awakening or a "realization" hardly possible. The line between wakefulness and sleeping, control and impotence becomes blurred. Perhaps the real question is no longer if we can wake up, but if we can direct the dream into a meaningful direction before it turns irrevocably into a nightmare.

We can only imagine what the young people in Noemi Pfister's painting *Sleepover (Tinfoil Dreams)* (2025; pp. 12–13) are dreaming. Their sleep is mystifying. The room in which they are lying takes on a mysterious depth due to the blue tones and the skewed perspective. Shoes are strewn on the floor along with piles of unopened Amazon packages. A Kendrick Lamar *DAMN.* poster on the wall shows the rapper with a thoughtful expression. The table in the center of the room is littered with an empty bag of chips and black cans of Monster Energy. How can it be that after drinking so many energy drinks they sleep as deeply as if they had taken a narcotic? An older woman in a gray coat, equipped with sunglasses, a luxurious handbag, and a dog wearing a jacket, stands at the edge of the scene. Outside the window, a meteor shower is taking place.

The composition of Pfister's painting and the motifs depicted evoke associations with the painting *The Astonishment of the Mask Wouse* (1899, Koninklijk Museum voor Schone Kunsten, Antwerp).[2] In Ensor's oeuvre, masks represent hypocrisy and loss of identity, concealing the true nature of the figures and their alienation from themselves and their surroundings. There are similar dynamics in Pfister's painting. The woman hides behind status symbols that serve as protection as well as a façade. Although her gaze is empty, her alertness contrasts strongly with the tranquility that fills the nocturnal space. Pfister seems to ask if this sleeping is a privilege or if it is already symptomatic of overload. Are young people afraid of waking up? The opposite of sleep is not alertness but insomnia, a condition of incessant sensory overload, of being driven, and the fear of missing out.[3] The woman seems like a threat to the young people: an authority figure that confronts them with the seriousness of life.

In addition to art-historical references, Pfister layers social media posts and further developments of her sketches in her works. Apart from Ensor's painting, *Sleepover (Tinfoil Dreams)* references a second image: a low-resolution picture from Instagram showing a bedroom with teenagers sleeping on the floor.[4] Super Mario is still running on the flickering monitor, as if they had simply fallen asleep after playing all night. Pfister derives the idea of layering from the digital behavior of our age. Hours spent scrolling on our smartphones often induces a drugged state. Dissociated from physical reality, this numbing resembles a dreamlike condition in which irreconcilable events are lined up in a sequence that nonetheless makes sense.

It may seem daring to transfer to the present Borges's idea of a dream in which every realization turns out to be a deception. If, however we view the dream of modernism, which for decades was celebrated as a promise, we must conclude that it increasingly resembles a failed utopia. The protagonists that we created for this dream were once pure and powerful. Although they were beacons that showed us the way to the future, negative consequences already began to grow rampantly in their shadows early on.

The ideals of modernism are increasingly coming under pressure: the belief in the ability of humans to understand the world and solve its problems through reason yields to (digital) propaganda. Nearly every narrative can be fed into the brains of human beings. Freedom of thought and action, which is stabilized by achievements such as democracy and human rights, is being increasingly challenged in a fundamental way. Productivity and competition as a promise for prosperity do not only lead to the excessive gains of the economic elite, but also to unstoppable warming of the planet. We have begun to run away from the achievements of modernism, and we are losing our orientation.

The loss of critical distance is also reflected in the concept of "dark ecology" developed by philosopher Timothy Morton. His observations are devoted to developments such as climate change that are too massive to comprehend in their totality. For this reason, Morton recommends that we accept the ecological crises and adapt a stance of coexisting with nature founded on humility and exchange with all entities of the world. This means living with uncertainty and recognizing darkness as part of our existence. Morton argues that we need a more comprehensive understanding of coexistence.[5]

In this sense, the young people in the painting *Happily Aging & Dying* (2022; pp. 98–99) seem to comply with the fragility of the world. They take it as a given. The teenagers are self-sufficient and smoke their joints thoughtfully. They linger in the dark sublimity of a world that does not exist separately from us but takes us away with it. Above their heads, mysterious warriors ride off to face unknown rivals. We can practically hear rampant horses and the sound of wind instruments in the distance. Pfister here refers to a folktale existing in many parts of Europe that tells of supernatural hunters who hunt in the sky. They are considered harbingers of catastrophes such as wars, droughts, and sickness. Pfister's story takes place on a stage consisting of the dried-out ground. The hardened surface of the earth is covered with cracks.

Happily Aging & Dying combines different time layers and cultural narratives. While the young people and their e-scooters exist in the here and now, their surroundings, the desiccated ground, and the mysterious warriors reflect historical and ecological relationships that extend beyond their being together. The picture suggests that we can no longer look at the ecological crisis from the outside, since it is part of the framework in which past and present, myth and reality, individual and environment coexist. With this psychologically charged scene, which reflects power structures and social reality, Pfister encourages viewers to think about their own position in the world.[6] Whether sleeping, being driven away, suffering, uncomplaining, absent, or forgotten, the people and their destinies in her paintings are familiar to us.

Pfister's works not only make it possible to identify. They also create a critical distance to that which is depicted. Instead of giving answers, her works urge viewers to engage in self-reflection. This productive ambivalence runs through Pfister's entire oeuvre. For example, the painting *Formen in Aufruhr (After I.W.)* (Forms in Turmoil [After I.W.], 2023; p. 17) depicts a scene in which opposites are interwoven.[7] The personification of wind blows three white balloons into the sky. The balloons seem to be connected to the wind's hands, in which there lies an open pocketknife. The wind may push the balloons in a certain direction, but it can cut off the connections at any time and leave them to their fate. The picture is characterized by the tension between impotence and the readiness to use violence, although the composition and colors seem balanced.

The fragile balance in Pfister's work, which might tip at any moment, allows us to make an incredible association with a dream by American songwriter Dion McGregor. In the early 1960s, McGregor did not have a permanent address and moved from sofa to sofa in various apartments around New York. Despite this vagrant lifestyle, he always slept deeply and had many dreams. His hosts soon observed that he spoke in his sleep and told grotesque but plausible stories in the wee hours of the morning.

Troubled by the realization that McGregor was relating his dreams, one of his housemates began to record the wild anecdotes. He realized that the dreams did not oppose reality but were intertwined with it. In the following dream, McGregor elatedly lists the names of the passengers who are taking a trip to the moon in a hot-air balloon. As the journey begins, spirits are high:

this is the first balloon flight . . .
everybody is in . . .
everyone in their seats . . .
rise slowly, rise slowly . . .
three and half weeks to get to the moon . . .

The balloon in McGregor's dream then encounters a flock of sharp-beaked storks.[8]

1   Jorge Luis Borges, "The Circular Ruins" [1944], in *Collected Fictions*, trans. Andrew Hurley (New York: Viking, 1998), 96–100.
2   James Ensor (1860–1949) was a Belgian painter, graphic artist, and draftsman. His work can be categorized as Symbolism that anticipates Expressionism and Surrealism.
3   This statement takes cues from ideas that philosopher Jonathan Crary discusses in his book *24/7: Late Capitalism and the Ends of Sleep* (London and New York: Verso, 2013). Crary describes how capitalism increasingly undermines sleep and forces people into a state of permanent availability and overstimulation.
4   See the Instagram profile @misfihtss (accessed on March 26, 2025).
5   See Timothy Morton, *Dark Ecology: For a Logic of Future Coexistence* (New York: Columbia University Press, 2016).
6   In this respect, Noemi Pfister's paintings follow the tradition of Portuguese artists Paula Rego (1935–2022).
7   "I.W." stands for painter and draftswoman Ilse Weber (1908–1984).
8   Dion McGregor, "The Flight," 2:00–3:17 min, https://www.youtube.com/watch?v=ryiIK3ZPrnc (accessed on March 6, 2025).

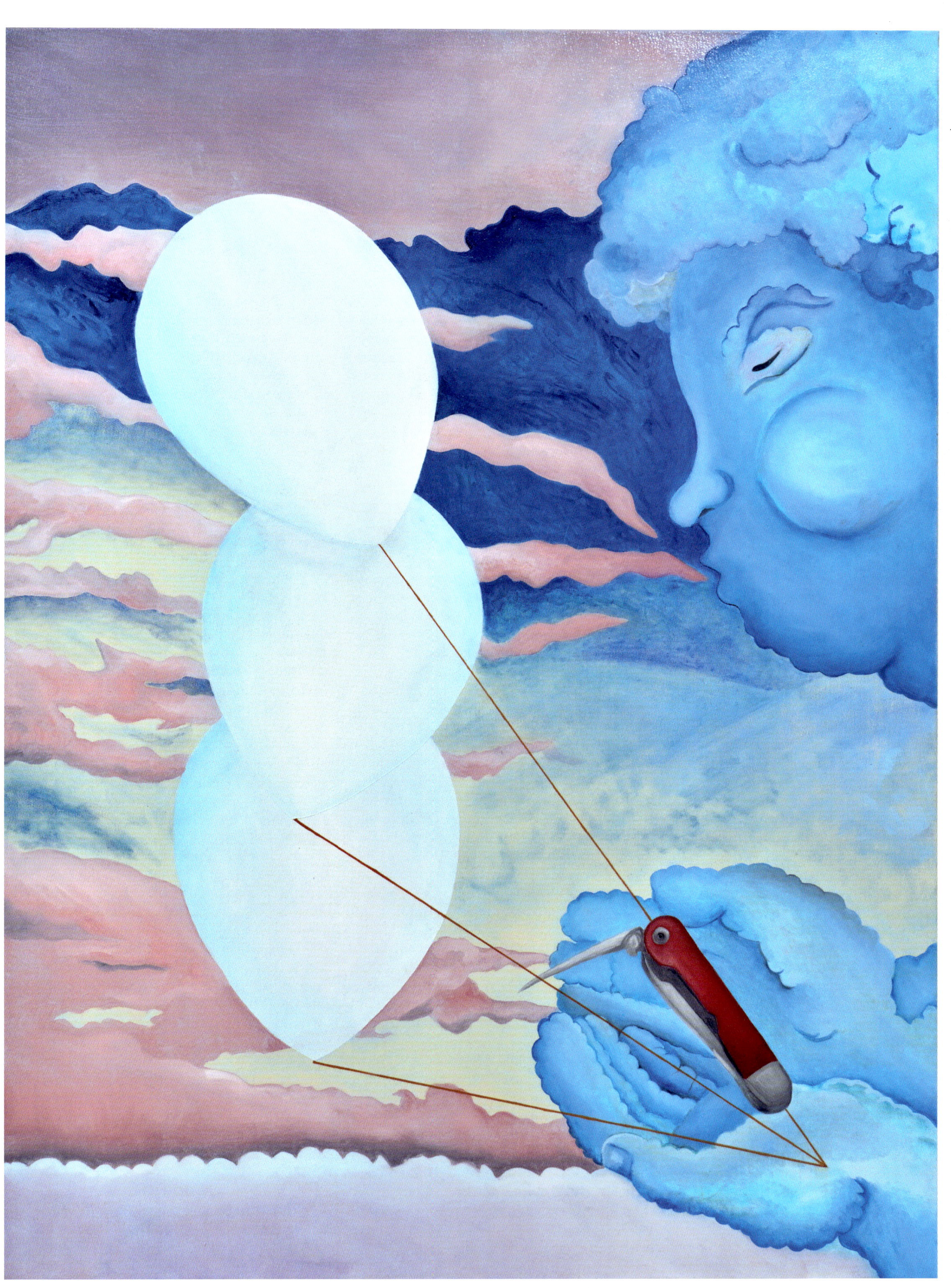

Formen in Aufruhr (After I.W.), 2023   125×90 cm   17

Schlaflos. Wenn das Gemälde zurückblickt
Damian Jurt

Nacht für Nacht lässt ein Magier in seinen Träumen einen Menschen entstehen. Mit jedem Traum vervollständigt er ihn schrittweise, er fügt das Skelett zusammen, bildet Organe und lässt ihm Haare wachsen. Dann lehrt er ihn das Menschsein und verleiht ihm Zuversicht, bis er ihn schliesslich in die Welt entlässt. Als sich das Leben des Magiers dem scheinbaren Tod nähert, erkennt er mit erschütternder Klarheit, dass er selbst auch ein Traum ist: «Er schritt auf die Feuerfetzen zu. Sie bissen nicht in sein Fleisch, sie liebkosten und überfluteten ihn ohne Hitze und Brand. Erleichtert, erniedrigt, entsetzt begriff er, daß auch er nur ein Scheinbild war, daß ein anderer ihn träumte.»[1]

Die Erzählung «Die kreisförmigen Ruinen» des Schriftstellers Jorge Luis Borges aus dem Jahr 1944 reflektiert eine Wirklichkeit als unentrinnbaren Traum. Das Erwachen führt nur in eine weitere Schicht des Traums und die eigentliche Erkenntnis besteht darin, dass das Erwachen selbst nichts anderes als eine Illusion ist. Borges' Text kann als Denkfigur für die Gegenwart dienen, in der jedes Erwachen den Übergang in eine neue Unsicherheit, in eine Wirklichkeit ohne festen Boden markiert: Betrachten wir unsere Welt, in der Klimawandel, geopolitische Instabilität und technologische Umwälzungen so allumfassend und durchdringend sind, dass uns eine Aussenperspektive entgleitet, scheint ein Aufwachen, ein «Erkennen» kaum mehr möglich. Die Grenzen zwischen Wachsein und Schlaf, Kontrolle und Ohnmacht verschwimmen. Vielleicht ist die eigentliche Frage nicht mehr, ob wir erwachen können, sondern wie wir den Traum noch in eine sinnvolle Richtung lenken können, bevor er endgültig zum Albtraum wird.

Wovon die Jugendlichen in Noemi Pfisters Gemälde *Sleepover (Tinfoil Dreams)* (2025; S. 12–13) träumen, können wir nur erahnen. Ihr Schlaf wirkt unergründlich. Sie liegen in einem Raum, der durch die Blautöne und die verzogene Perspektive eine rätselhafte Tiefe erhält. Auf dem Boden liegen verstreut Schuhe und stapeln sich ungeöffnete Amazon-Pakete. Ein Poster zu Kendrick Lamars Album *DAMN.* zeigt den Rapper mit nachdenklichem Gesicht. In der Mitte des Raumes auf dem Tisch liegen eine leere Chipstüte und schwarze Dosen des Energydrinks «Monster». Wie kommt es, dass sie nach all den Energydrinks so tief schlafen, als hätten sie ein Narkotikum genommen? Eine ältere Frau im grauen Mantel, ausgestattet mit Sonnenbrille, bekleidetem Hund und luxuriöser Handtasche, steht am Rand der Szenerie. Draussen, vor dem Fenster regnet es Meteoriten.

Die Komposition und die Motive von Pfisters Bild wecken Assoziationen zum Gemälde *Die Verwunderung der Maske Wouse* von James Ensor (1889, Koninklijk Museum voor Schone Kunsten, Antwerpen).[2] In Ensors Œuvre stehen Masken für Heuchelei und Identitätsverlust, welche die wahre Natur der Figuren und deren Entfremdung von sich selbst und ihrer Umwelt verbergen. Im Gemälde von Pfister zeigt sich eine ähnliche Dynamik. Die Frau verbirgt sich hinter Statussymbolen, die zugleich Schutz und Fassade sind. Obschon ihr Blick ins Leere geht, steht ihre Wachheit in starkem Kontrast zur Ruhe, die den nächtlichen Raum erfüllt. Noemi Pfister scheint zu fragen, ob dieses Schlafen noch ein Privileg oder bereits ein Symptom der Überforderung ist. Fürchten sich die Jugendlichen vor dem Aufwachen? Das Gegenteil von Schlaf ist nicht mehr Wachsein, sondern Schlaflosigkeit, ein Zustand der permanenten Reizüberflutung, des Getriebenseins und der Angst, den Anschluss zu verlieren.[3] Die Frau wirkt wie eine Bedrohung für die Jugendlichen. Eine autoritäre Figur, die sie mit der Ernsthaftigkeit des Lebens konfrontiert.

Noemi Pfister überlagert in ihren Arbeiten neben kunsthistorischen Verweisen auch Posts aus den sozialen Medien und Weiterentwicklungen ihrer Skizzen. In *Sleepover* verbirgt sich ergänzend zum Gemälde von James Ensor ein weiteres Bild. Es stammt von einem Instagram-Kanal und zeigt in geringer Auflösung ein Jugendzimmer, in dem Teenager auf dem Boden schlafen. Auf dem flimmernden Monitor läuft noch Super Mario, als wären sie nach einer durchspielten Nacht einfach eingeschlafen.[4] Die Idee der Schichtung sieht Pfister auch im digitalen Verhalten unserer Zeit. Das stundenlange Scrollen auf dem Handy vermag uns zuweilen in einen berauschten Zustand versetzen. Dissoziiert von der physischen Wirklichkeit gleicht diese Betäubung einem traumähnlichen Zustand, in dem sich unvereinbare Ereignisse aneinanderreihen und dennoch einen Sinn ergeben.

Es mag kühn wirken, Borges' Idee eines Traums, in dem jede Erkenntnis zur Täuschung wird, auf unsere Gegenwart zu übertragen. Betrachten wir jedoch den Traum der Moderne, der über Jahrzehnte als Verheissung gefeiert wurde, müssen wir feststellen, dass er immer mehr einer gescheiterten Utopie gleicht. Die Protagonisten, die wir für diesen Traum erschufen, waren einst rein und kraftvoll. Von ihnen ging ein Licht aus, das uns den Weg in die Zukunft wies, auch wenn in ihren Schatten bereits früh negative Konsequenzen wucherten.

Die Ideale der Moderne geraten zunehmend unter Druck: Der Glaube an die menschliche Fähigkeit, durch Vernunft die Welt zu verstehen und ihre Probleme zu lösen, weicht (digitaler) Propaganda. Nahezu jedes Narrativ kann in die Hirne der Menschen eingespeist werden. Die Freiheit des Denkens und Handelns, die durch Errungenschaften wie Demokratie oder Menschenrechte gesichert wurde, wird immer grundlegender herausgefordert. Produktivität und Wettbewerb als Versprechen für Wohlstand führen nicht nur zur masslosen Bereicherung einer Wirtschaftselite, sondern auch zur unaufhaltsamen Klimaerwärmung. Inzwischen sind wir auf der Flucht vor den Errungenschaften der Moderne und verlieren die Orientierung.

Den Verlust der kritischen Distanz reflektiert auch das Konzept der «Dark Ecology» des Philosophen Timothy Morton. Seine Überlegungen widmen sich Entwicklungen wie dem Klimawandel, die zu gross sind, um sie in ihrer Gesamtheit zu begreifen. Er schlägt daher vor, dass wir die ökologischen Krisen akzeptieren und eine Haltung der Koexistenz zur Natur einnehmen sollen, die auf Demut und Austausch mit allen Entitäten der Welt beruht. Das bedeutet, mit Ungewissheit zu leben und Dunkelheit als Teil unserer Existenz anzuerkennen. Morton argumentiert, dass wir ein umfassenderes Verständnis von Koexistenz brauchen.[5]

In diesem Sinn scheinen sich auch die Jugendlichen im Gemälde *Happily Aging & Dying* (2022; S. 98–99) der brüchigen Welt nicht zu widersetzen. Sie nehmen sie als gegeben hin. Die Teenager genügen sich selbst und ziehen gedankenverloren an ihren Joints. Sie verweilen in der dunklen Erhabenheit einer Welt, die nicht getrennt von uns existiert, sondern uns mit sich forträgt. Über ihren Köpfen reiten rätselhafte Krieger unbekannten Rivalen entgegen. In der Ferne meinen wir, entfesselte Pferde und Laute von Blasinstrumenten zu hören. Noemi Pfister verweist hier auf eine in Teilen Europas verbreitete Volkssage, die von übernatürlichen Jägern erzählt, die über den Himmel jagen. Sie gelten als Vorboten für Katastrophen wie Kriege, Dürren oder Krankheiten. Die Bühne, auf der sich Pfisters Erzählung abspielt, ist ein ausgetrockneter Boden. Risse überziehen die hart gewordene Erdoberfläche.

Happily Aging & Dying verschränkt verschiedene Zeitebenen und kulturelle Narrative. Die Jugendlichen und ihre E-Scooter existieren zwar im Hier und Jetzt, ihr Umfeld, der ausgetrocknete Boden und die geheimnisvollen Krieger reflektieren aber historische und ökologische Beziehungen, die über ihr Zusammensein hinausreichen. Das Bild evoziert, dass wir nicht mehr von Aussen auf ökologische Krisen blicken können, da sie Teil eines Gefüges sind, in dem Vergangenheit und Gegenwart, Mythos und Realität, Individuum und Umwelt gleichzeitig existieren. Mit der psychologisch aufgeladenen Szene, in der sich Machtverhältnisse und gesellschaftliche Wirklichkeit spiegeln, regt Noemi Pfister dazu an, über unsere eigene Position in der Welt nachzudenken.[6] Die Schlafenden, die Getriebenen, die Leidenden, die Geduldigen, die Abwesenden, die Vergessenen – die Menschen und ihre Schicksale in den Gemälden sind uns vertraut.

Pfisters Werke ermöglichen aber nicht nur Identifikation. Sie schaffen auch eine kritische Distanz zum Dargestellten. Ihre Werke geben keine Antworten, sondern fordern zur Selbstreflexion auf. Diese produktive Ambivalenz zieht sich durch Pfisters gesamtes Schaffen. So zeigt auch das Gemälde *Formen in Aufruhr (After I. W.)*[7] (2023; S. 17) eine Szene, in der die Gegensätze miteinander verwoben sind. Die Verkörperung des Windes treibt drei weisse Luftballone in den Himmel. Sie scheinen mit den Händen des Windes verbunden zu sein, in denen ein geöffnetes Taschenmesser liegt. Der Wind mag die Ballone zwar in eine bestimmte Richtung treiben, aber er kann die Verbindung zu ihnen jederzeit kappen und sie ihrem Schicksal überlassen. Im Bild liegt eine Spannung zwischen Ohnmacht und Gewaltbereitschaft,

obschon Komposition und Farbgebung
ausgewogen wirken.

Die fragile Balance in Pfisters Werk, die
jederzeit kippen kann, lässt eine erstaunliche
Assoziation zu einem Traum des Song-
writers Dion McGregor zu. Der Musiker ist
Anfang 1960er-Jahre ohne festen Wohnsitz
und pendelt zwischen den Sofas verschie-
dener Wohnungen in New York hin und her.
Trotz des unsteten Lebens ist sein Schlaf
tief und traumreich. Bald bemerken seine
Gastgeber, wie er in den frühen Morgen-
stunden groteske, aber nachvollziehbare
Erzählungen von sich gibt. Aufgewühlt von
der Erkenntnis, dass es sich dabei um die
Wiedergabe seiner Träume handelt, beginnt
ein Mitbewohner, die ungezügelten Anek-
doten aufzuzeichnen. Er realisiert, dass
McGregors Träume nicht im Gegensatz zur
Wirklichkeit standen, sondern mit ihr
verflochten sind. Mit beschwingter Stimme
zählt McGregor in folgendem Traum die
Namen der Passagiere auf, die in einen Heiss-
luftballon steigen, um zum Mond zu
reisen. Als der Flug beginnt, ist die Stimmung gehoben:

this is the first balloon flight [...]
everybody is in [...]
everyone in their seats [...]
rise slowly, rise slowly [...]
three and half weeks to get to the moon [...]

Dann trifft der Ballon in McGregors Traum
auf einen Schwarm von Störchen mit
scharfen Schnäbeln.[8]

1   Jorge Luis Borges, «Die kreisförmigen
Ruinen» [1944], in: ders., *Fiktionen.*
Erzählungen 1939–1944, Frankfurt am Main
1992, S. 46–52, hier S. 52.
2   James Ensor (1860–1949) war ein bel-
gischer Maler, Grafiker und Zeichner. Ensors
Werk lässt sich dem Symbolismus zuord-
nen und als Vorgriff auf Expressionismus und
Surrealismus lesen.
3   Diese Aussage greift Ideen auf, die der
Philosoph Jonathan Crary in seinem Buch
24/7. Schlaflos im Spätkapitalismus (Berlin
2014) diskutiert. Crary beschreibt, wie
der Kapitalismus den Schlaf zunehmend
untergräbt und Menschen in einen Zustand
permanenter Erreichbarkeit und Reizüberflutung zwingt.
4   Siehe dazu das Instagram-Profil
@misfihtss, abgerufen am 26.3.2025.
5   Siehe Timothy Morton, *Dark Ecology.*
For a Logic of Future Coexistence,
New York 2016.
6   Noemi Pfisters Bilder ordnen sich damit
in eine Tradition etwa der portugiesischen
Künstlerin Paula Rego (1935–2022) ein.
7   «I. W.» steht für die Malerin und
Zeichnerin Ilse Weber (1908–1984).
8   Dion McGregor, «The Flight»,
2:00–3:17 min, https://www.youtube.com/
watch?v=ryilK3ZPrnc, abgerufen am
6.3.2025.

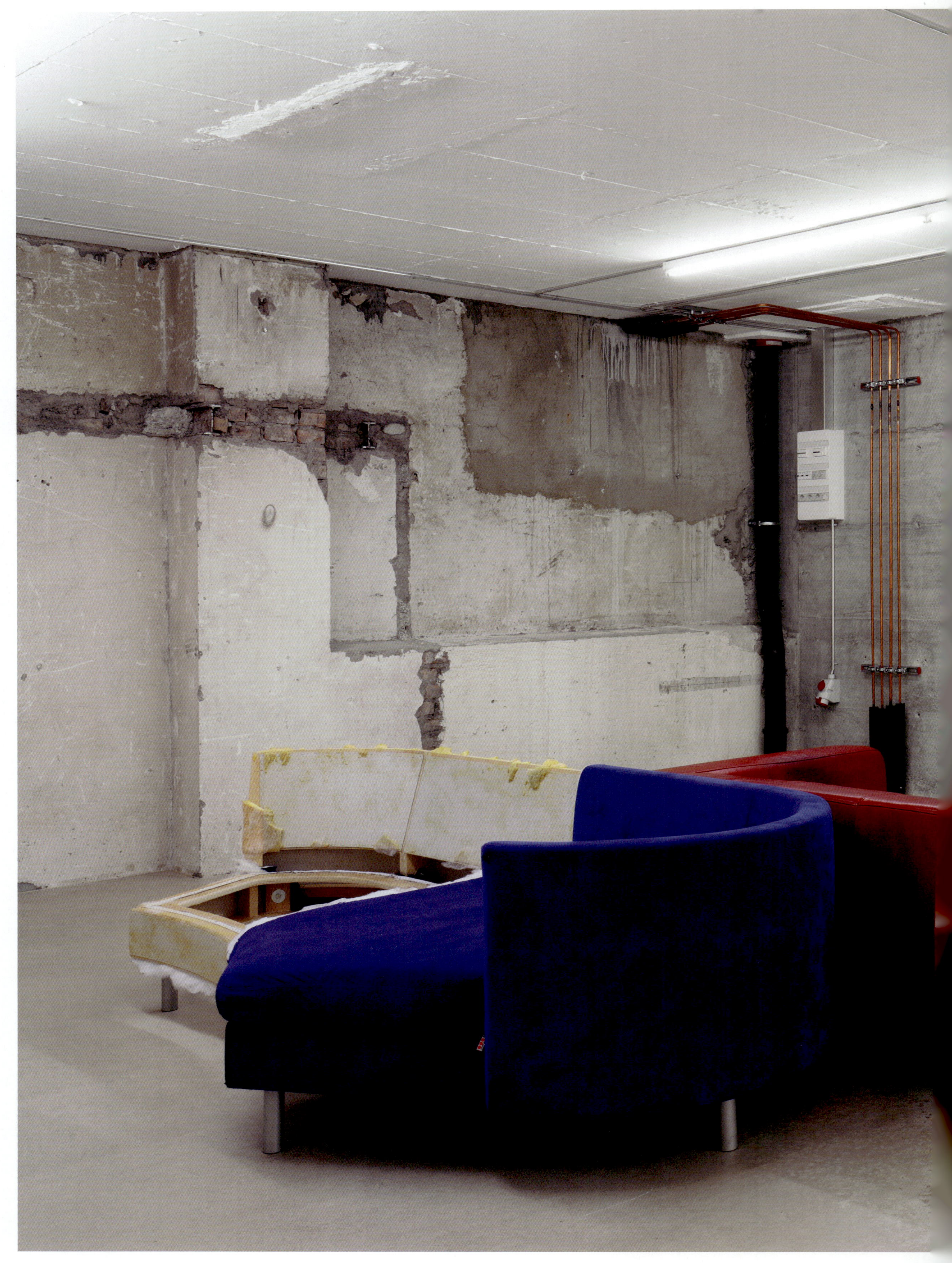

Melting Point, 2024   For, Basel

Noemi Pfister, *Anonymous Artists*, 2024
20 Virginie Sistek, *Monogamie*, 2024

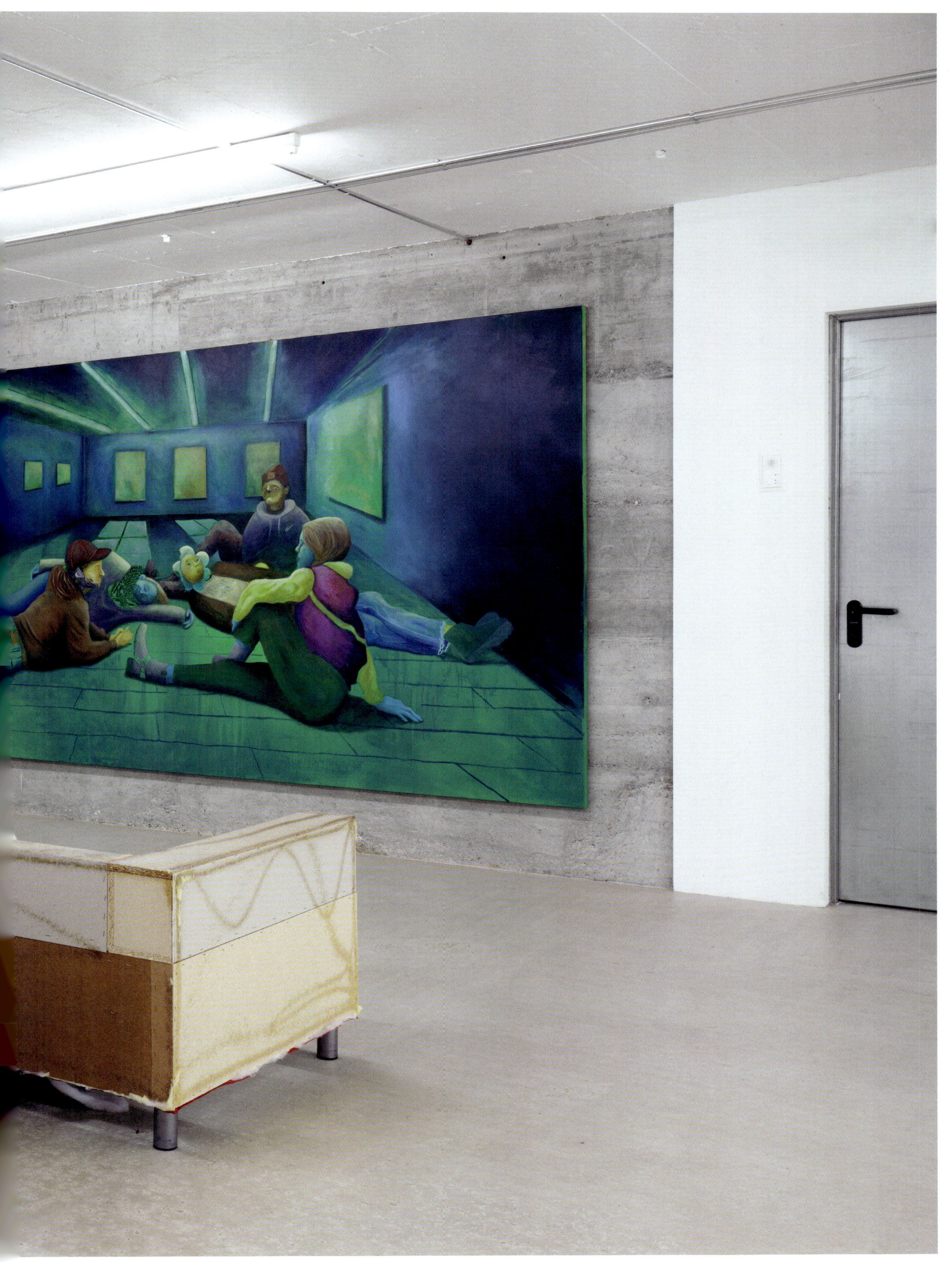

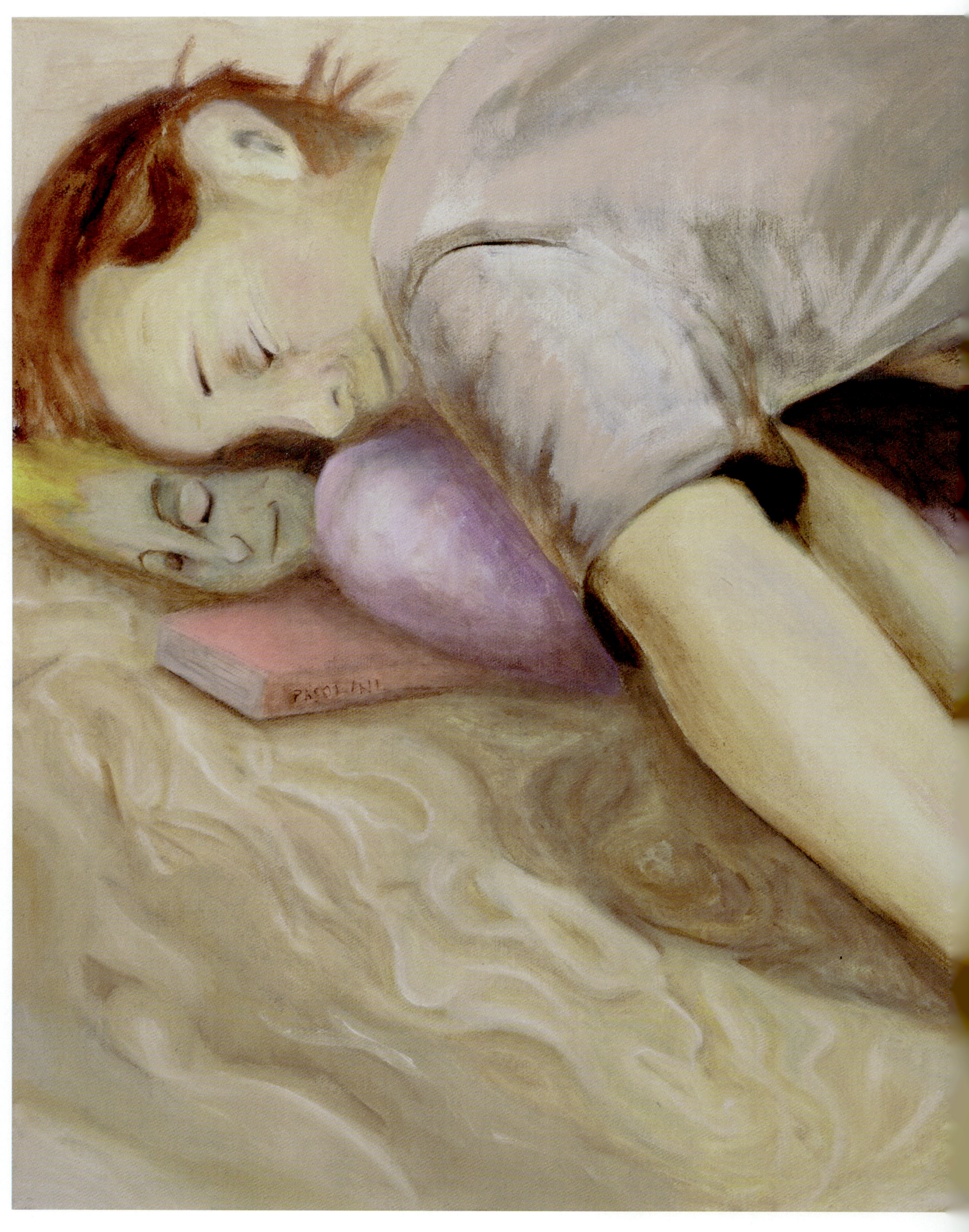

Ragazzi di vita, 2024   63 × 97 cm

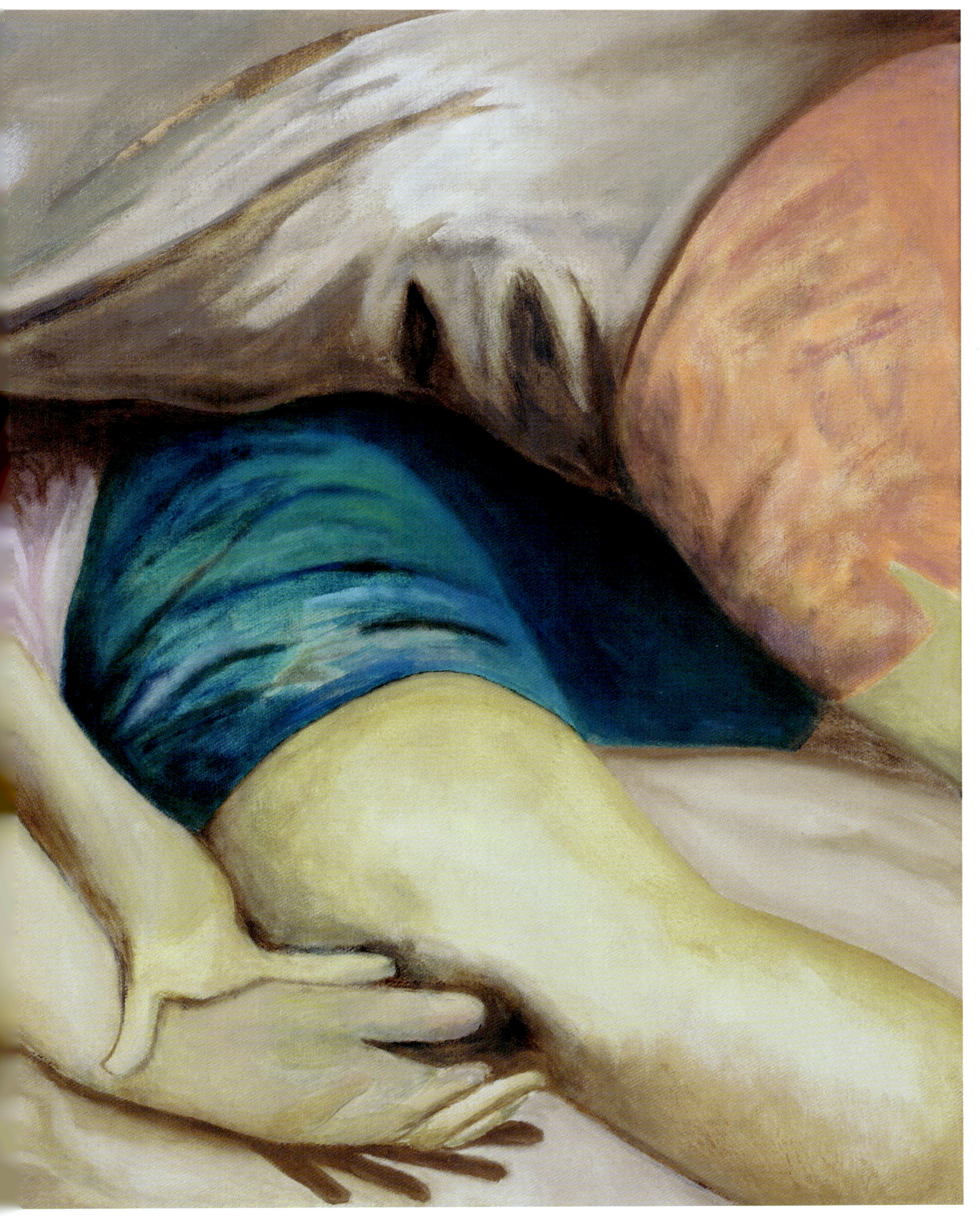

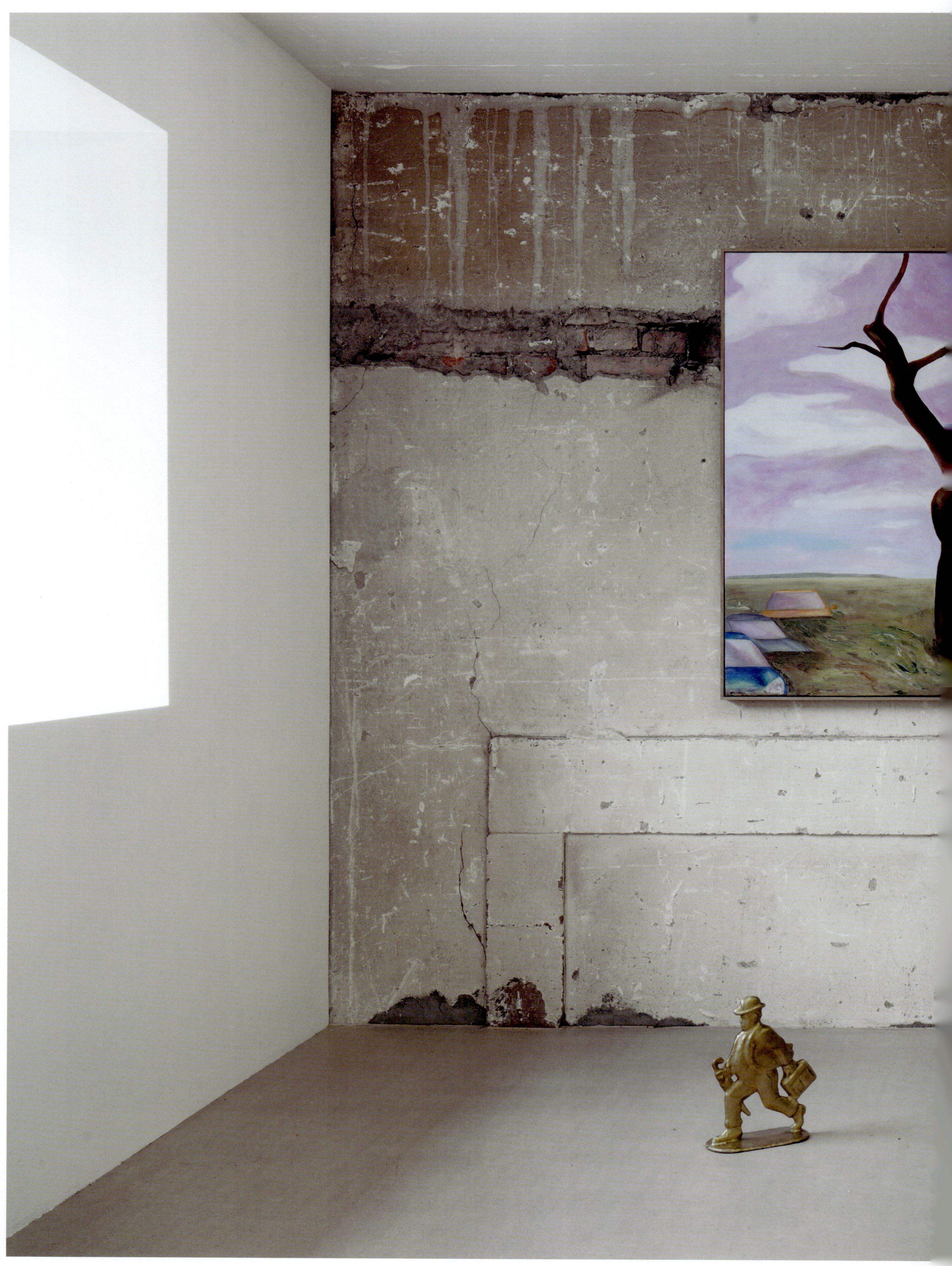

Melting Point, 2024   For, Basel

Noemi Pfister, *Great Things End, Small Things Endure*, 2024
24 Baker Wardlaw, *The Partners*, 2023

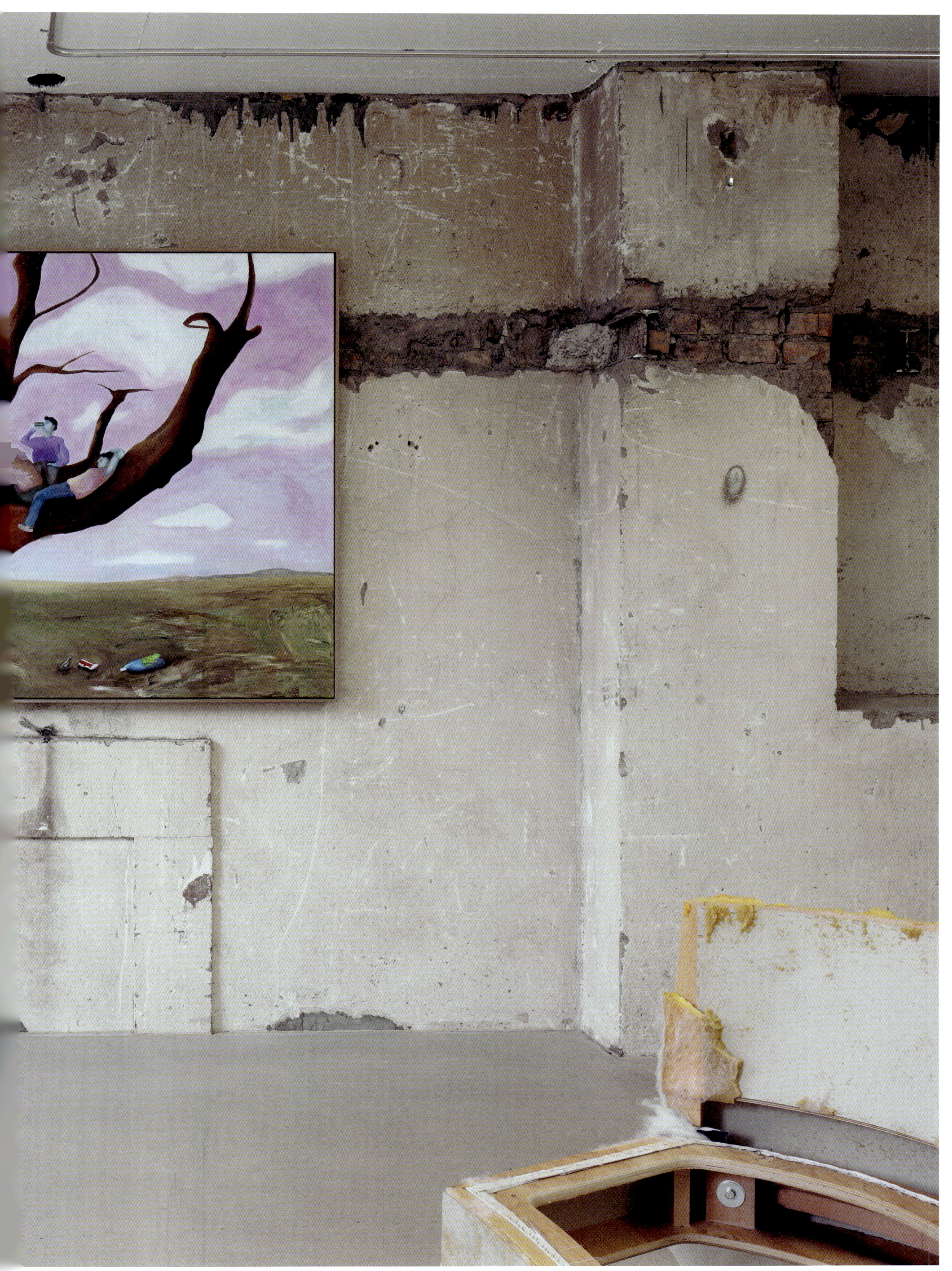

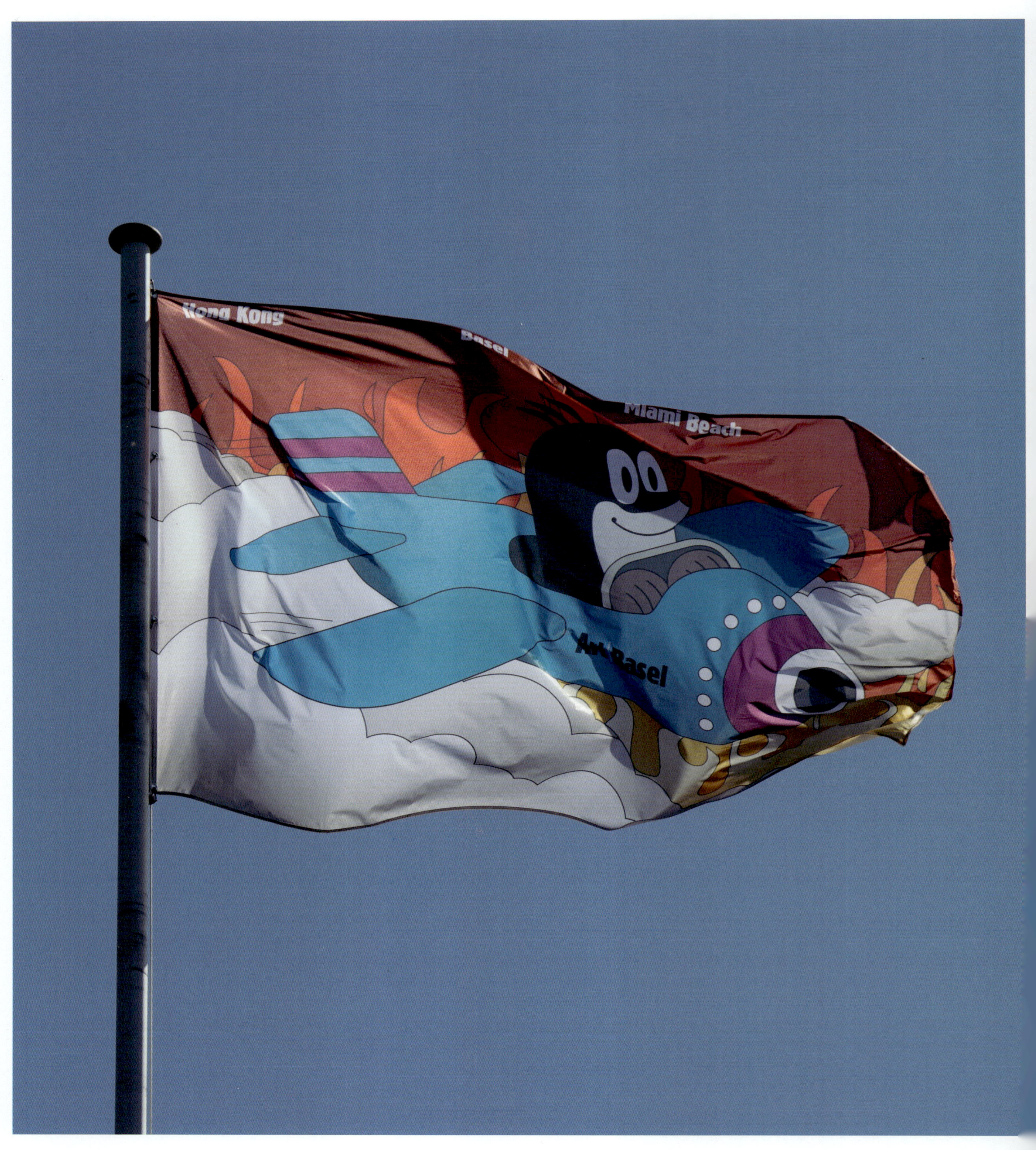

Art Basel Odyssey, 2024   160×240 cm

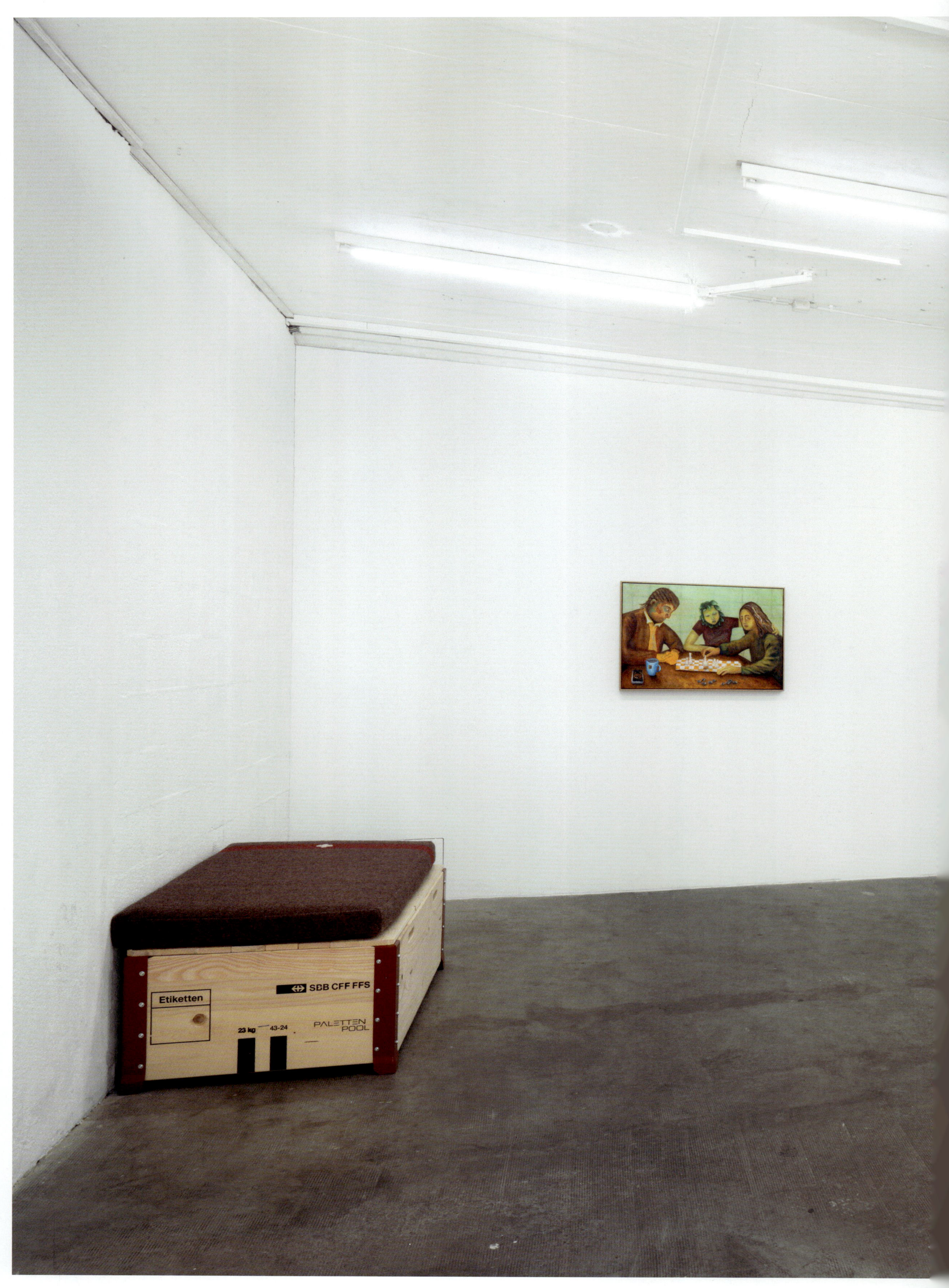

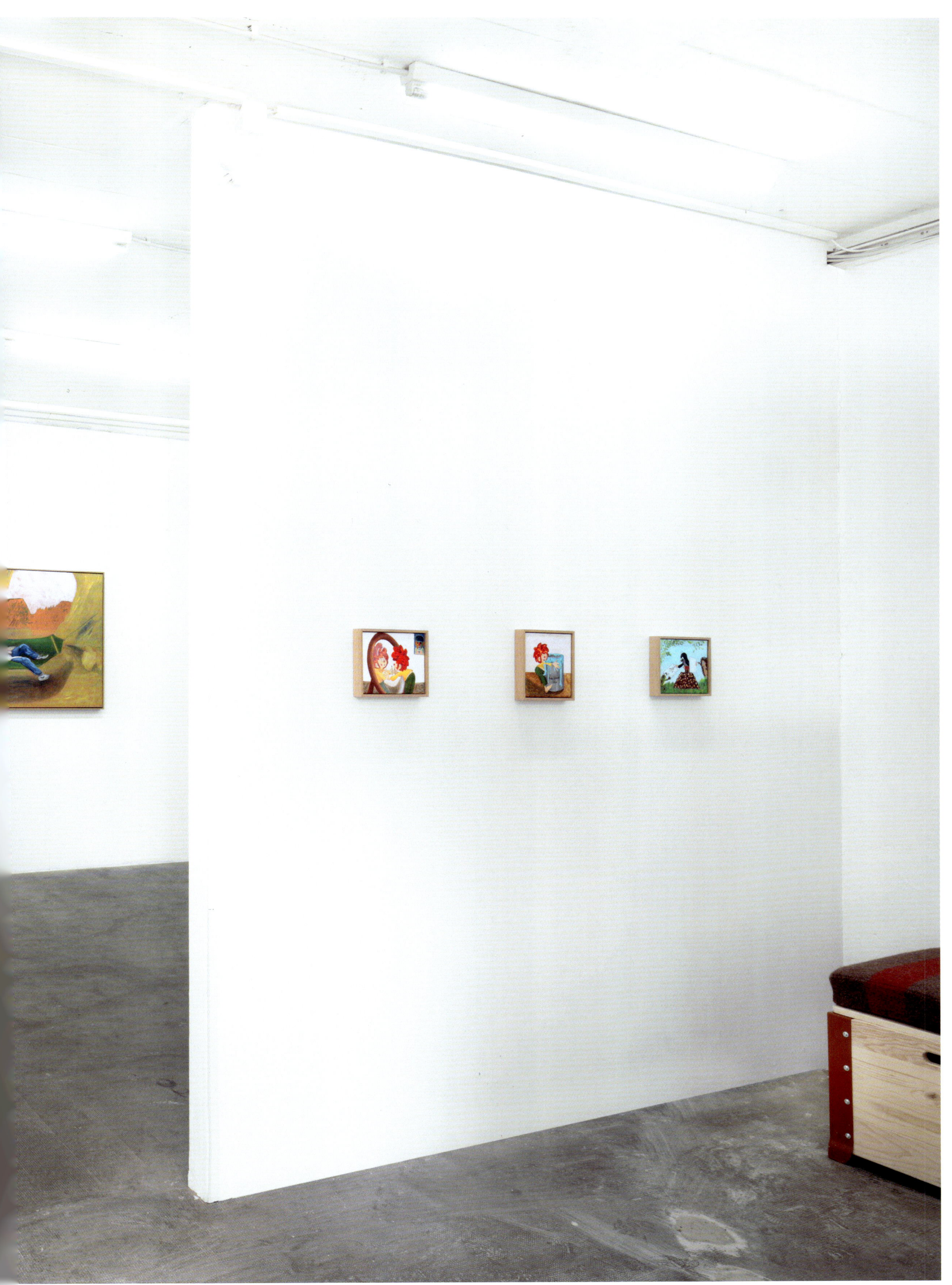

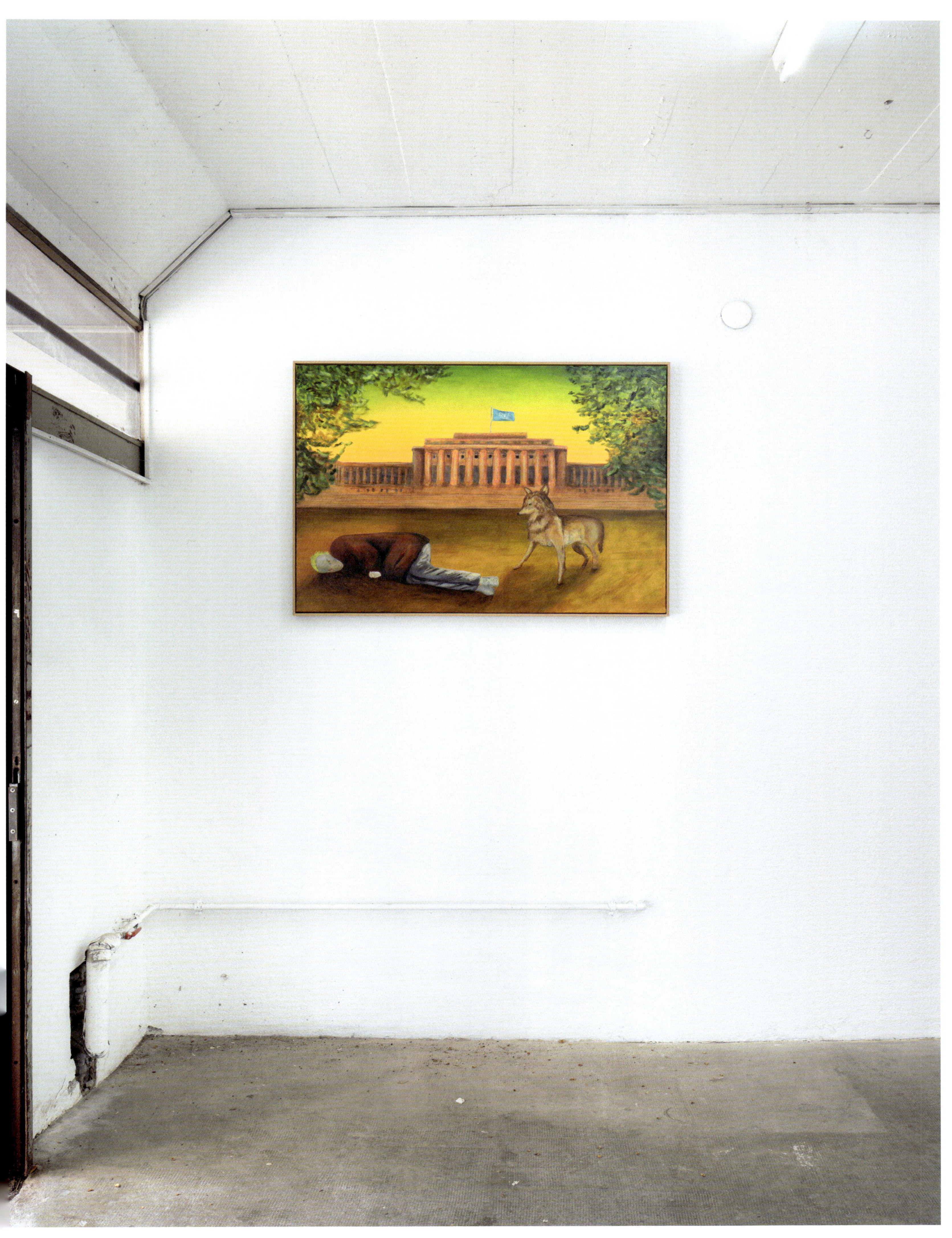

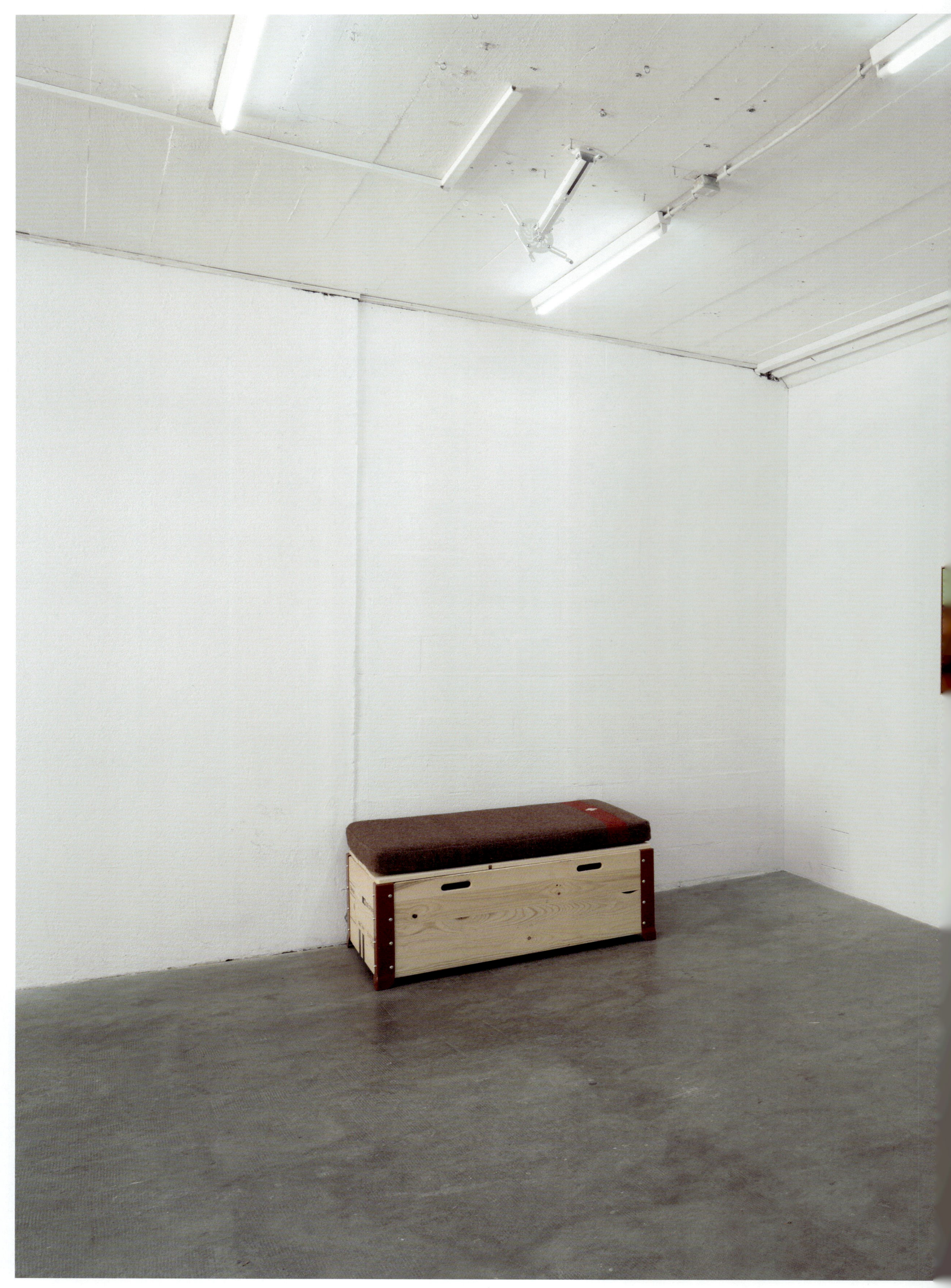

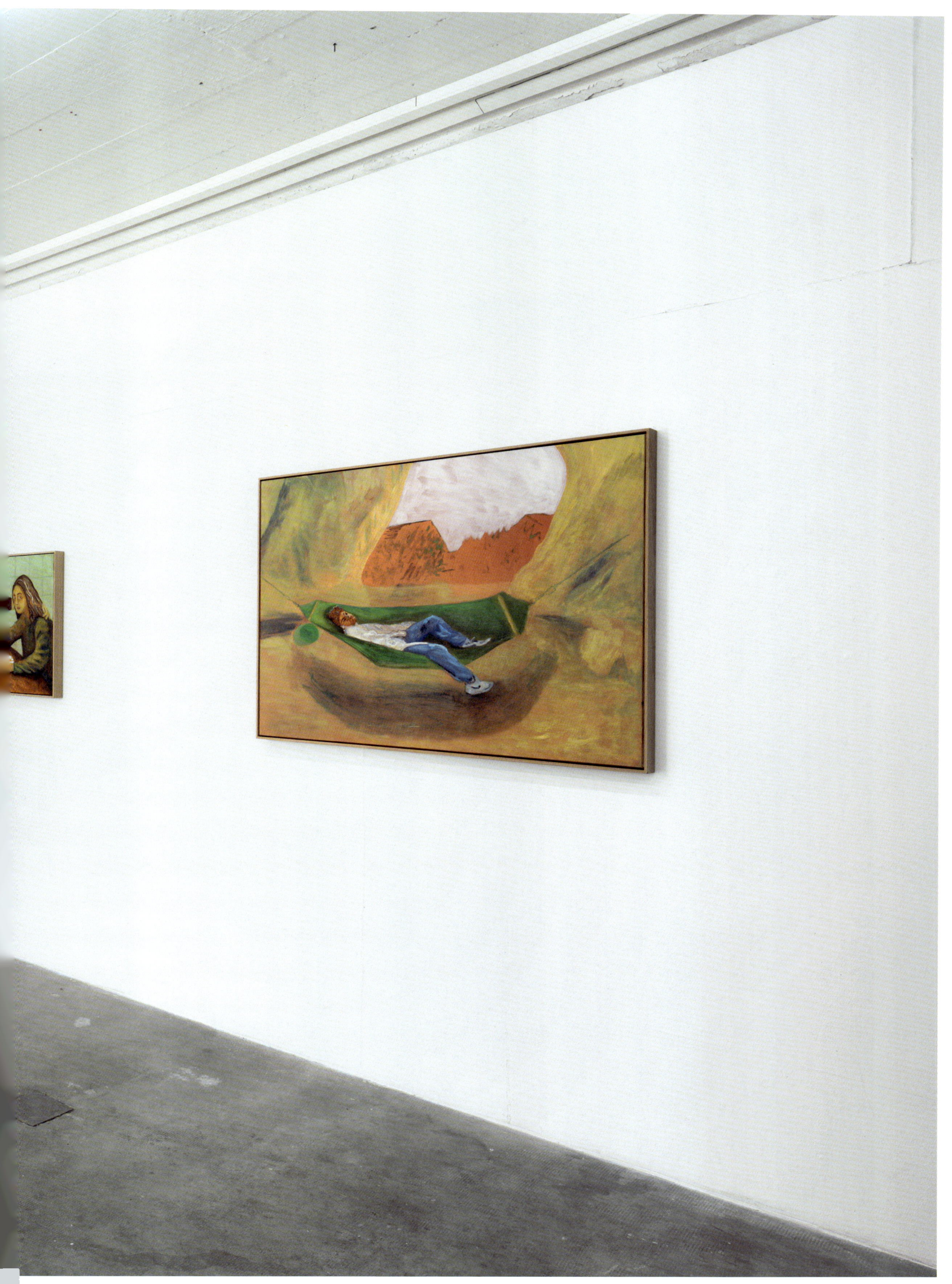

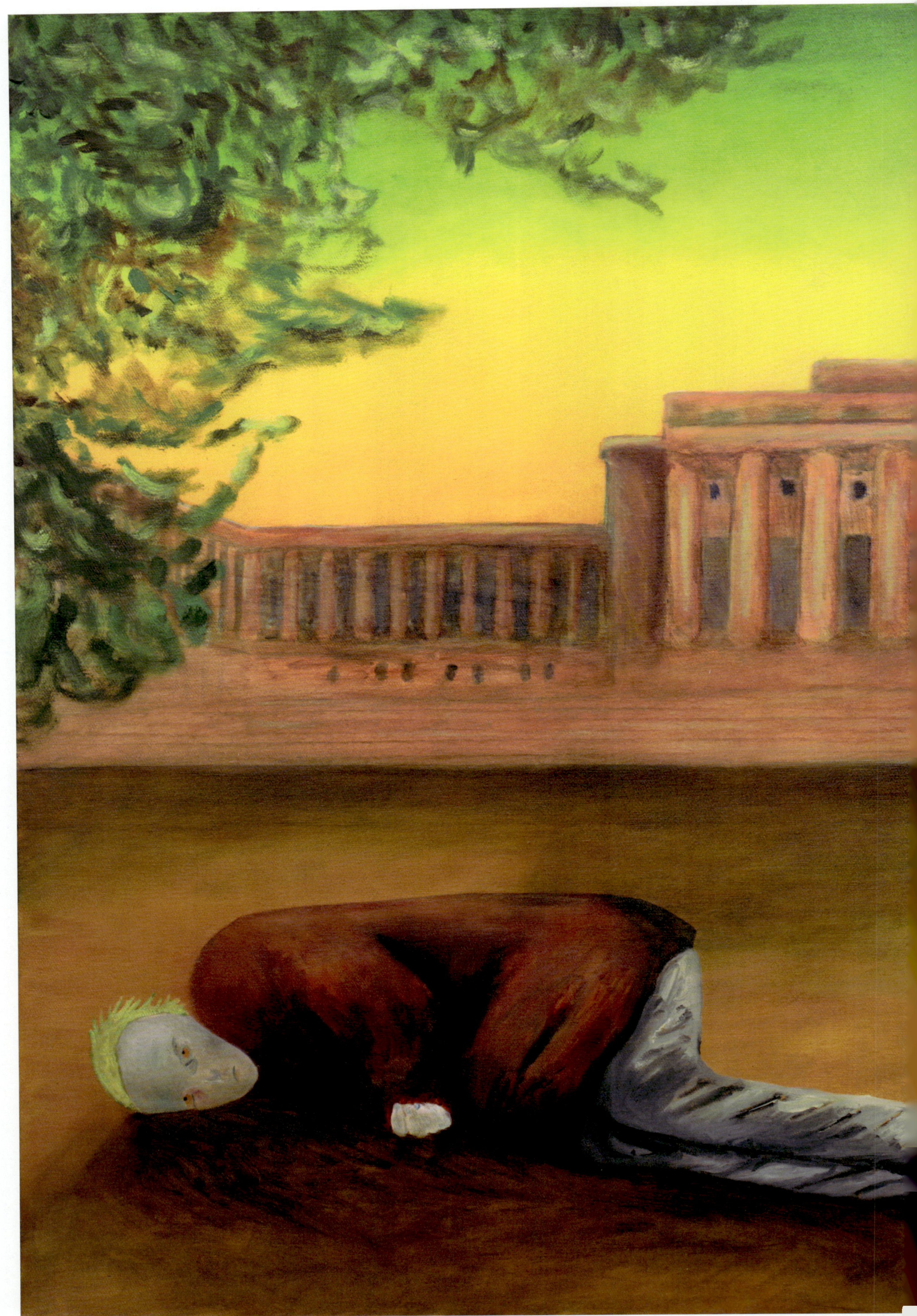

Città ideale, 2024   90.5×125 cm

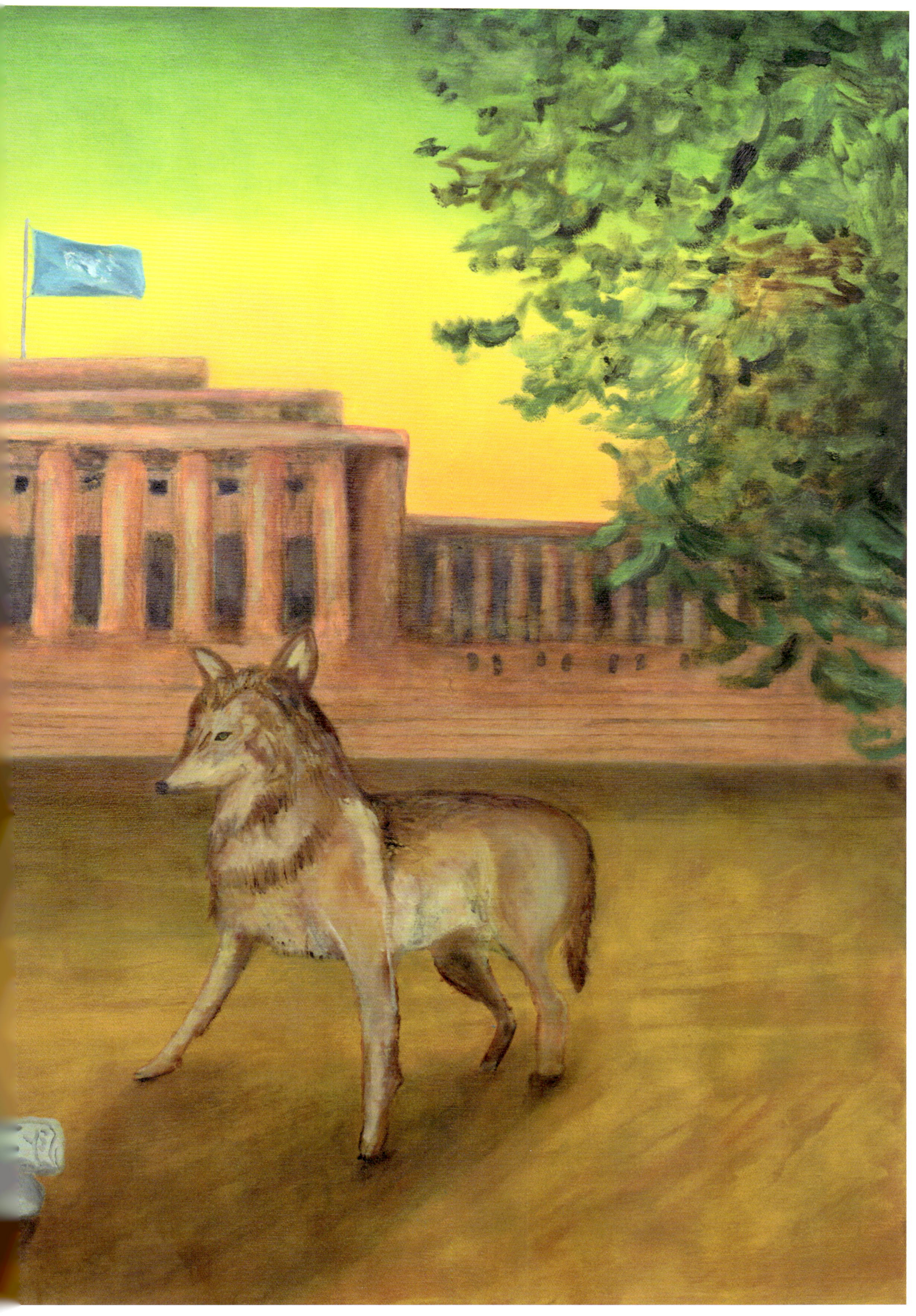

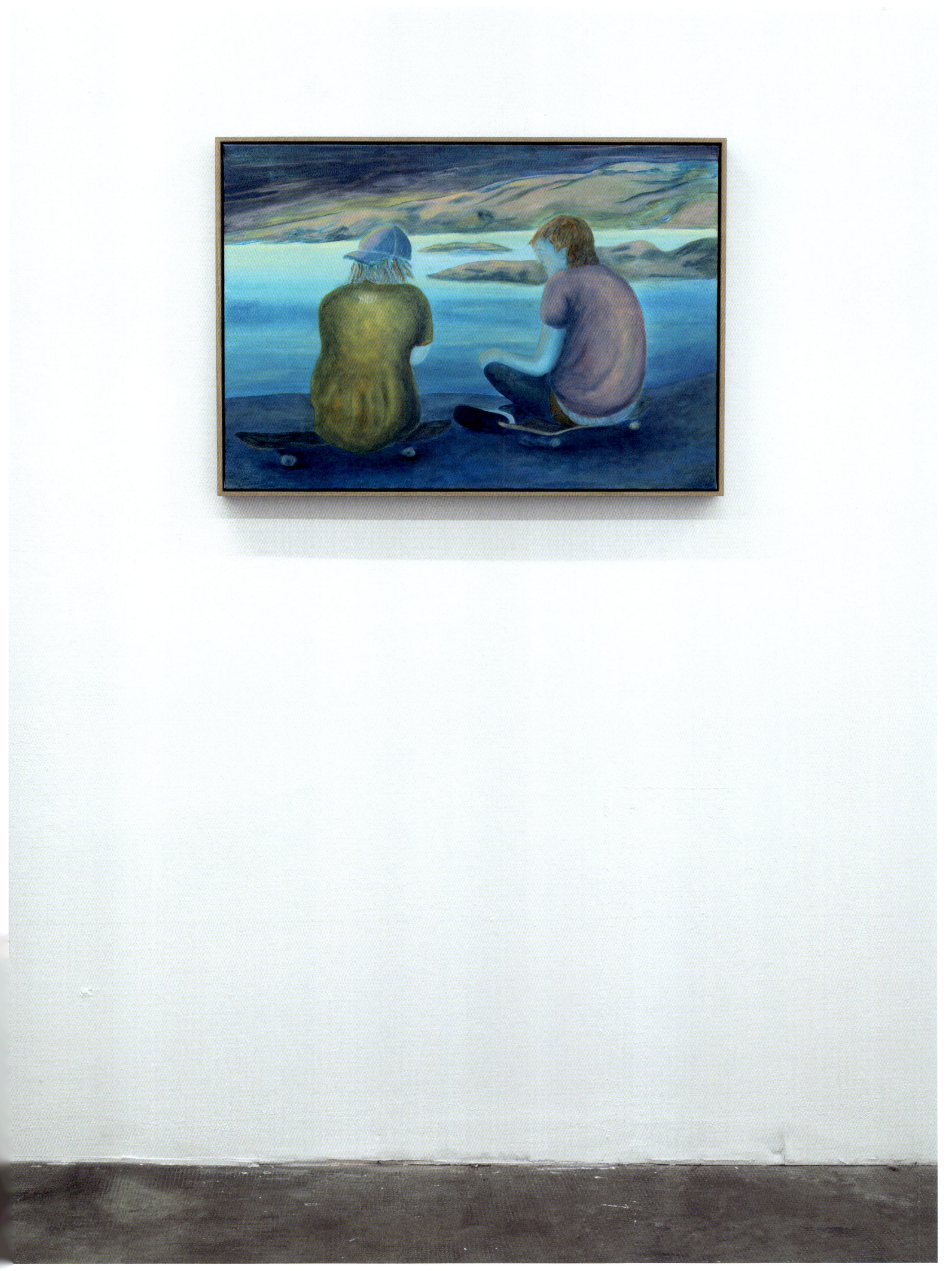

Till the Morning Rises, 2024   60.3×80.2 cm   37

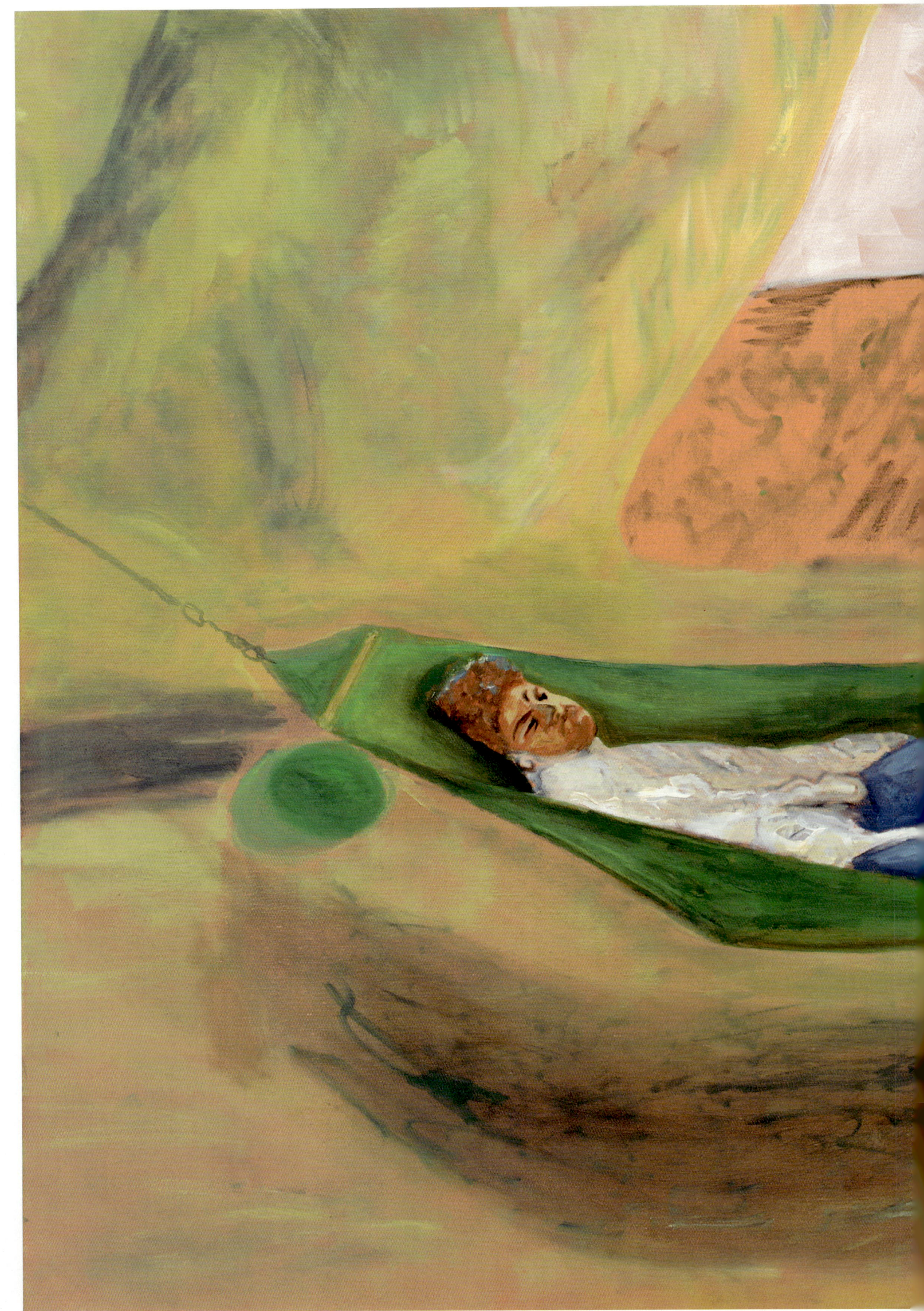

Emma Kunz' Grotte, 2024   90.5×125 cm

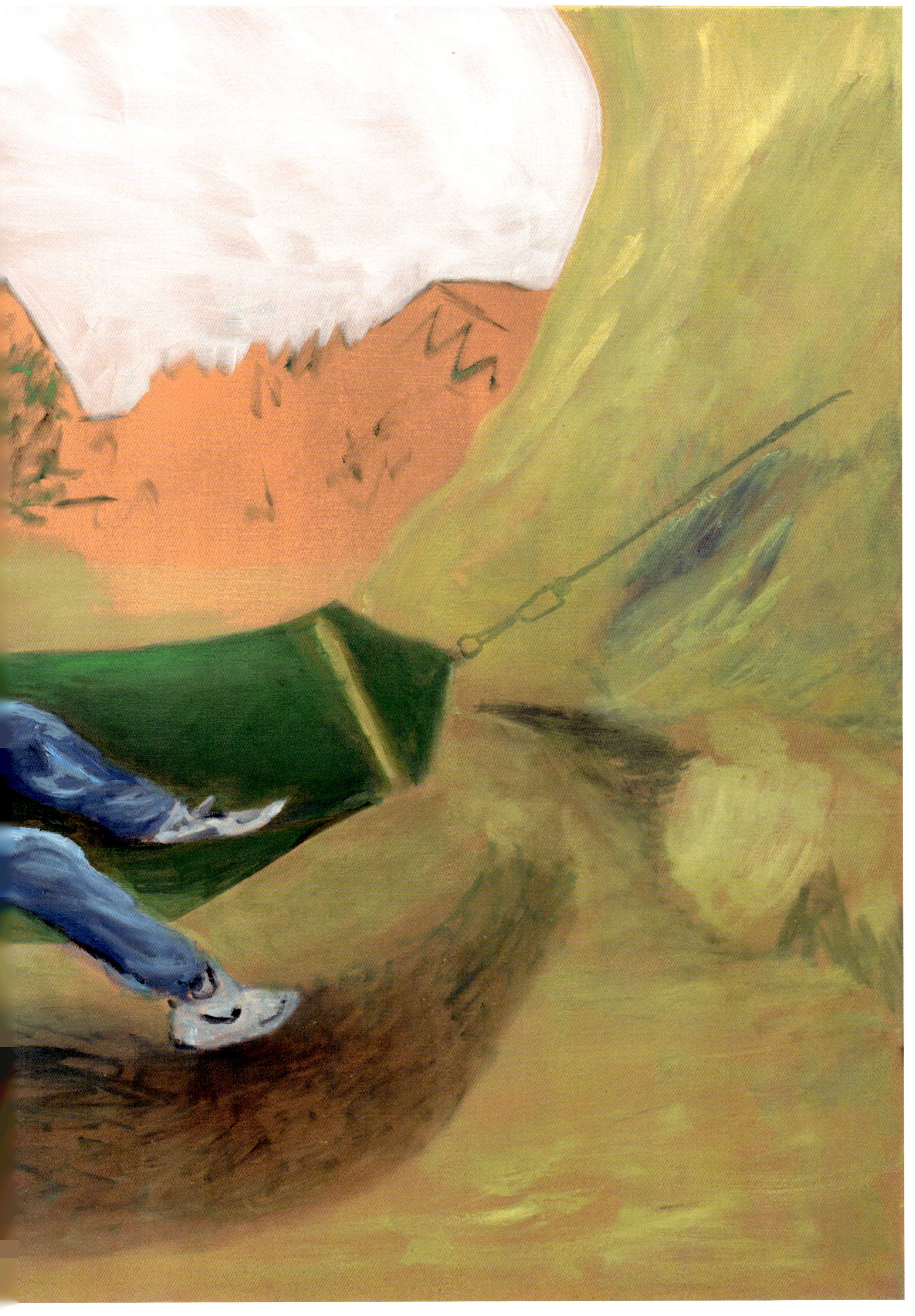

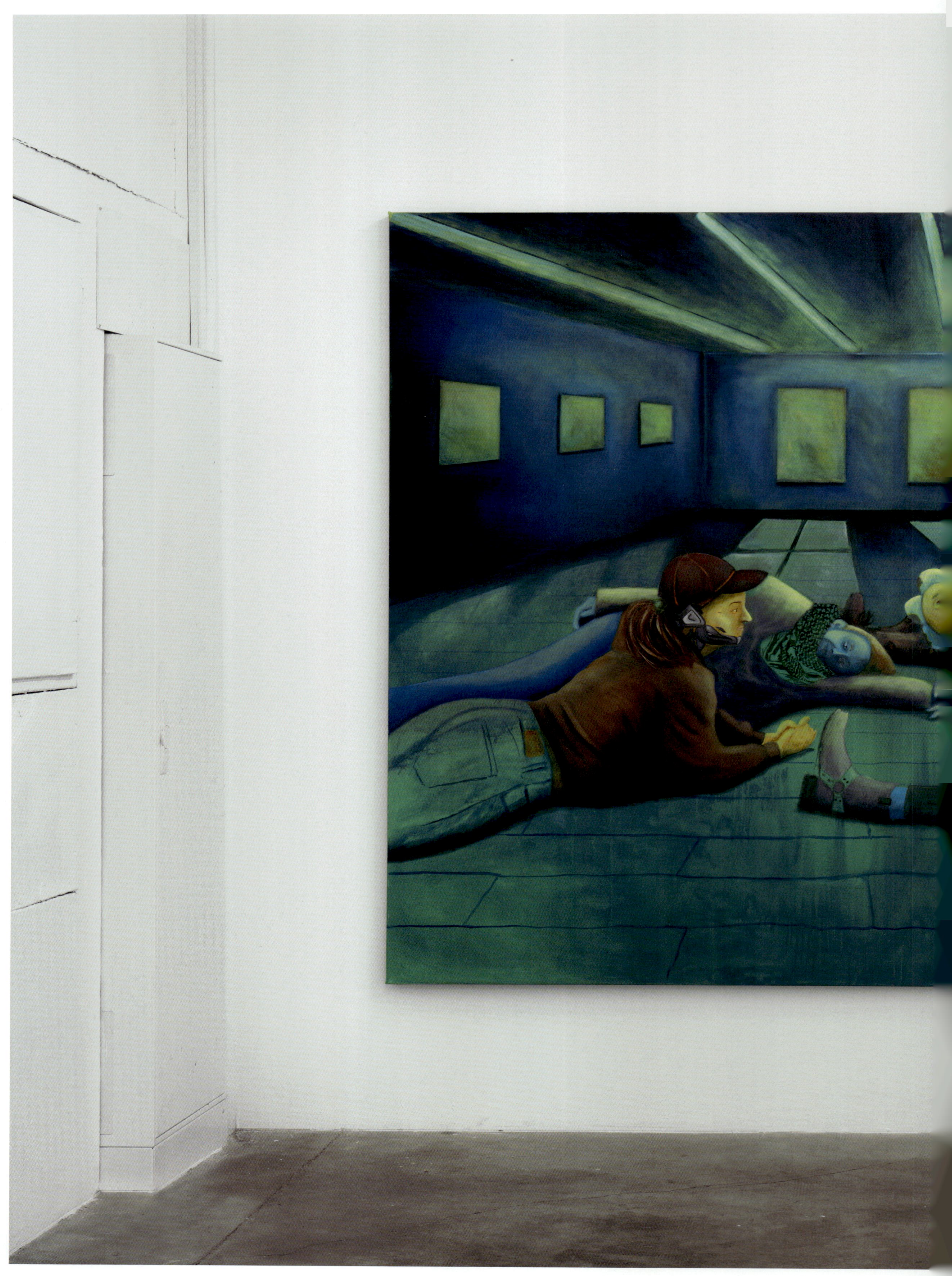

Anonymous Artists, 2024   195×306 cm

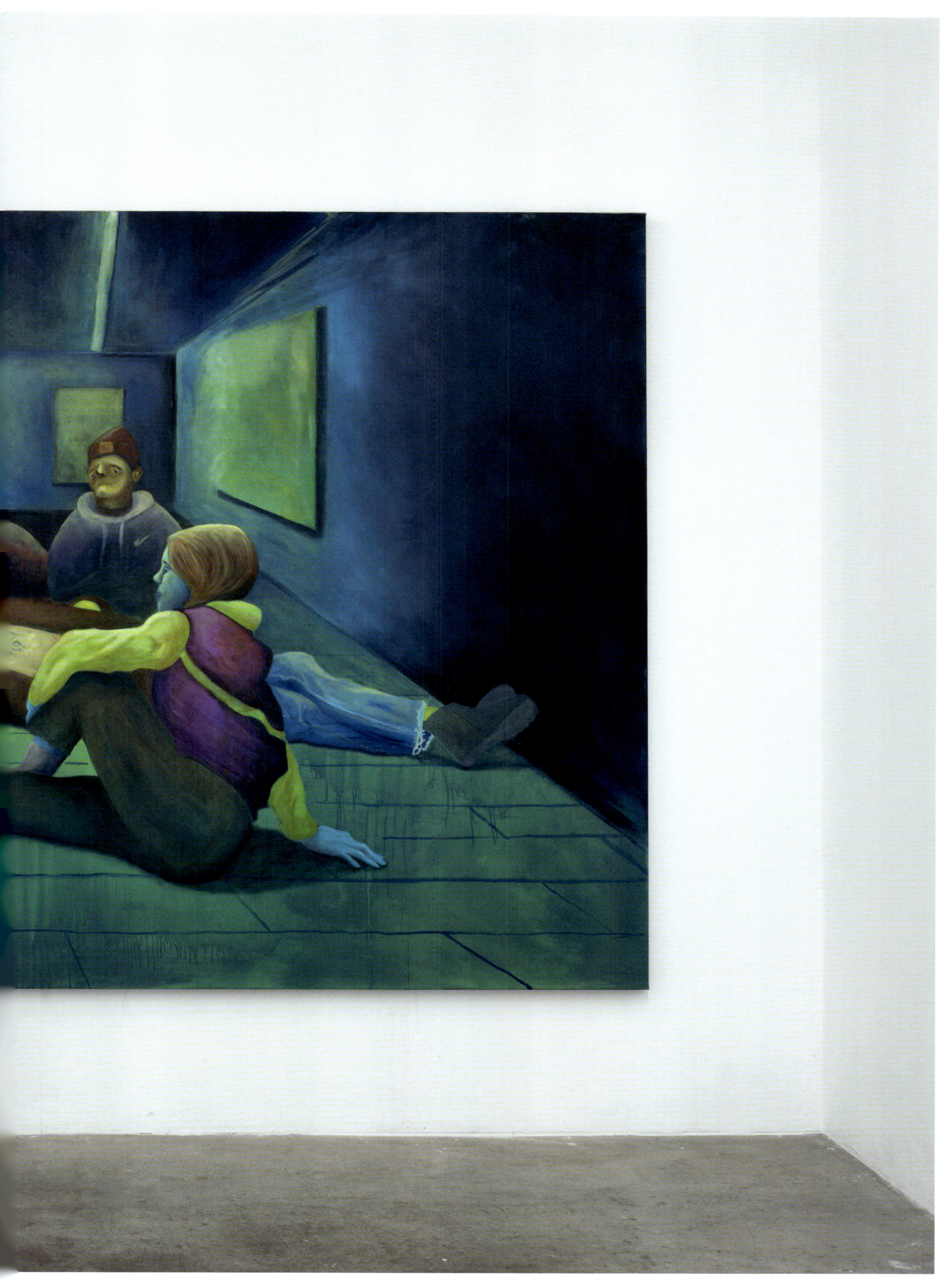

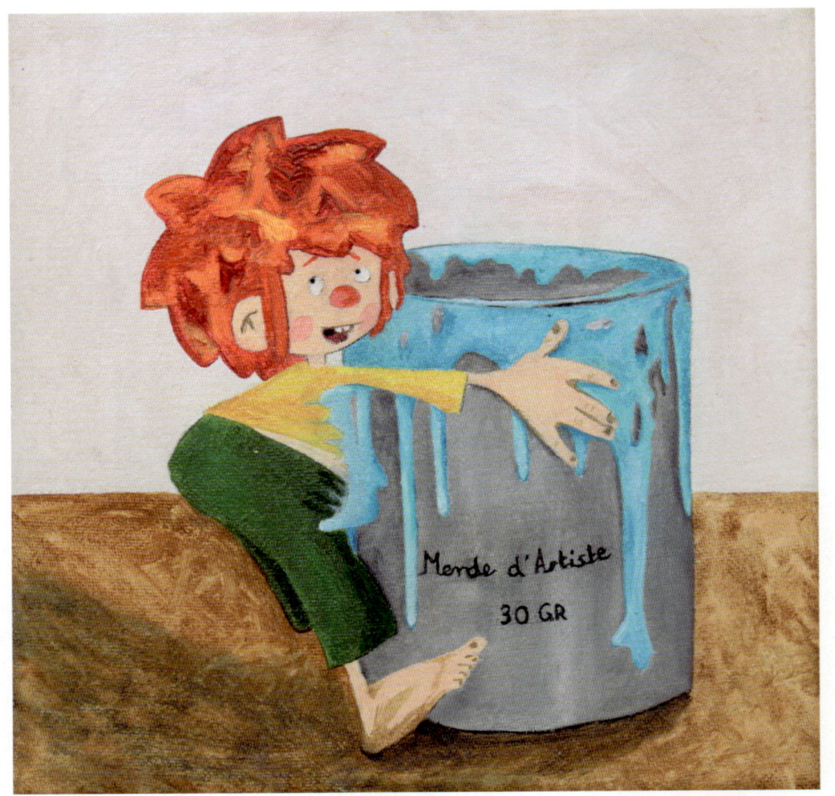

Merde d'Artiste, 2024   20×20 cm

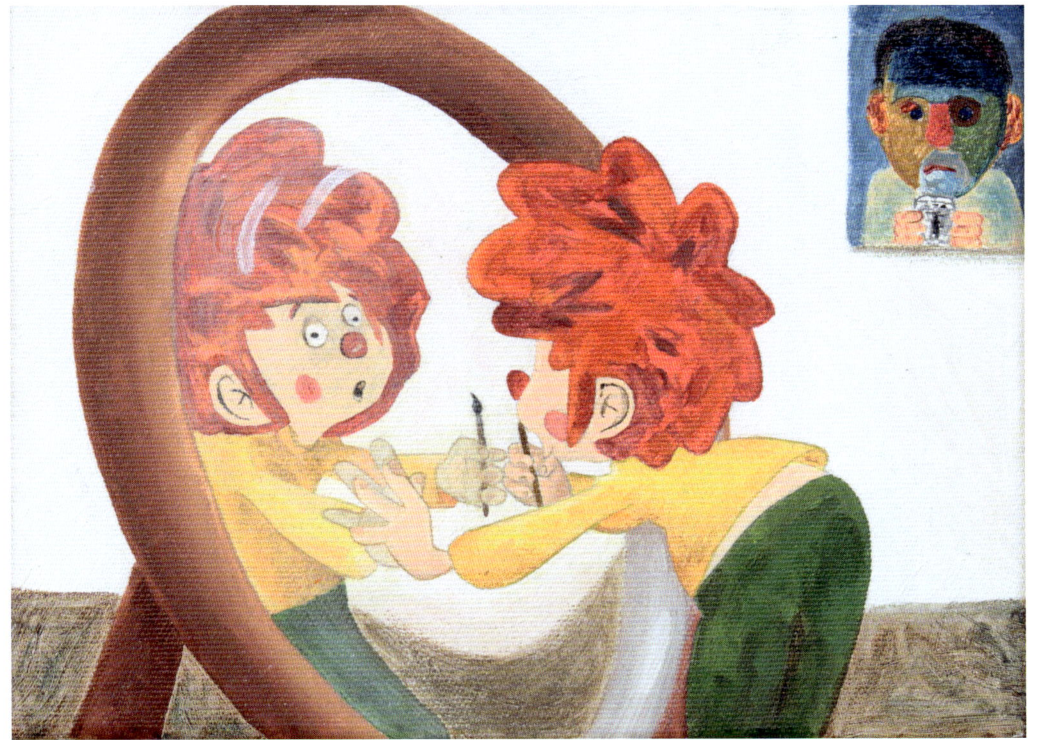

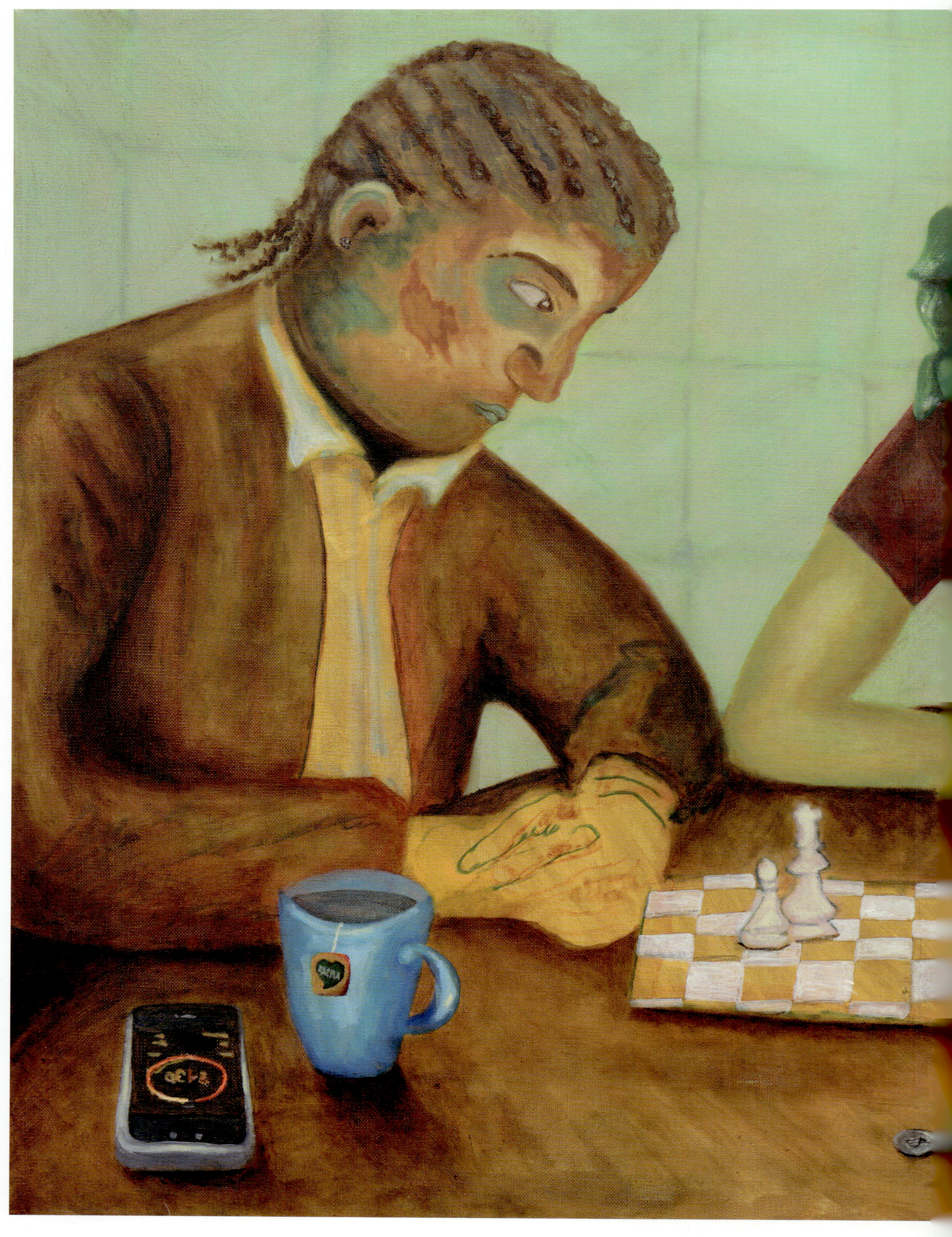

No Counterpart, 2024   61×95 cm

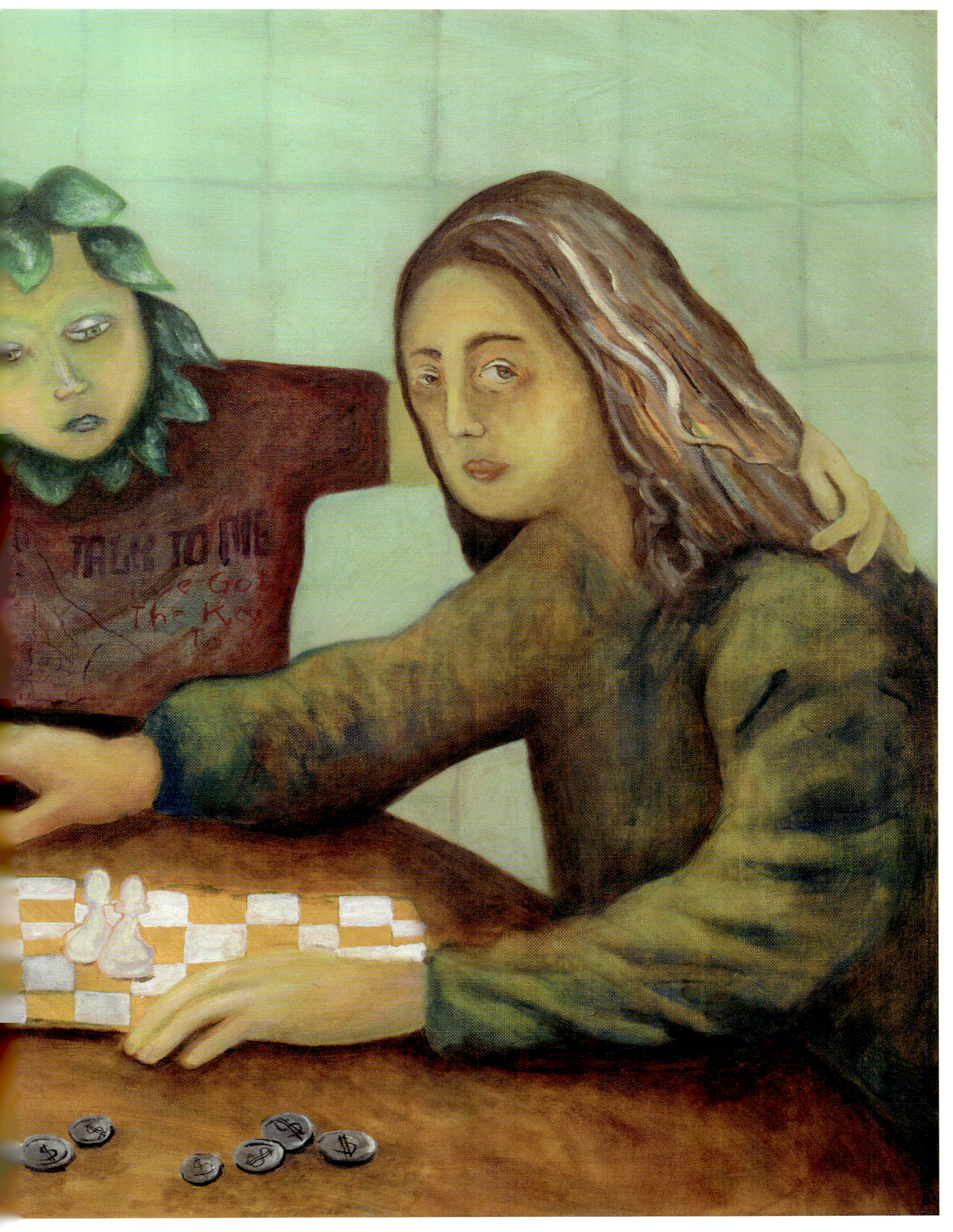

TALK TO ME
I've Got
Th- Key
To

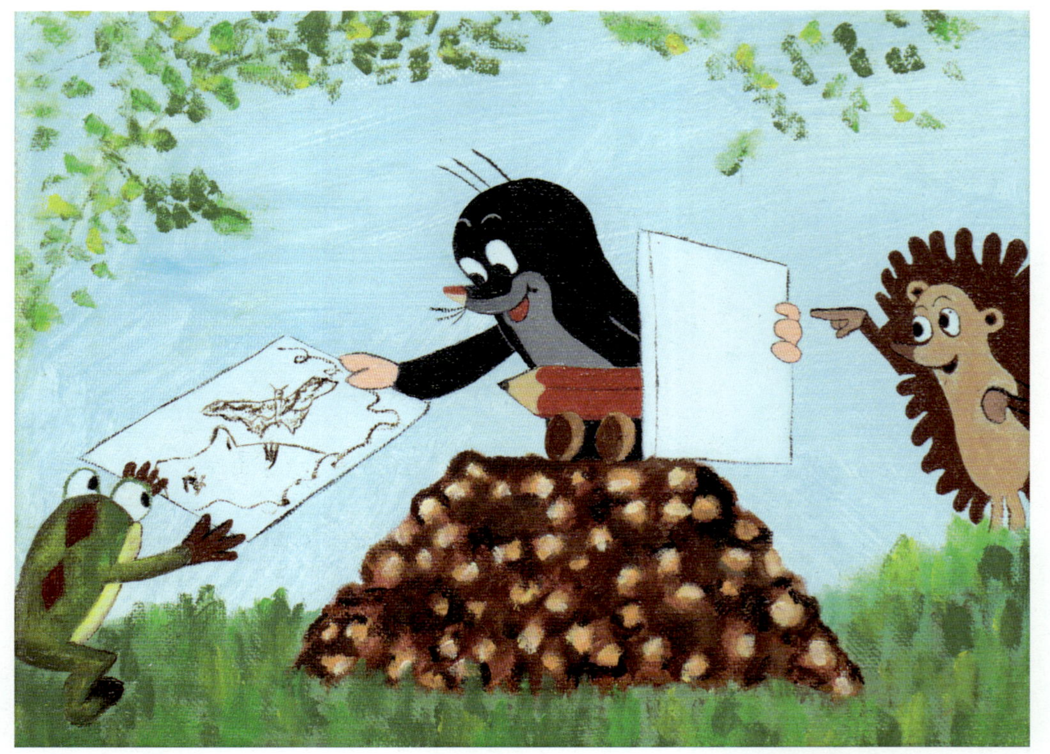

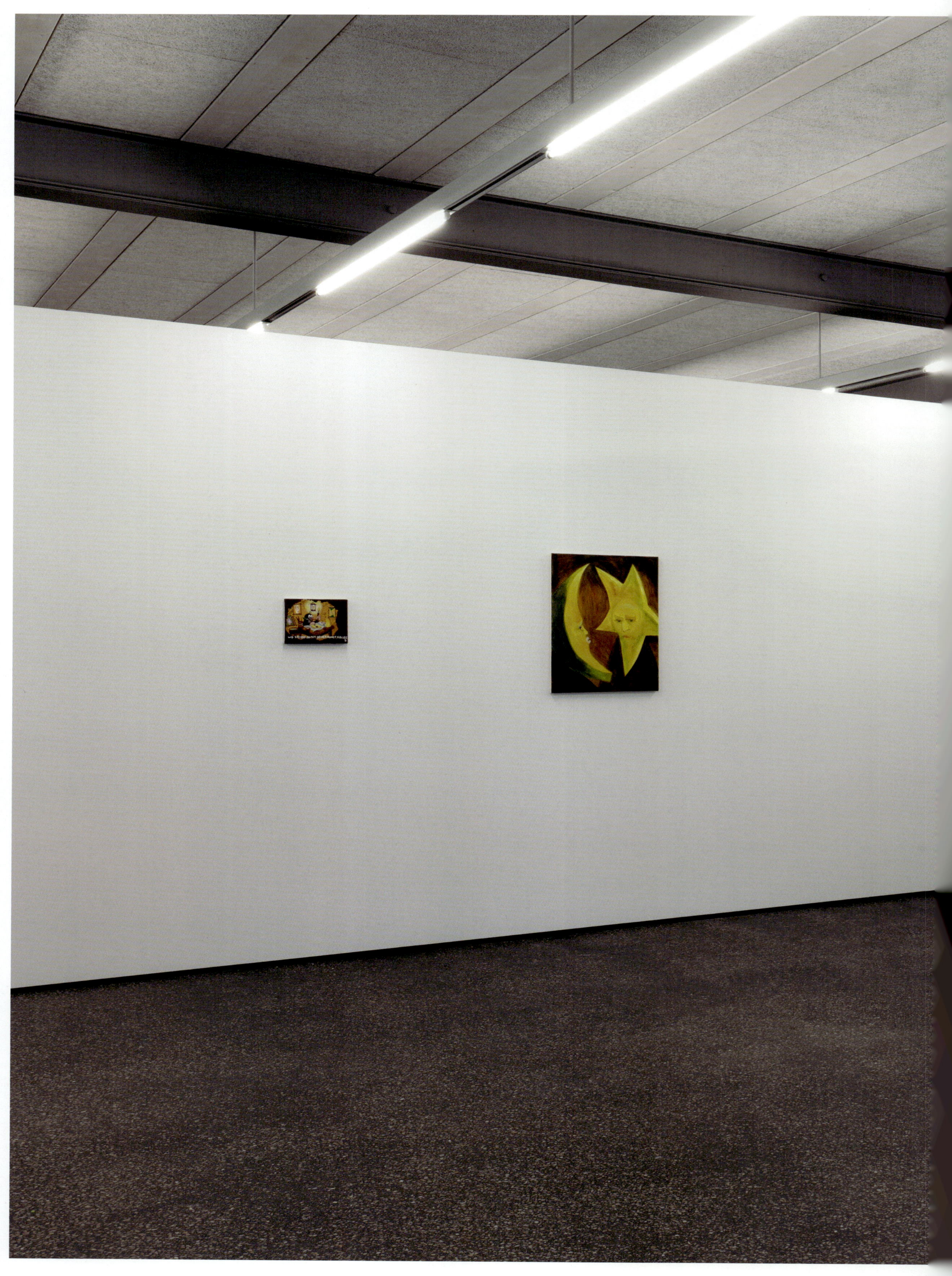

Mirror Mirror on the Wall, 2024   Alte Fabrik, Rapperswil   48

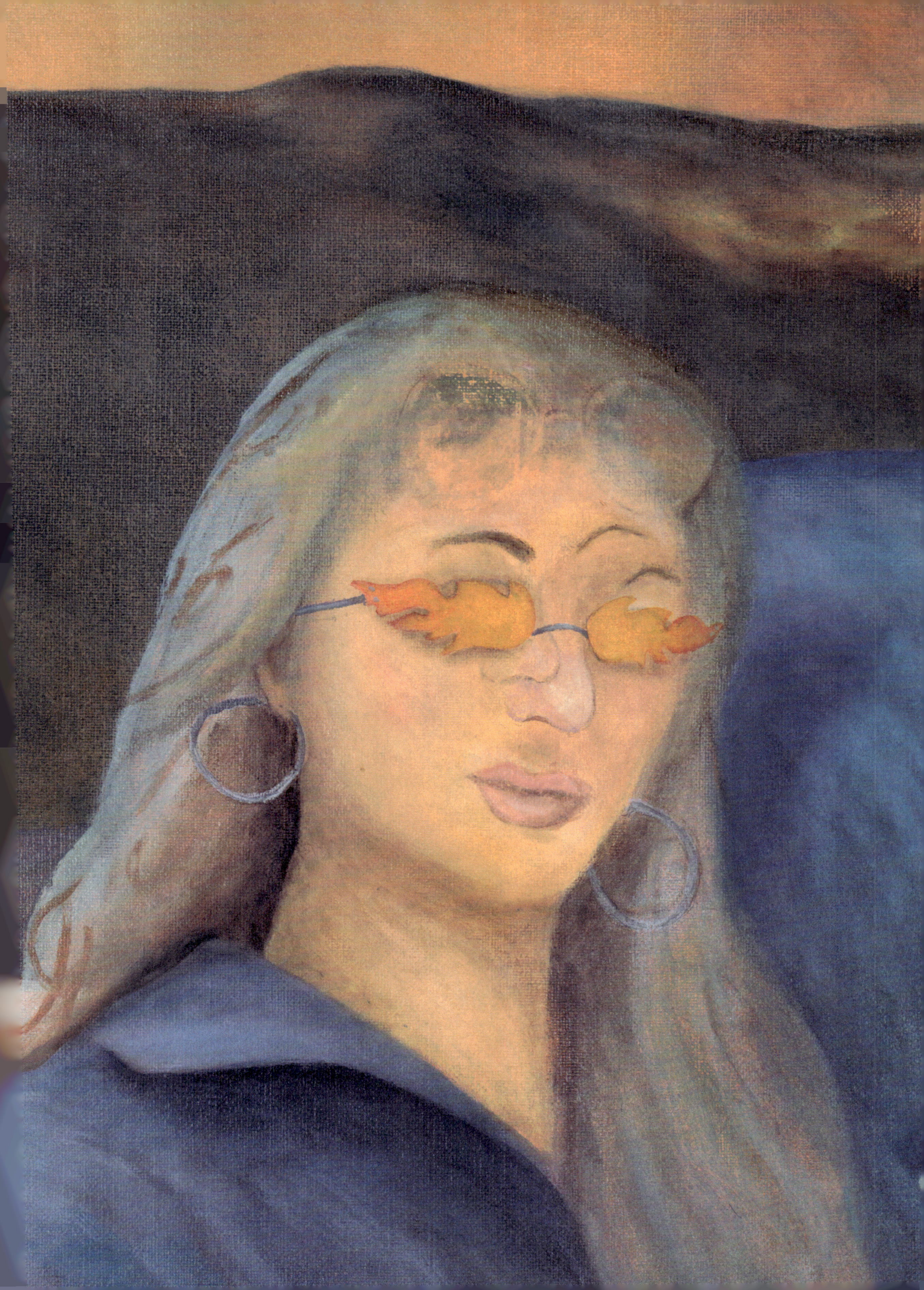

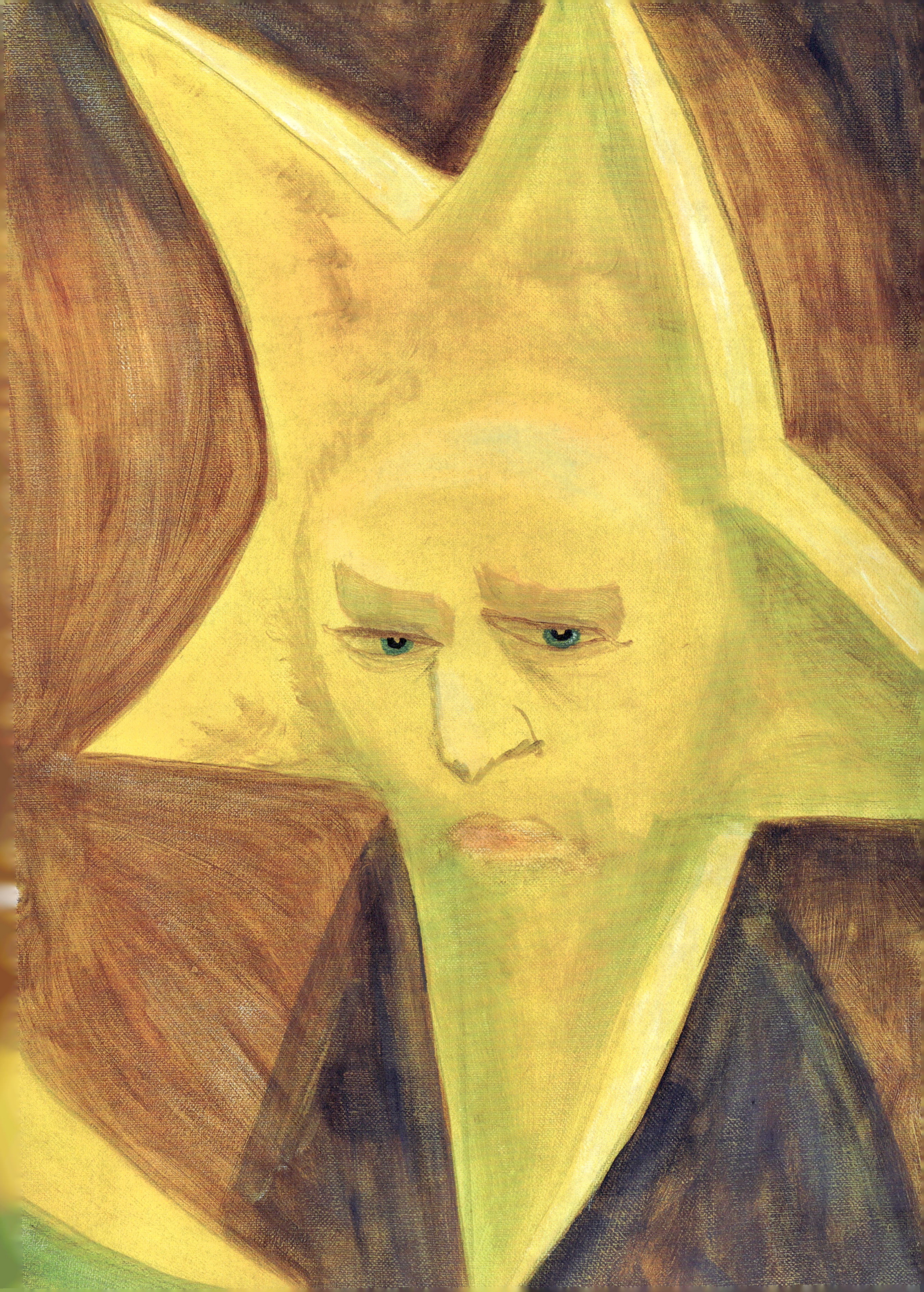

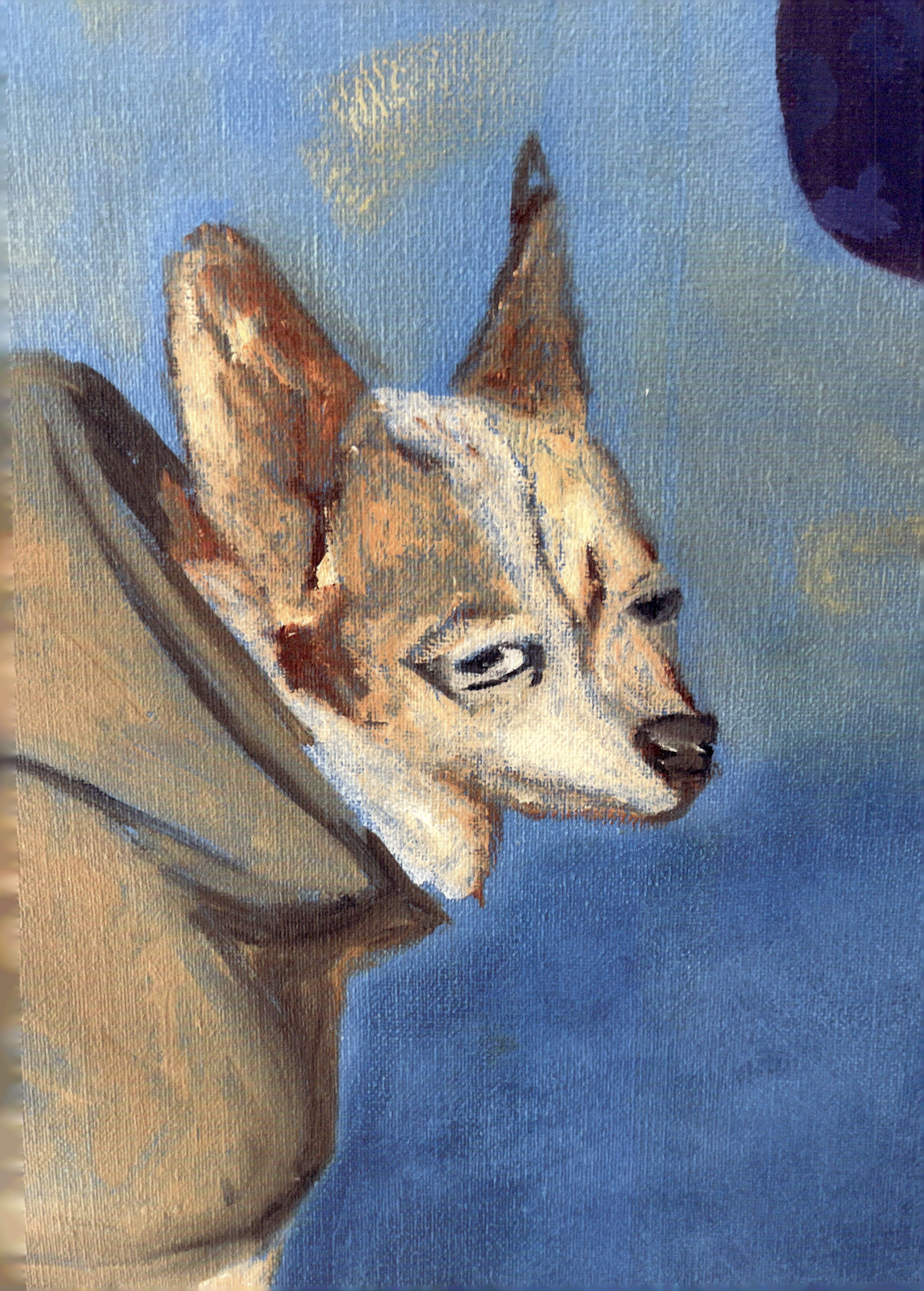

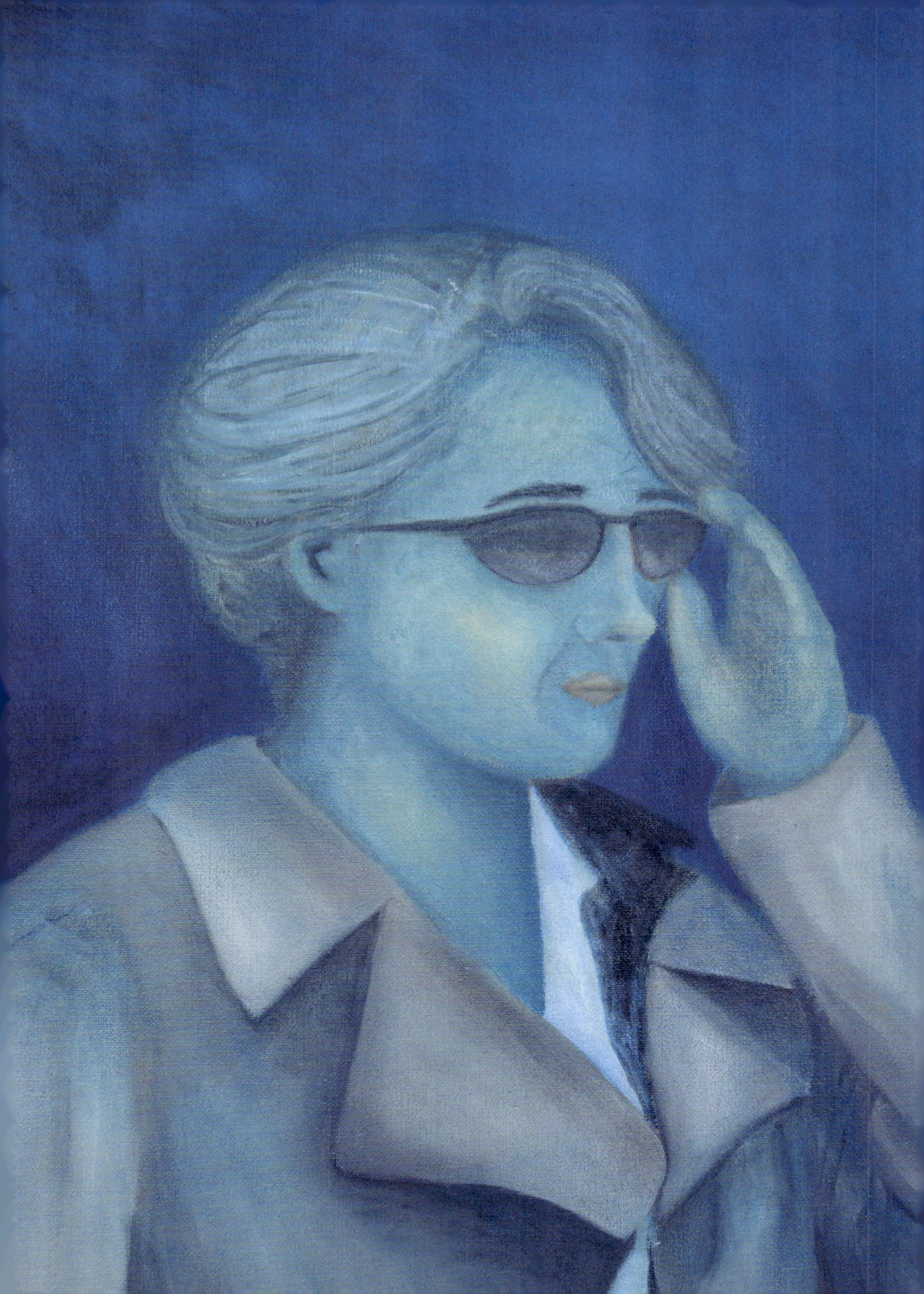

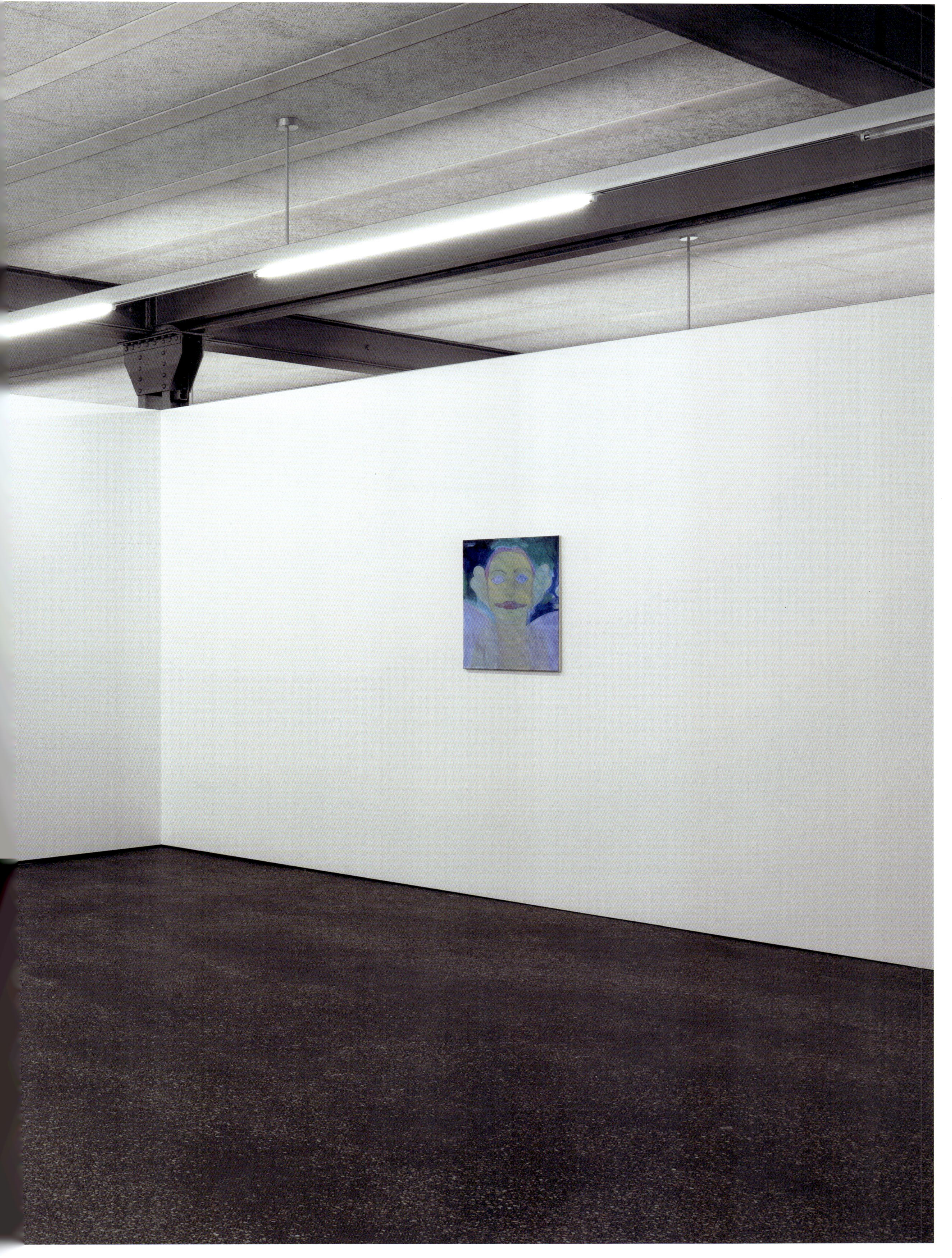

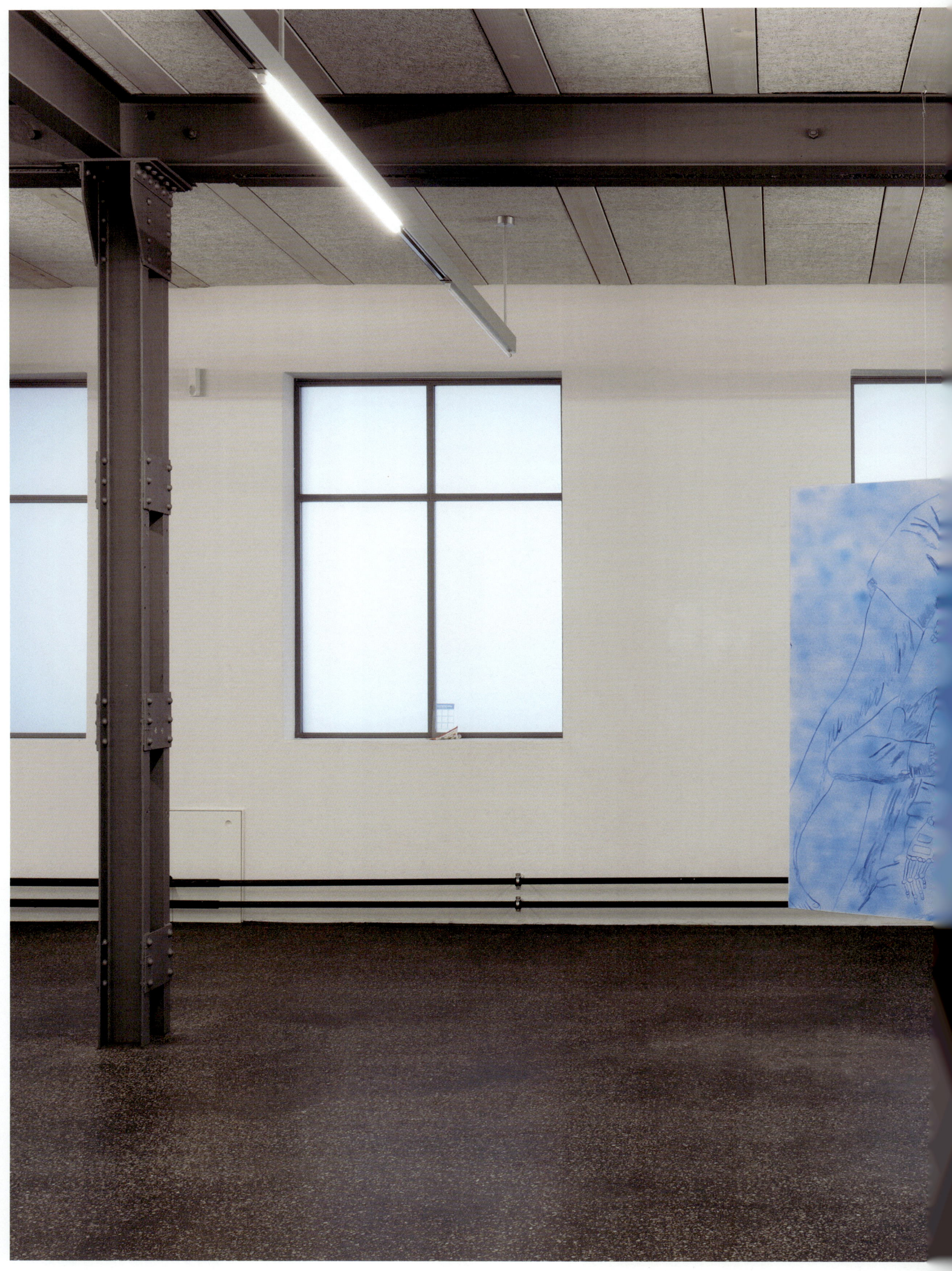

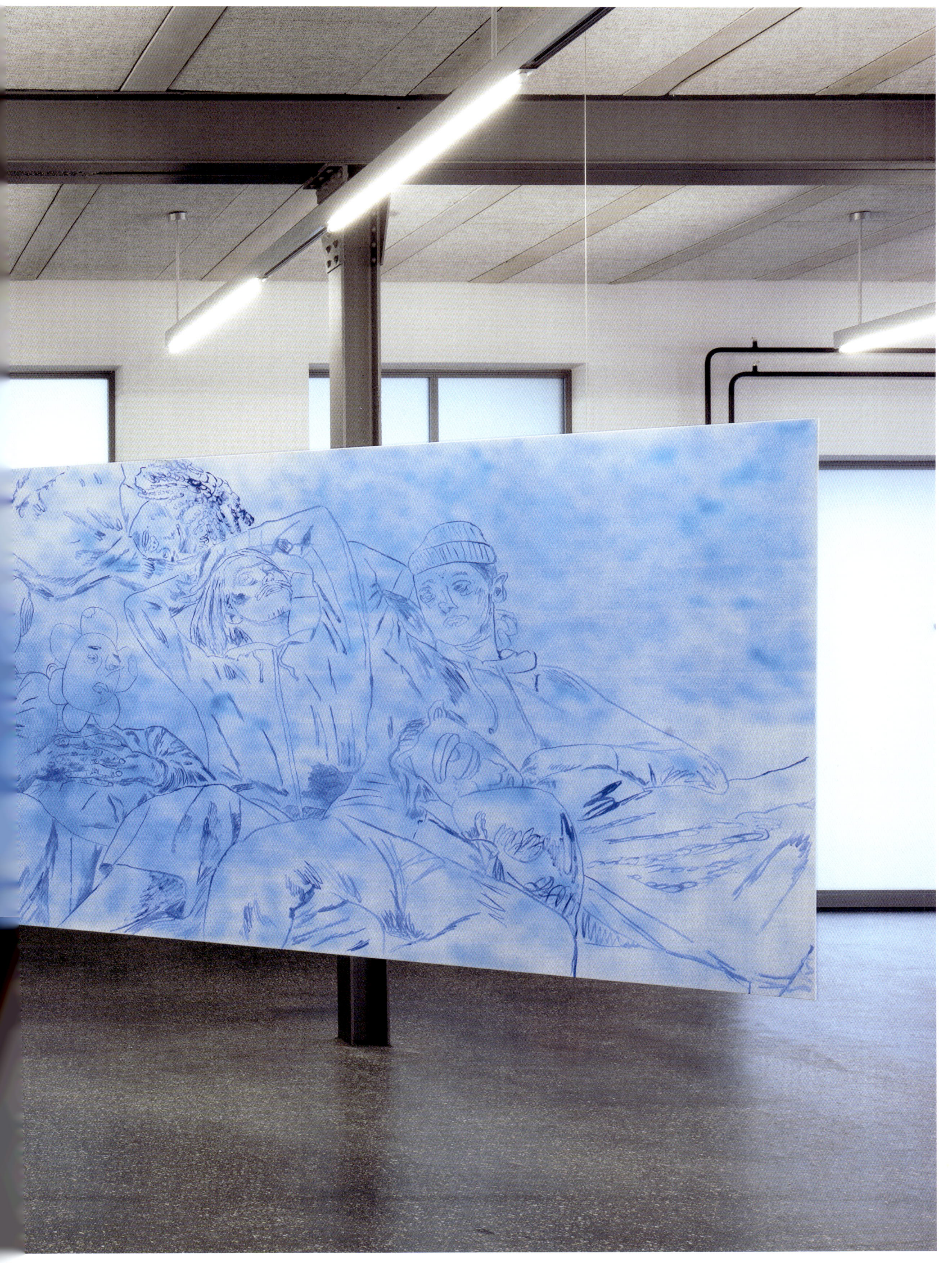

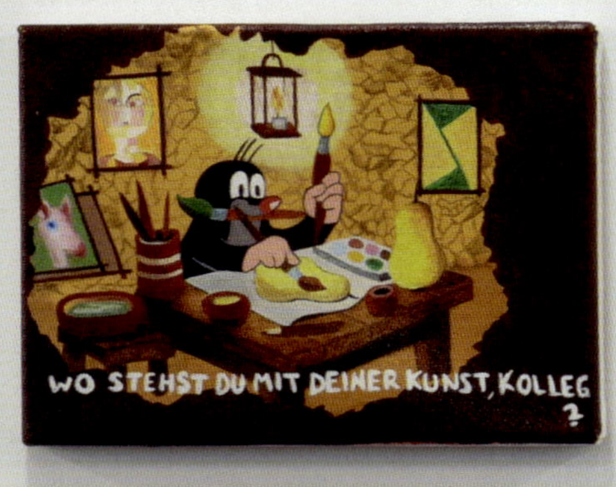
WO STEHST DU MIT DEINER KUNST, KOLLEG?

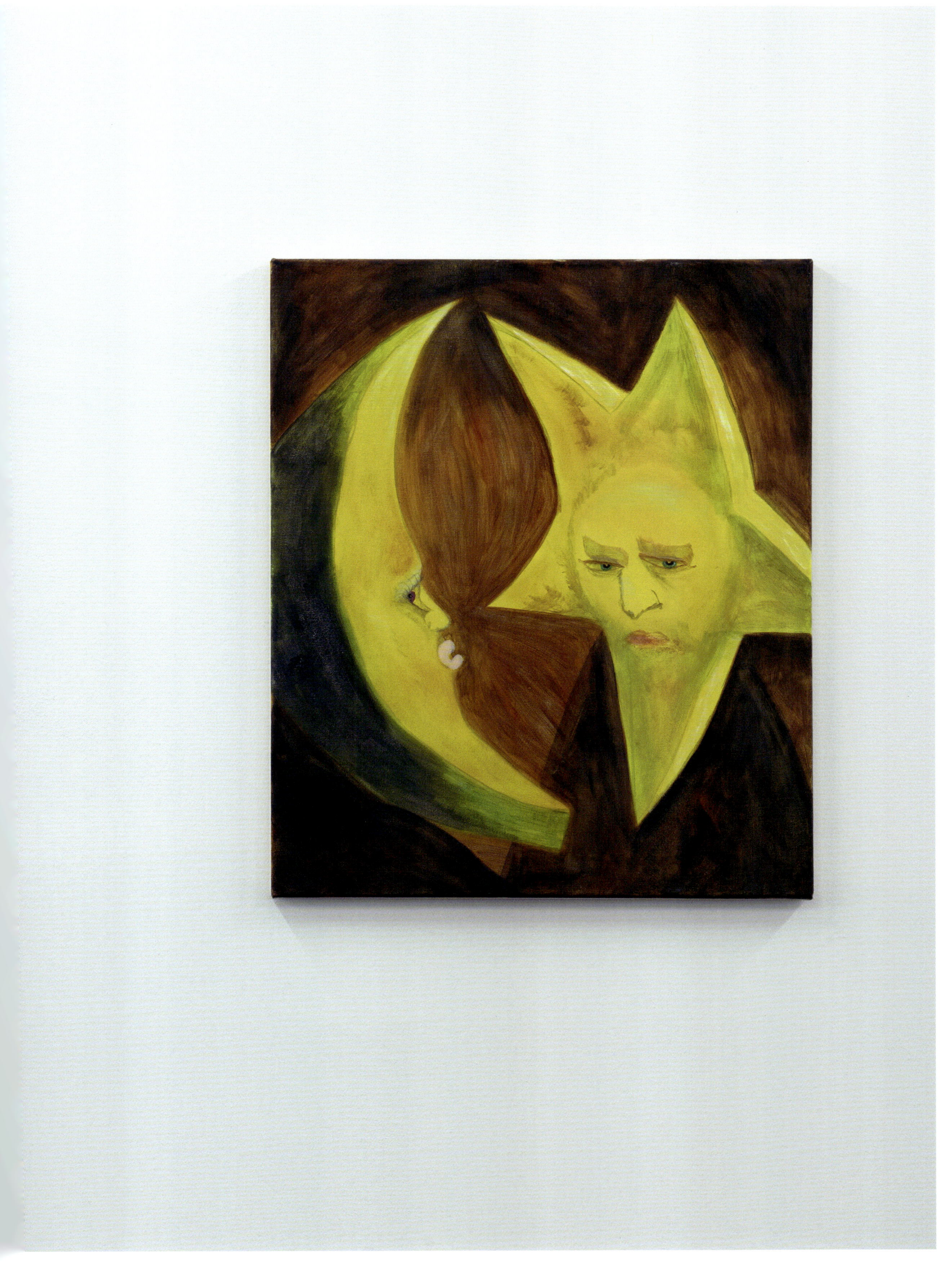

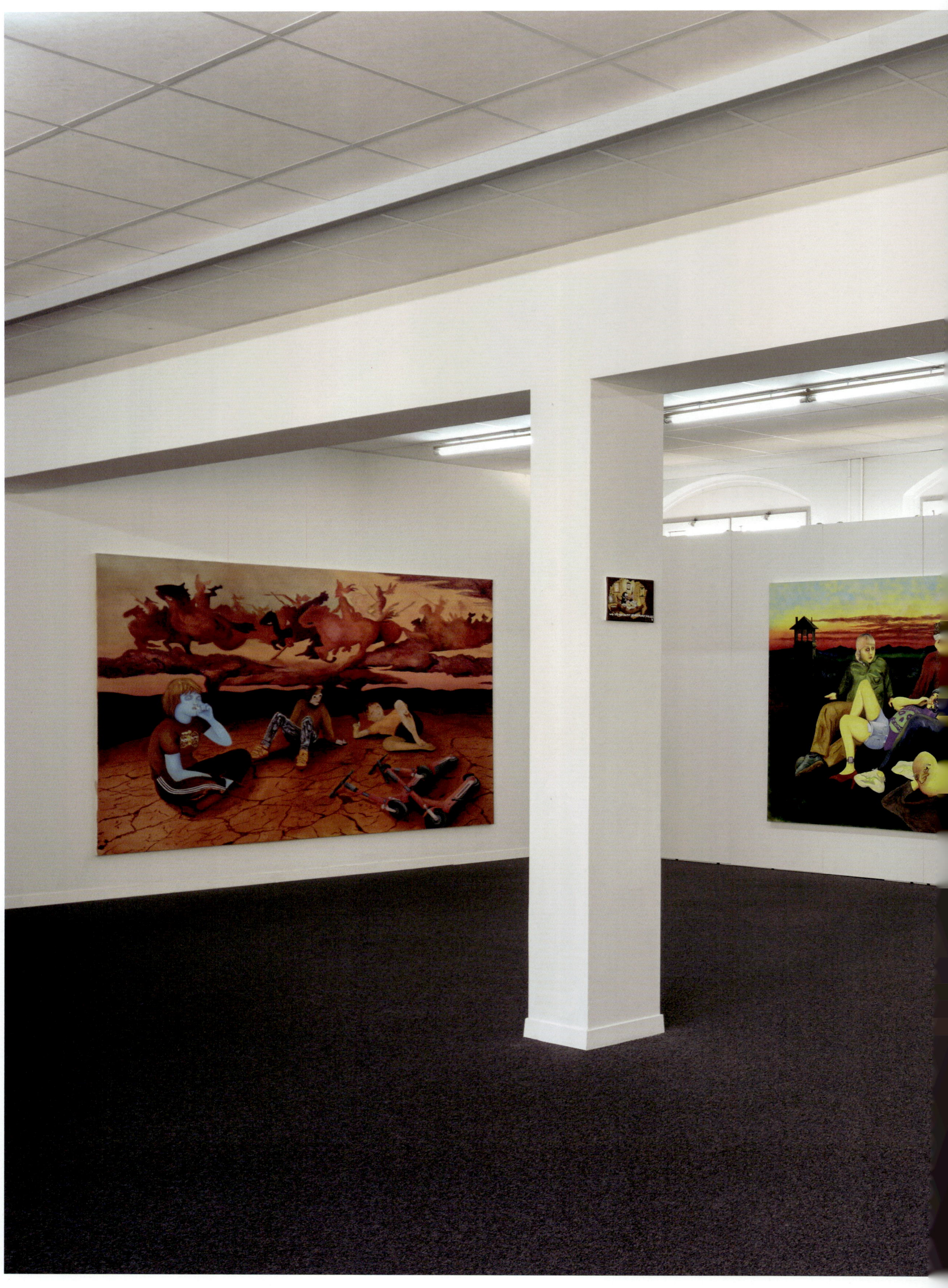

Fixing the Shoes with Glue, So Many Times, 2023

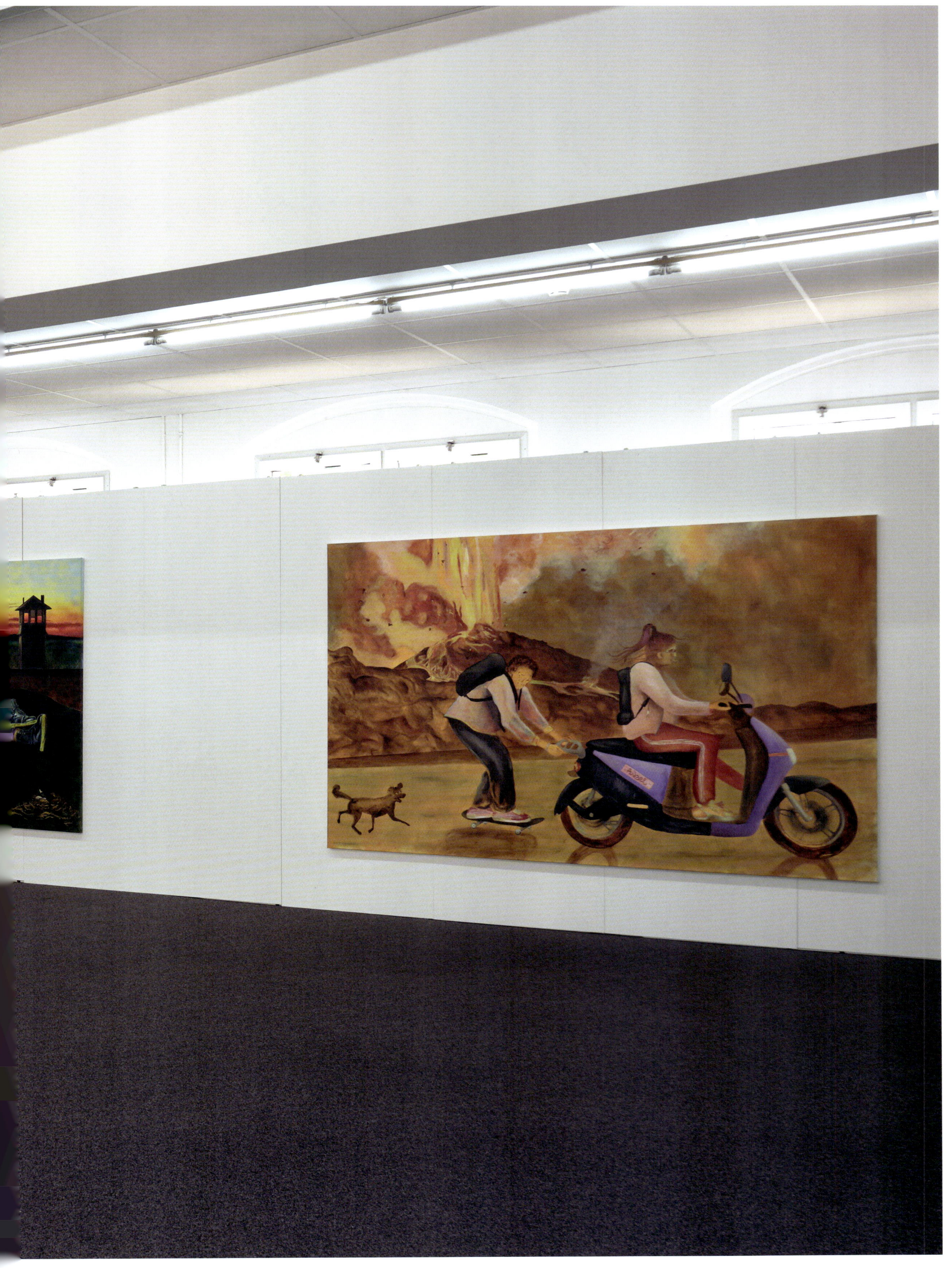

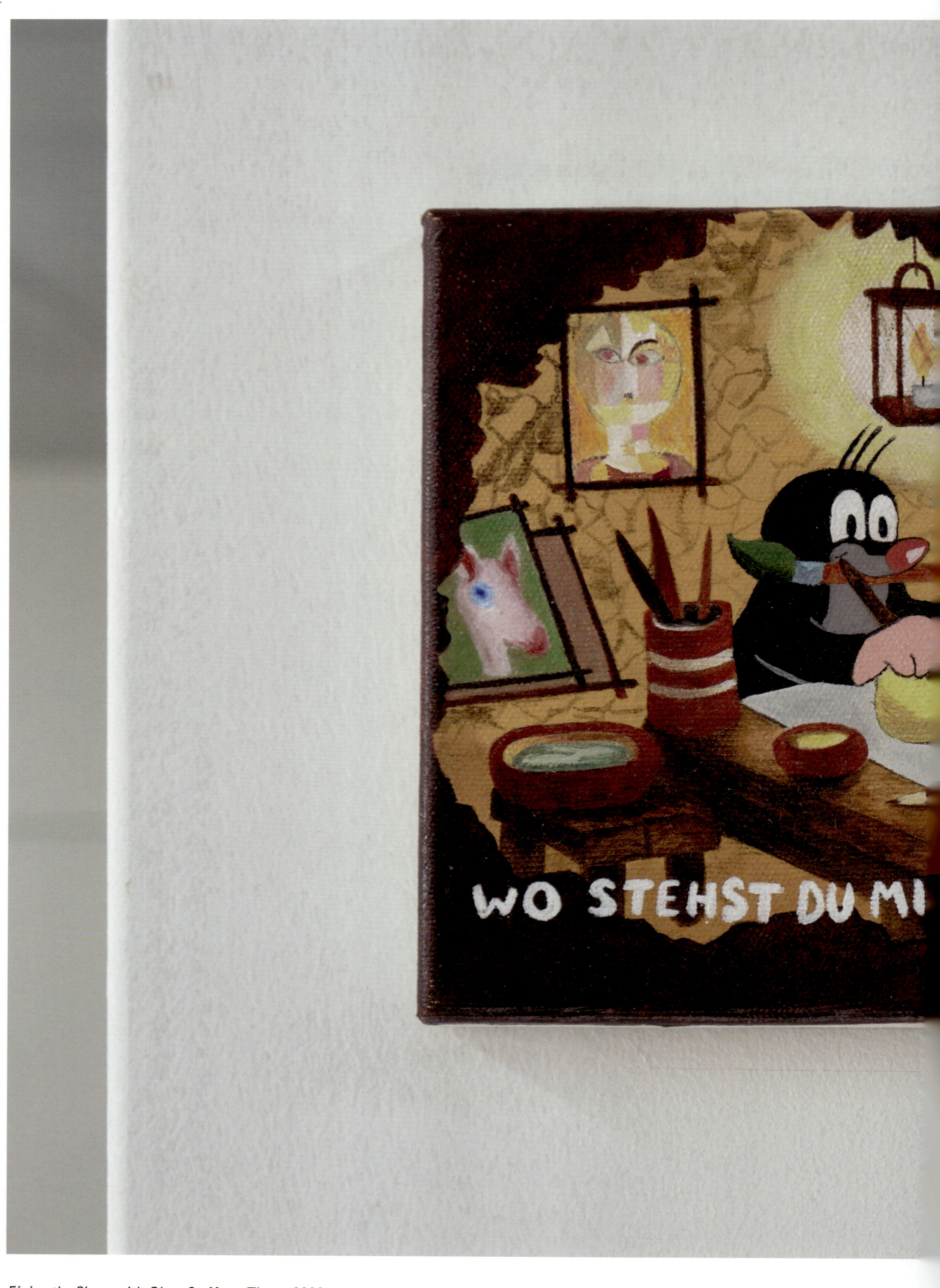

WO STEHST DU MI

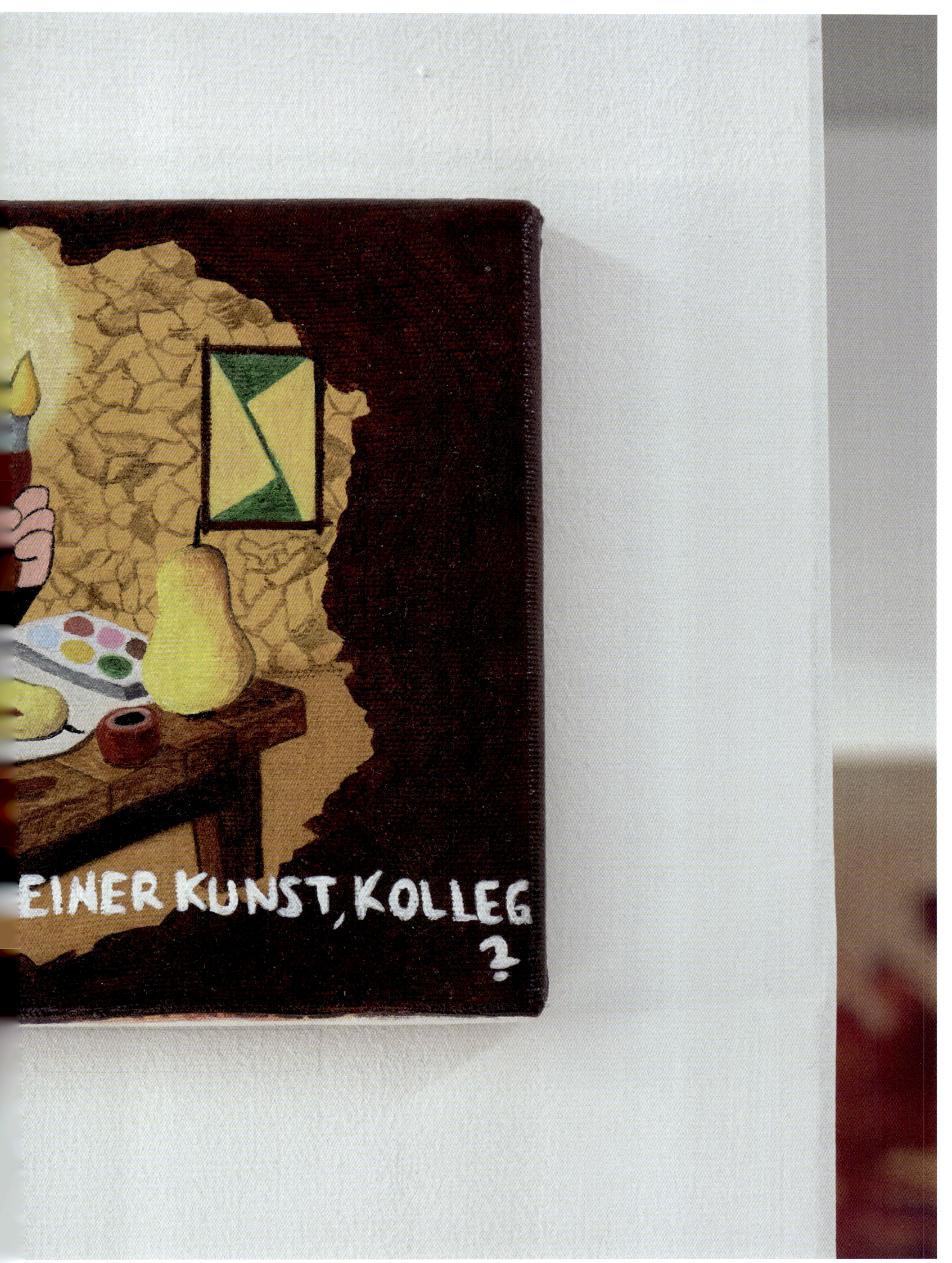
EINER KUNST, KOLLEG
?

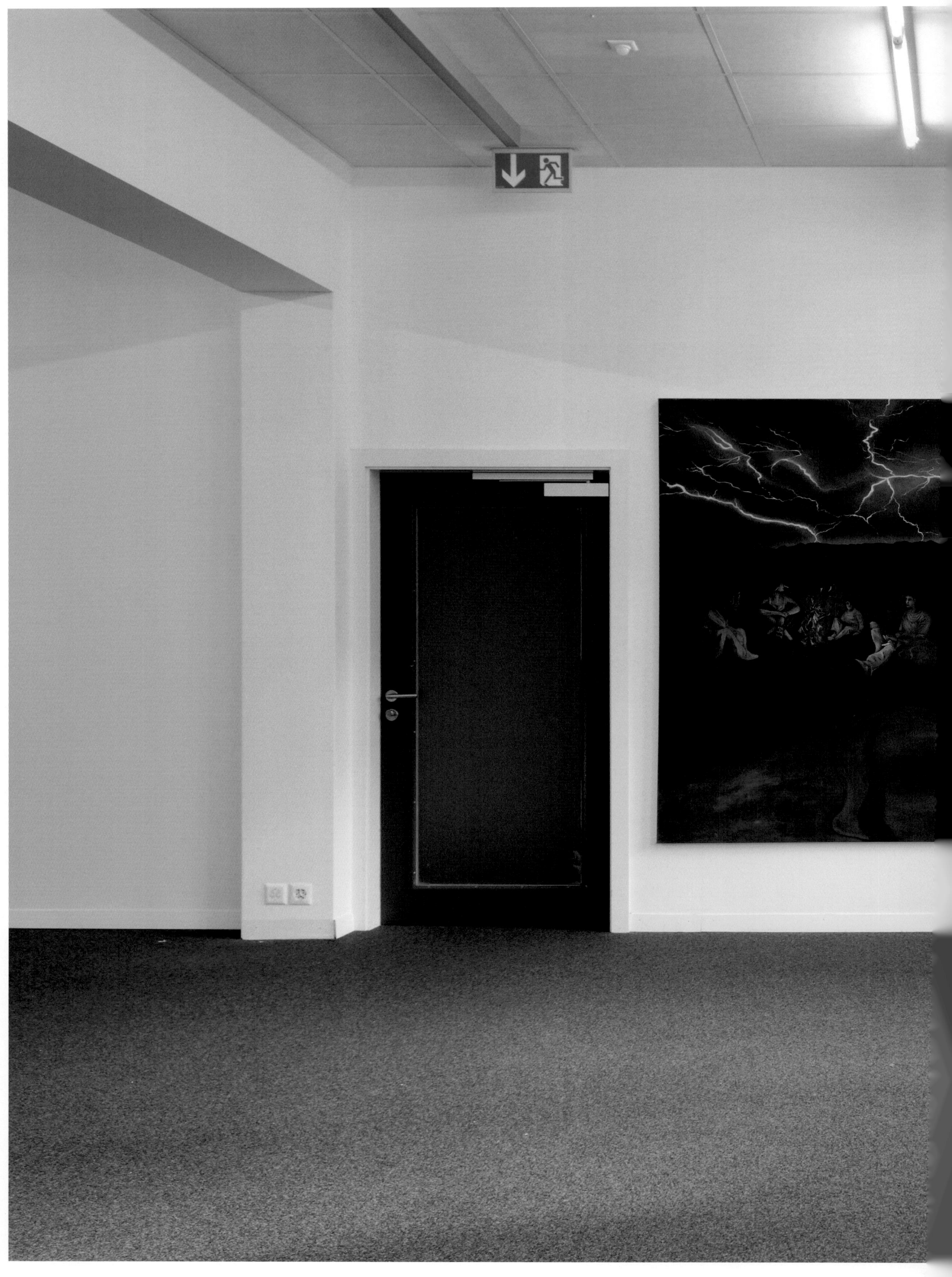

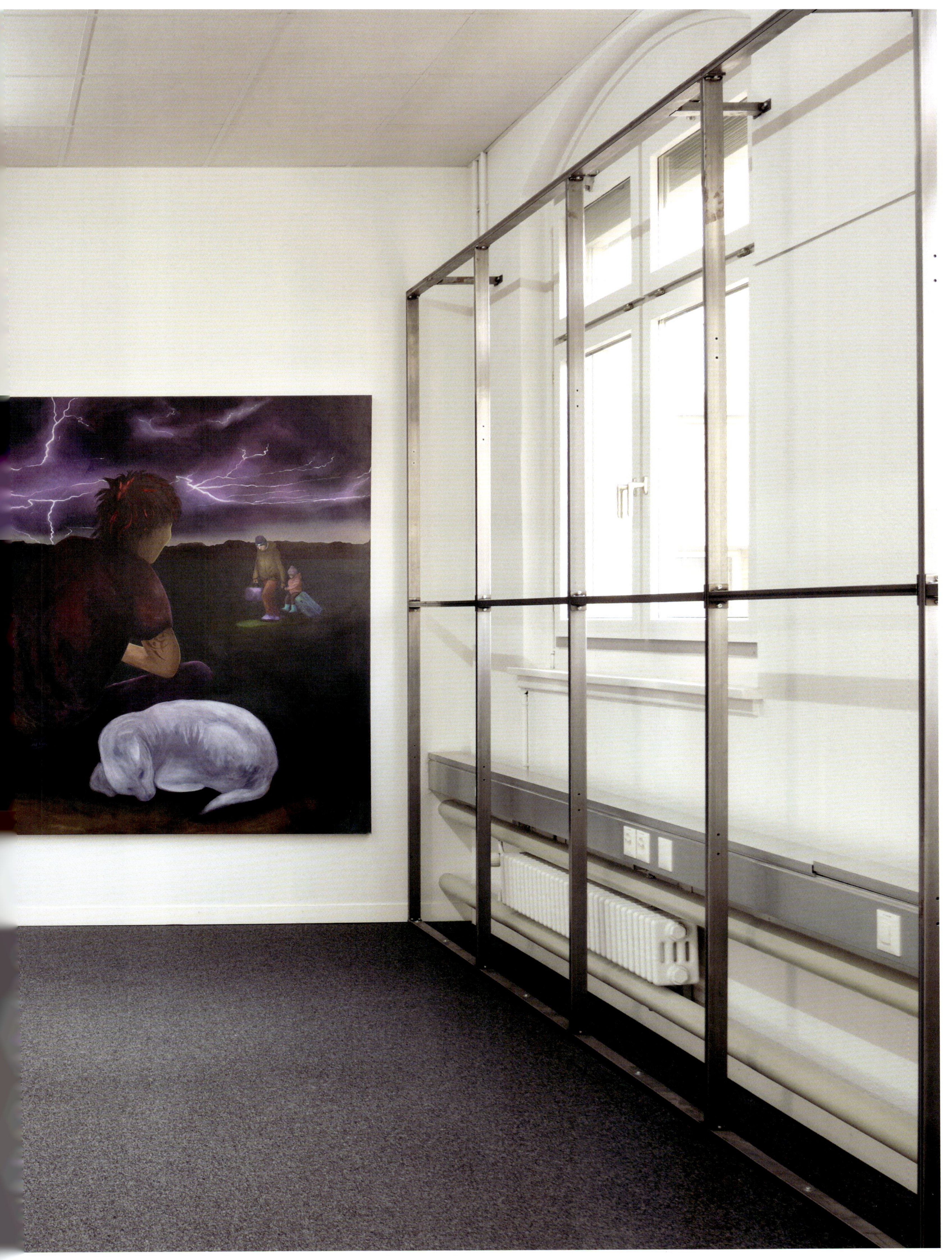

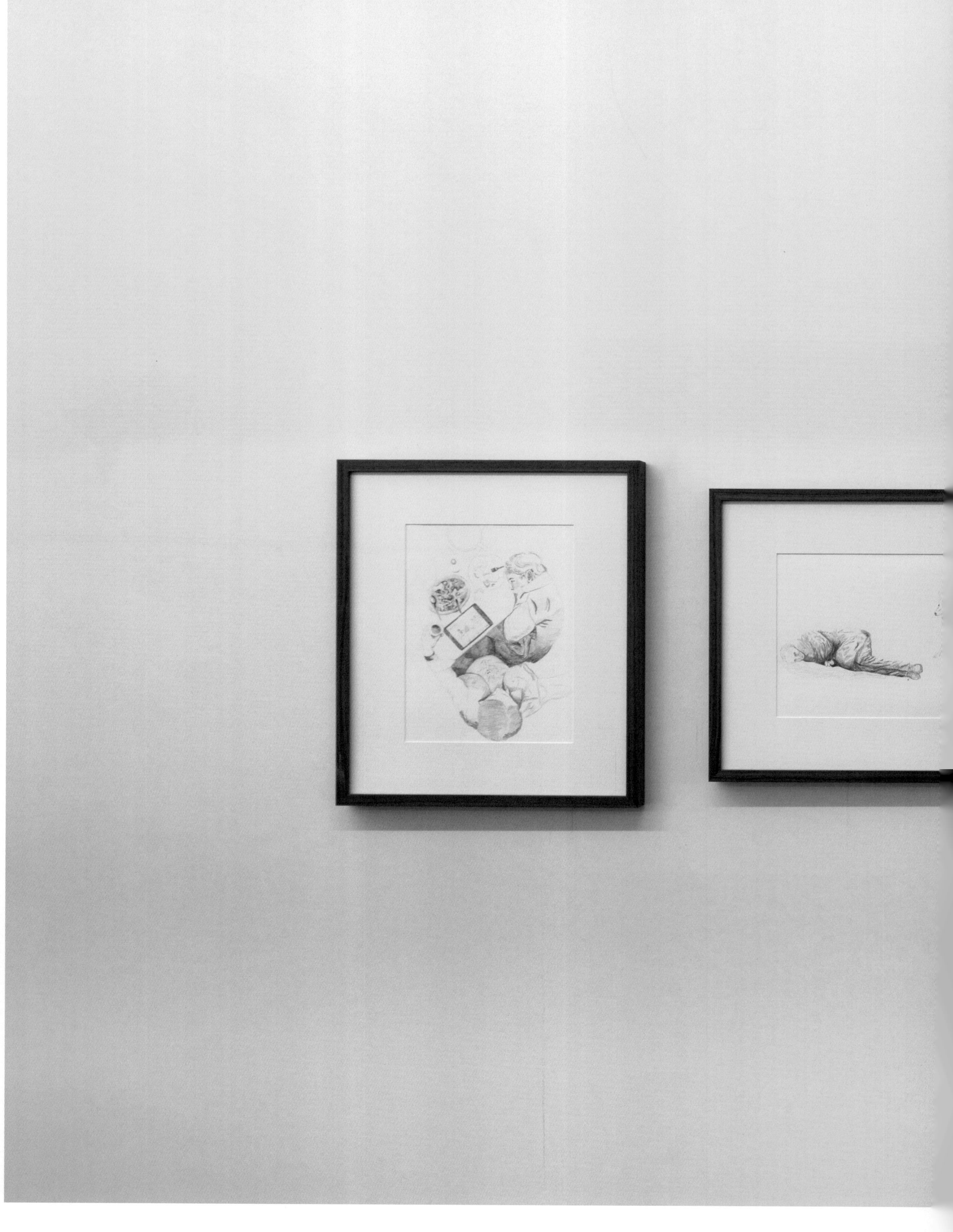

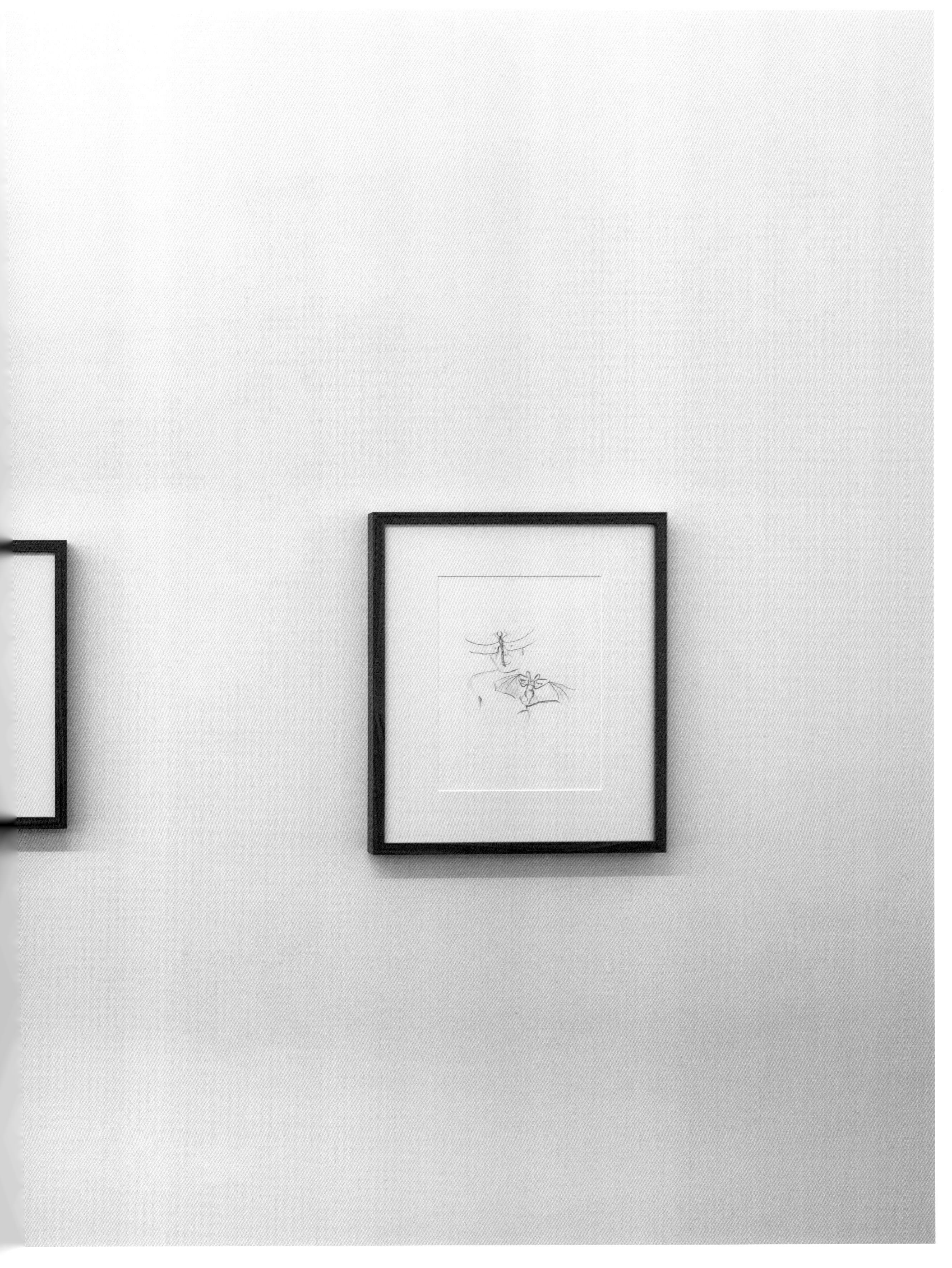

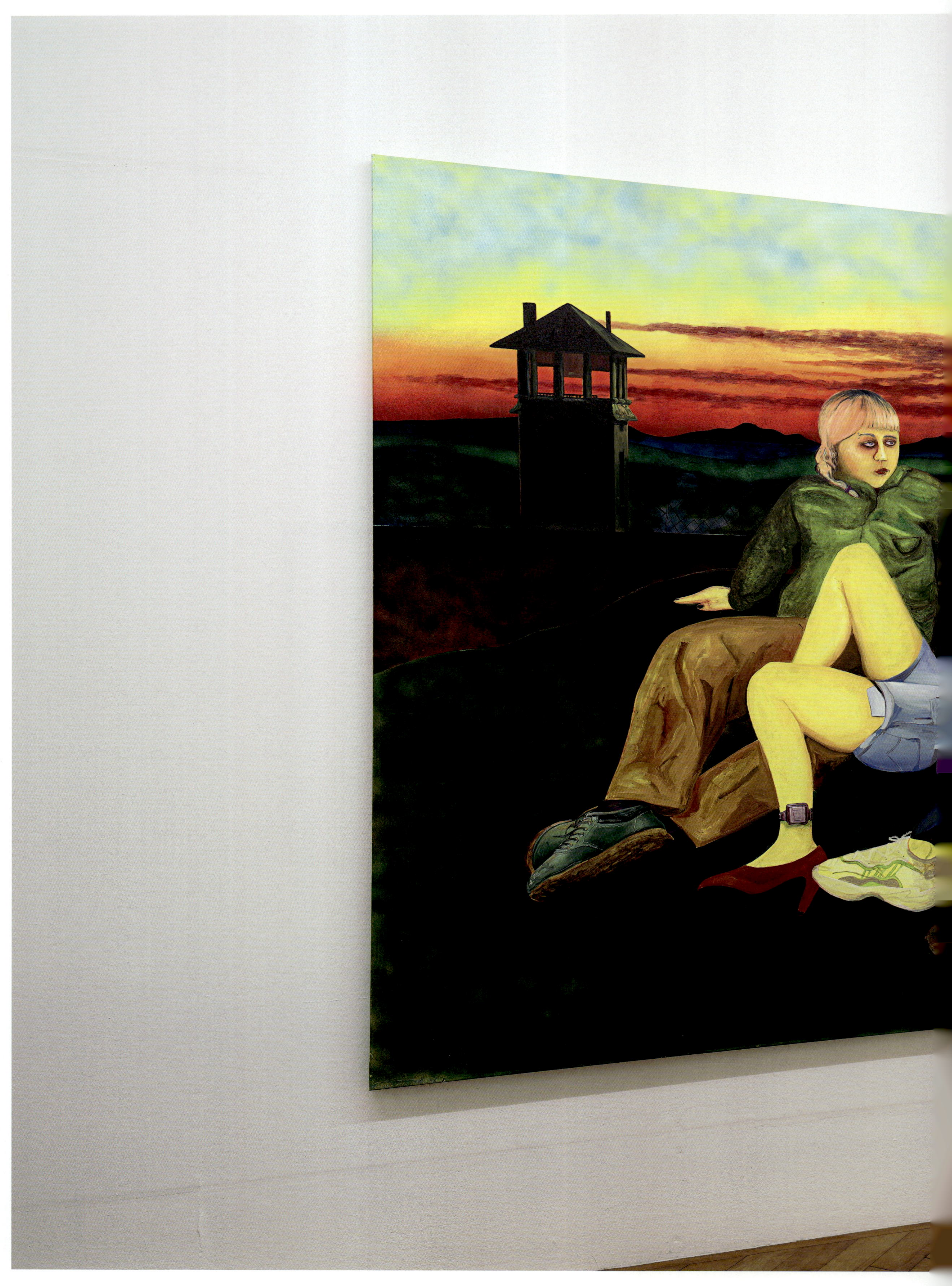

Vom Körper im Digitalen Leben, 2024   Kunsthaus Langenthal   70

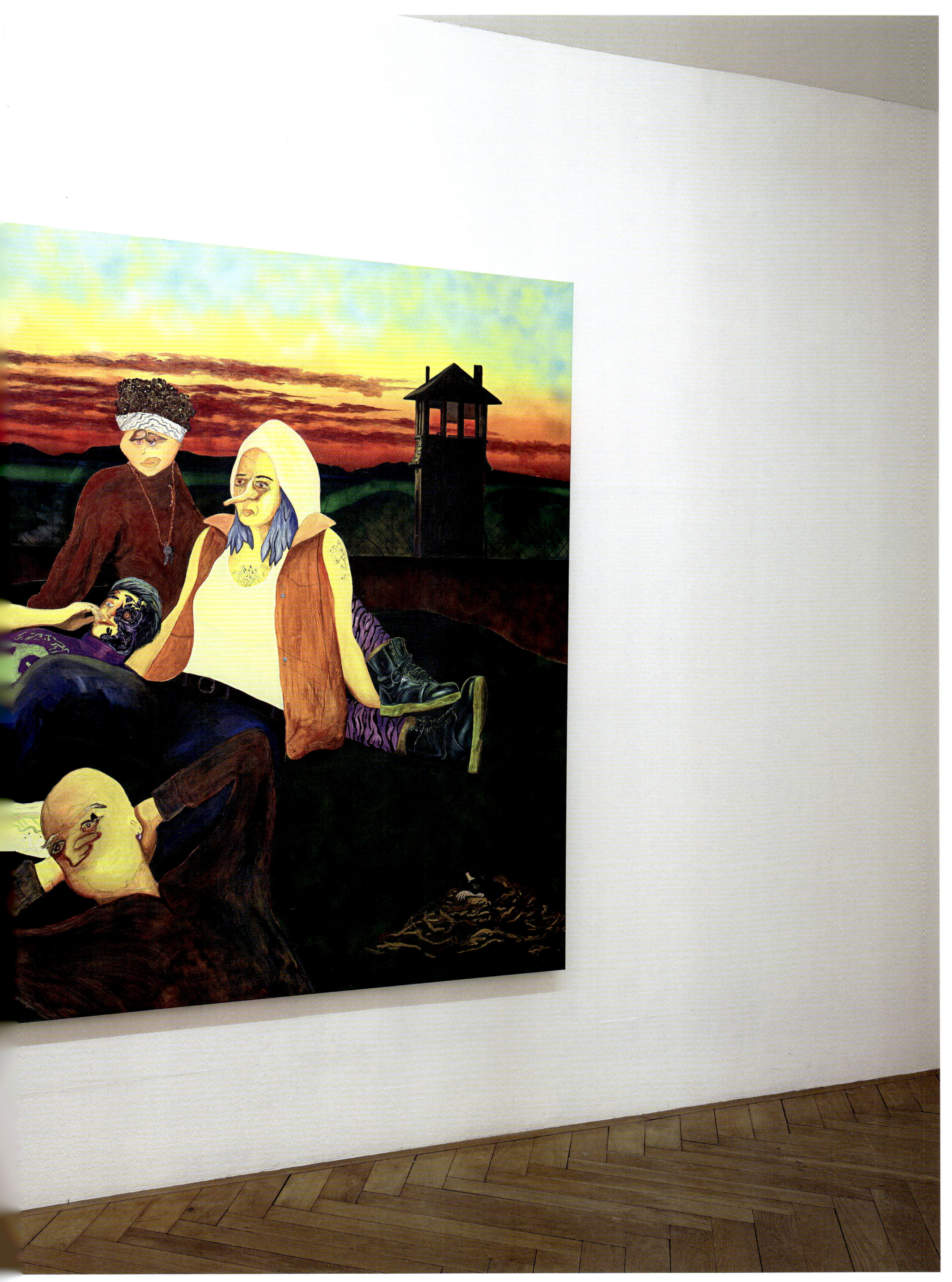

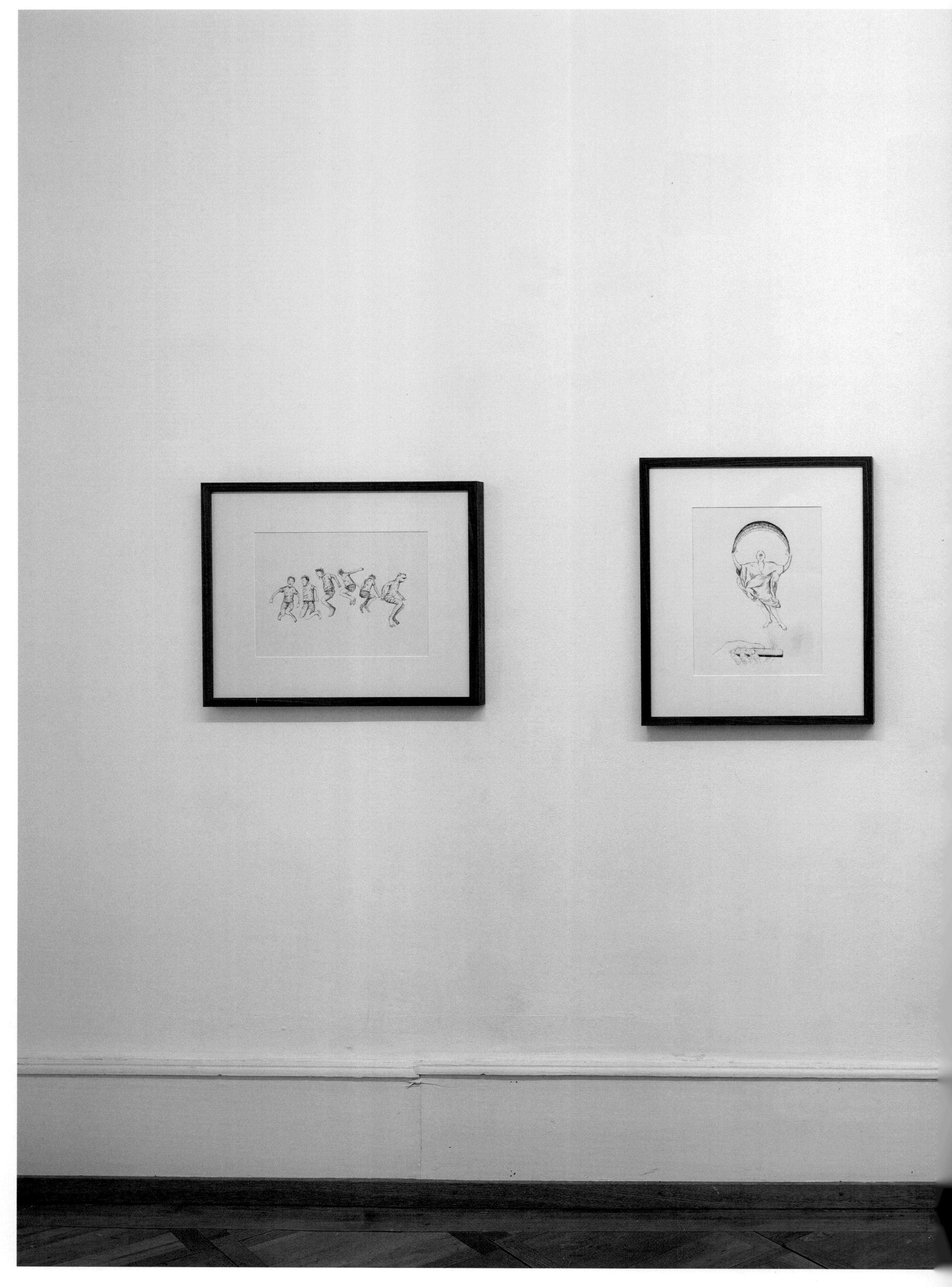

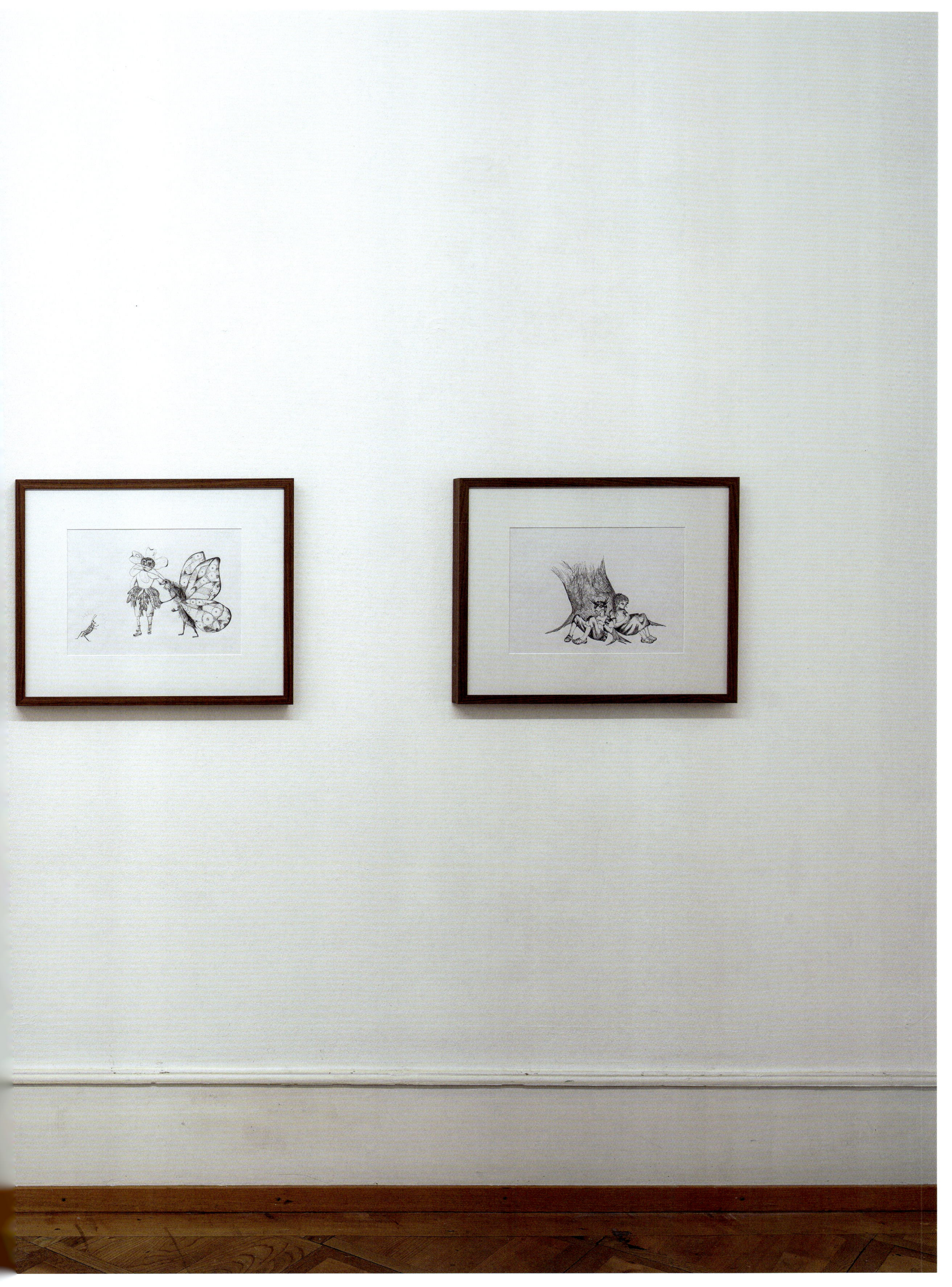

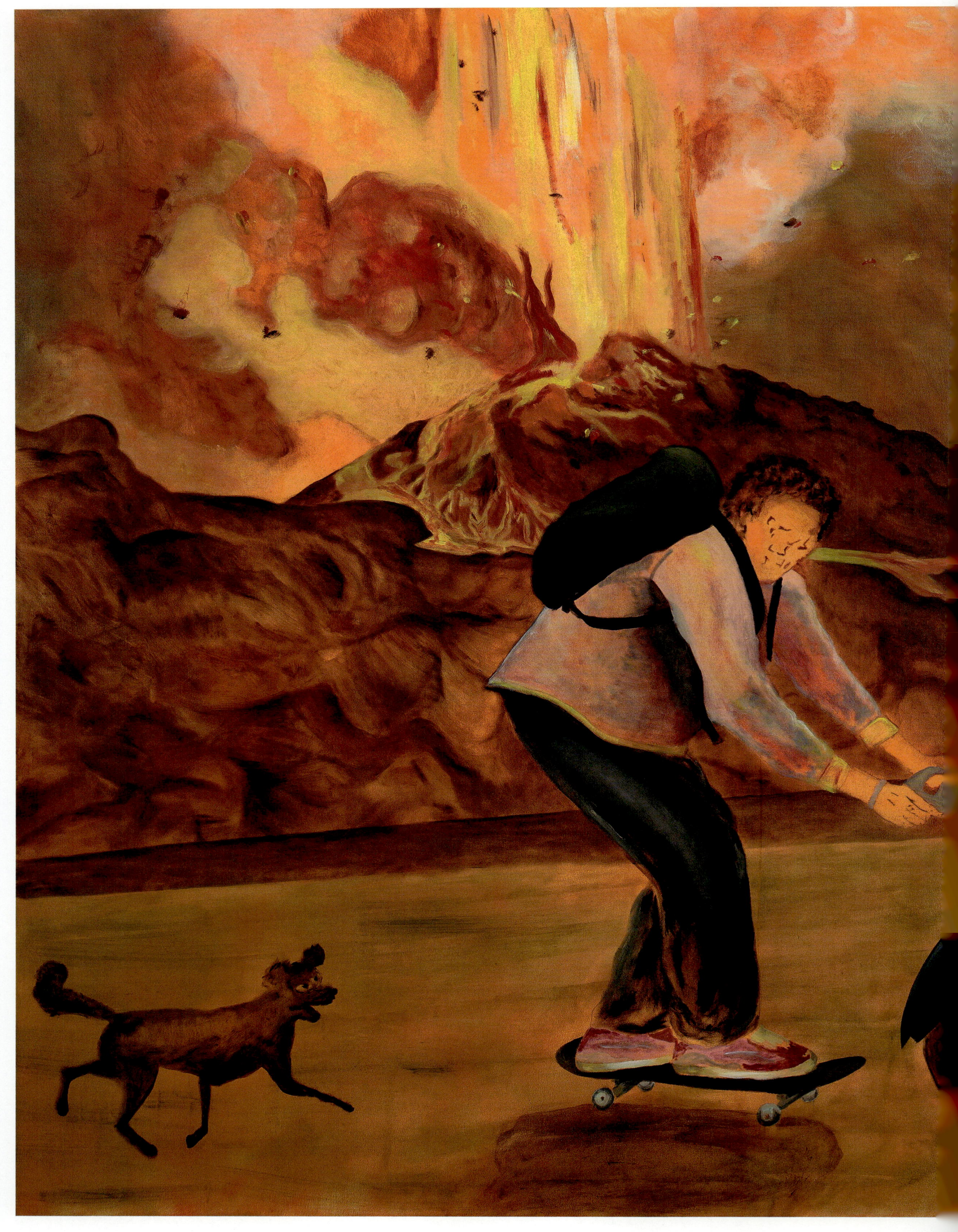

Crashing Sky, 2023   195×306 cm

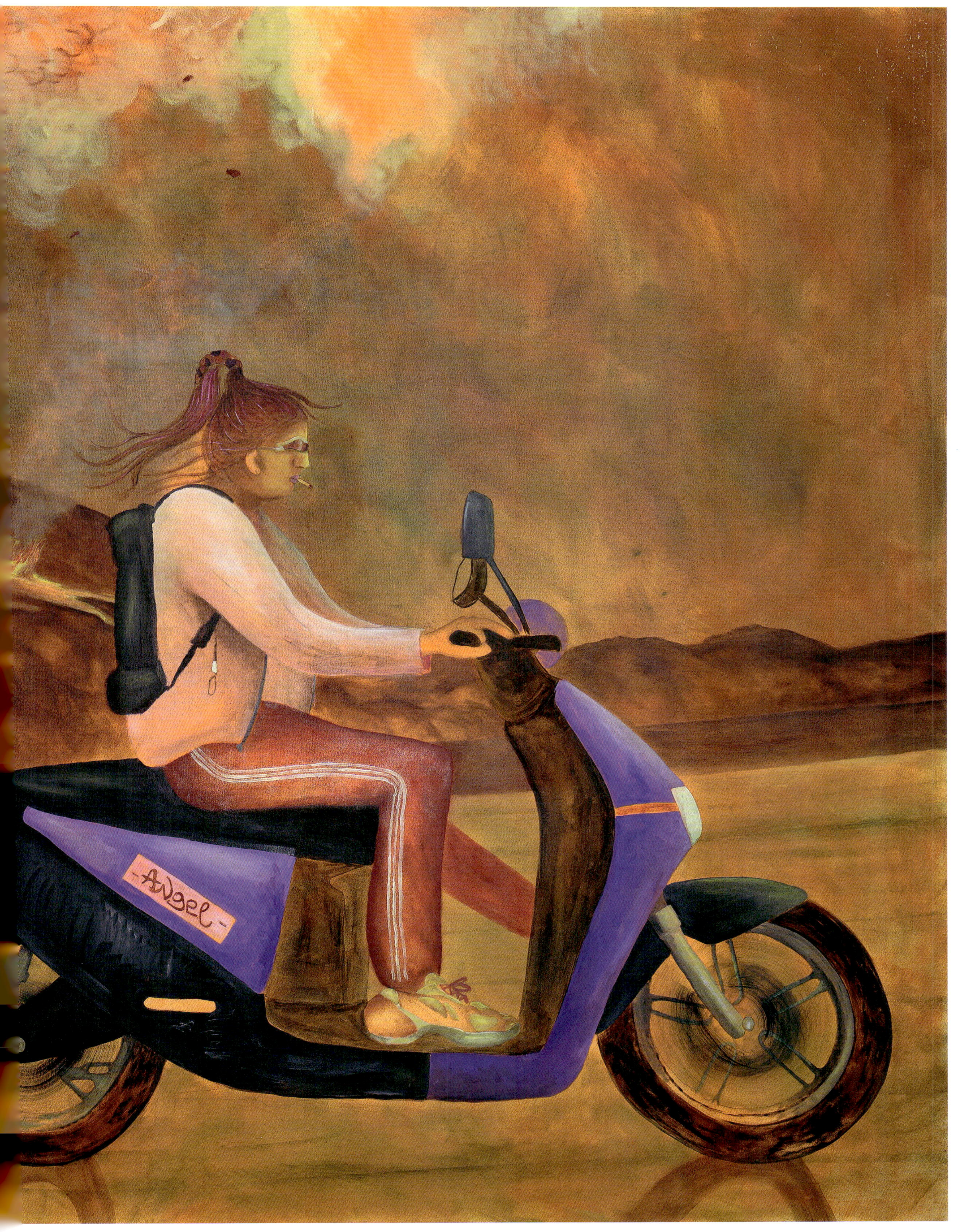

-ANGEL-

"I'm not gonna die," repeats Jennie emphatically, the character played by the young Chloë Sevigny, seated in the back seat of a taxi and staring blankly into the distance as the lights of Manhattan pass by. She has just learned that she is HIV positive, infected by a boy who indulges in sex as if it were a hunting game. Against the background noise of the city, she whispers the sentence over and over again, a last attempt to deflect the impending reality. It is one of the most moving scenes in Larry Clark's film *Kids* (1995), in which the narrative nearly comes to a standstill—and the alleged immortality of youth implodes. Innocence suddenly mutates into uncanniness, the purported ordinariness of everyday life is transformed into something menacing, and ignorance becomes painful knowledge. Clark's radical coming-of-age film quickly entered the canon of this genre: this raw, almost documentary representation of youthful excess and precariousness shows young people who seem lost yet exuberant, vulnerable yet provocative. The film is characterized by a seemingly youthful lightness that turns out to be deceptive. This leaves viewers to ponder the question of how you survive growing up.

This question is also an important theme in Noemi Pfister's paintings, which often feature scenes of young people. Her figures move in constellations that are shaped by charged relationships and floating states—caught in the bubble of "immortal youth." Her large-format paintings become stages for scenes that are characterized by a strange ambivalence; they also allow viewers to immerse themselves. *Crashing Sky* (2023; pp. 74–75) evokes an apocalyptic mood, with a couple riding past an erupting volcano: she is perched on a moped and he stands behind her on a skateboard, casually holding onto the moped's luggage rack. A panting dog chases them—*totally chill-n-real*. In *Great Things End, Small Things Endure* (2024; pp. 24–25), a laid-back group of young people hang out drinking in a tree, while under them the earth is washed away—a few cars are still recognizable in the brownish-green swamp below them. The group of young artists in *Anonymous Artists* (2024; pp. 40–41) also seems relaxed, sitting on the ground and apparently "doing nothing." We are not privy to their conversations; are they discussing the lack of acknowledgment and visibility in the art world, their hopes of having an artistic breakthrough, or the establishment that they strive to eliminate—and that they would one day like to belong to *no matter what*?

The abovementioned paintings are distinguished by their grand scale: many of Pfister's works are formats measuring 306 by 195 centimeters, a size in art history that was usually reserved for history paintings. Pfister consciously uses these dimensions to depict "everyday" contemporary scenes in a monumental framework to create a contrast between content and form. As a proponent of Realist history painting, Gustave Courbet (1819–1877) broke with the conventions of his era by depicting everyday scenes on a monumental scale. In his picture *A Burial at Ornans* (1849–50), he shows a country funeral with unspectacular yet vividly characterized figures, a far cry from the heroic depictions of history painting.[1] *After Dinner at Ornans* (1849), on the other hand, presents a seemingly banal scene: men sitting at a table, a fiddler, a sleeping guest—an intimate moment that is strengthened by the centrally positioned *Rückenfigur*, a figure shown from behind.[2] Featuring a *Rückenfigur* as the central motif was more than just a small formal breech of taboo. The gesture of turning away from the viewers was intended to enable them to have a new perspective on the event—the critical stance of an observer who turned away from the historicizing and idealizing depictions of Neoclassicism.[3] The motif of *Rückenfigur* can consequently be described as a moment of demarcation, or an alienating effect. Pfister places herself within the tradition of Realism by allowing us to take on the role of observer in her "histories." However, she expands the tradition by using ironic and grotesque elements that allow us to interpret her large-format pictures not only as a reflection of social and artistic realities but also as commentaries on the present.

Pfister's painting practice is also related to more recent art history: she works in the tradition of "bad" painting, as defined by curator Maria Tucker in 1978, and takes the liberty of constantly breaking with convention. One example is her tiny paintings that she intersperses in her exhibitions as apparent "disturbances." Measuring around twenty by twenty centimeters, they work with childhood imagery such as Pumuckl, a cartoon figure who was created in 1962 and broadcast on German television starting in 1973, or the little mole, a Czechoslovakian cartoon character from the late 1950s. In *Painting in the Age of Social Media* (2024; p. 43) we see a slightly confused Pumuckl peering at himself in a mirror with a paintbrush in hand; in the background on the wall hangs the now iconic picture *The Breakup* (2011) by American painter Nicole Eisenman (b. 1965), in which a deeply entranced man stares at his smartphone.[4] Representing a commentary on our society in reference to social media and artistic self-portraits—a reference *gone wrong* to "Every human being is an artist," the motto of German artist Joseph Beuys (1921–1986)—Pfister combines her critical sense of humor in the painting with a tribute to a contemporary artist she appreciates. The small-format paintings open up a meta level on current painting discourse within the context of the exhibition. In *Wo stehst du mit deiner Kunst, Kolleg*?* (Where Do You Stand with Your Art, Man*?, 2023; pp. 64–65), the little mole carefully makes a "realistic" copy of a pear in his studio burrow, in which works painted in abstract, Cubist, and other styles hang in the background. The title of the painting is written along the bottom edge. In this way, this painting can be understood not only as a self-critical and humorous commentary, but also as a reflection of the history of painting with its rules and mechanisms of inclusion and exclusion. The title itself refers to *Wo stehst du mit deiner Kunst, Kollege?* (Where Do You Stand with Your Art, Colleague?, 1973), a painting by Jörg Immendorff (1945–2007), which Pfister's painting updates in a critical way.

Pfister's artistic work stands in the painting tradition of Maria Lassnig (1919–2014), Nicole Eisenman, Bod Mellor (b. 1970), Lucy Stein (b. 1979), and others artist who deliberately defy painting conventions in their oeuvres. Elegance, technical perfection, and harmonious compositions yield to an open visual language that oscillates between grotesque and humorous parody, illustrating a statement made by Lassnig in her diary: "Pictures should be more penetrating than elegant."

These visual languages, which are distinguished by their "expressive hysteria," allow these artists to express discomfort that is both personal and cultural through formal and content-related violation of the rules of traditional painting as well as allowing them to update themselves again and again. In her study *The Knotted Subject: Hysteria and Its Discontents*, cultural scholar Elisabeth Bronfen interprets this "much ado about nothing"—that is, the incessantly generated new symptoms that circle around the "nothing" that is inherent to hysteria—as a flexible self-conception. As such they should be taken seriously and viewed as a language that can express precisely this personal and cultural discomfort.[5] Bronfen does not base her observations on a gender-specific view of hysteria, which views all symptoms as an expression of an unsatisfied female sexual desire but reminds us that Sigmund Freund originally identified trauma—and not sex—as the root of hysteria. In this way, the conversion of psychic fears into physical symptoms can be interpreted as a staging of coded messages. In light of her own changes and mortality, hysterical people herald the vulnerability of the symbolic (the fallibility of paternal law and social connections), the vulnerability of identity (the uncertainty of sexual and ethnic ties as well as class affiliation), and ultimately the vulnerability of the body.

Personal, subjective, and social concepts of vulnerability are distilled in Pfister's bold paintings from the charged relationship between different categories of aesthetics and taste that through her combination and juxtaposition equally reflect the meaning of visual regimens and conventions of interpretation. Pfister's figures possess an ambiguity between ecstasy and emptiness, between pose and loss of control. Her figures often seem to simultaneously be protagonists and observers of their own existence who are caught in moments of overestimating themselves, of exuberance, of emptiness ... *but they're not gonna die.*

Lost Youth. Über die malerische Praxis von Noemi Pfister
Raphael Gygax

«*I'm not gonna die*», wiederholt eindringlich die Figur Jennie, gespielt von der jungen Chloë Sevigny, auf der Rückbank eines Taxis, die Lichter Manhattans ziehen vorbei, während ihr Blick ins Nichts starrt. Sie hat gerade erfahren, dass sie HIV-positiv ist, angesteckt von einem Jungen, der seine Sexualität wie ein Jagdspiel auslebt. Im Rauschen der Stadt flüstert sie den Satz immer und immer wieder, ein letzter Versuch, die drohende Realität abzuwenden. Es ist eine der bewegendsten Szenen von Larry Clarks Film *Kids* (1995), in der das Erzähltempo fast zum Stillstand kommt – und in der die vermeintliche Unsterblichkeit der Jugend in sich zusammenbricht. Die Unschuld schlägt ins Unheimliche um, das vermeintlich Alltägliche wandelt sich ins Bedrohliche, die Unwissenheit kippt in schmerzhafte Erkenntnis. Mit seinem radikalen Coming-of-Age-Film schuf Larry Clark ein Werk, das Eingang in den Kanon dieses Genres gefunden hat: In seiner rohen, fast dokumentarischen Darstellung jugendlicher Exzesse und Unsicherheiten zeigt Clark eine Jugend, die verloren und zugleich übermütig, verletzlich und herausfordernd wirkt. Der Film wird von einer vermeintlich jugendlichen Leichtigkeit durchzogen, die sich als trügerisch entpuppt. Am Ende bleibt die Frage: Wie überlebt man das Erwachsenwerden?

Diese Frage zieht sich auch durch das malerische Werk Noemi Pfisters, in dem die oftmals Szenen junger Menschen eine zentrale Rolle spielen. Ihre Figuren bewegen sich in Konstellationen, die von Spannungsverhältnissen und Schwebezuständen geprägt sind – gefangen in der Blase einer «unsterblichen Jugend». Ihre grossformatigen Bilder werden dabei zu Bühnenräumen, in denen sich Szenen abspielen, die von einer seltsamen Ambivalenz durchzogen sind; zugleich erlauben sie den Betrachter:innen, in sie einzutauchen. In *Crashing Sky* (2023; S. 74–75) spiegelt sich eine apokalyptische Stimmung: Ein Paar – sie auf einem Moped, er steht auf einem Skateboard und hält sich lässig am Gepäckträger fest – fährt vor einem ausbrechenden Vulkan vorbei. Ein Hund rennt ihnen hechelnd hinterher – *totally chill-n-real*. In *Great Things End, Small Things Endure* (2024; S. 24–25) hängt eine Gruppe Jugendlicher eher entspannt, trinkend in einem Baum, während unter ihnen die Erde weggeschwemmt wird, ein paar Autos sind noch im braungrünen Sumpf erkennbar. Entspannt wirkt auch die Gruppe junger Künstler:innen in *Anonymous Artists* (2024; S. 40–41), wie sie auf dem Boden sitzen und scheinbar «nichts tun». Ihre Gespräche bleiben für uns im Verborgenen – diskutieren sie über die fehlende Anerkennung und Sichtbarkeit in der Kunstwelt, über das Hoffen auf den künstlerischen Durchbruch oder über das Establishment, das sie niederreissen möchten und zu dem sie eines Tages gehören möchten, *no matter what*?

Die zitierten Bilder zeichnen sich durch ihre Masse aus – viele Arbeiten Pfisters haben das Format 306 × 195 Zentimeter, also eine Grösse, die in der Geschichte der Malerei typischerweise der Historienmalerei

vorbehalten war. Pfister nutzt diese Dimensionen bewusst, um «alltägliche», zeitgenössische Szenen in einem monumentalen Rahmen darzustellen und so einen Kontrast zwischen Inhalt und Form zu schaffen. Als Vertreter einer realistischen Historienmalerei brach Gustave Courbet (1819–1877) mit den Konventionen seiner Zeit, indem er Alltagsszenen in monumentalem Format darstellte. Im Bild *Ein Begräbnis in Ornans* (1849/50) zeigt er eine ländliche Beerdigung mit unspektakulären, aber eindringlich charakterisierten Menschen, weit entfernt von den heroischen Darstellungen der Historienmalerei.[1] *Nachmittag in Ornans* (1849) wiederum präsentiert eine scheinbar banale Szene: Männer an einem Tisch, ein Geigenspieler, ein Schlafender – ein intimer Moment, der durch die Rückenfigur im Zentrum noch verstärkt wird.[2] Die Rückendarstellung als zentrales Motiv war mehr als nur ein kleiner formaler Tabubruch. Die Geste des Sichabwendens von den Betrachter:innen sollte diesen einen neuen Blick auf das Geschehen ermöglichen, einen beobachtend-kritischen, der sich gegen die historisierenden und idealisierenden Darstellungen des Klassizismus wandte.[3] Die Rückendarstellung kann folglich als Moment einer Grenzziehung, eines Verfremdungseffekts beschrieben werden. Pfister stellt sich in die Tradition eines solchen Realismus, wenn sie uns zu Beobachter:innen ihrer «Historien» werden lässt. Sie erweitert diesen jedoch durch ironische und groteske Elemente, die ihre grossformatigen Bilder nicht nur als Reflexion über soziale und künstlerische Realitäten, sondern auch als Kommentar zur Gegenwart lesbar machen.

Pfisters malerische Praxis lässt sich aber auch in einer jüngeren Kunstgeschichte verorten: Sie steht in der Tradition des «Bad» Painting, wie es die Kuratorin Marcia Tucker 1978 definierte, und nimmt sich die Freiheit, Konventionen immer wieder zu durchbrechen – so etwa mit ganz kleinen Bildern um die 20 × 20 Zentimeter, die als vermeintliche «Störungen» in ihren Ausstellungen auftauchen und deren Motivik sich in der Kindheit verorten lässt. So tritt plötzlich der Pumuckl auf (eine 1962 erfundene Figur, die ab 1973 im deutschen Fernsehen zu sehen war) oder der kleine Maulwurf, eine tschechische Zeichentrickfigur aus den späten 1950er-Jahren. In *Painting in the Age of Social Media* (2024; S. 43) sehen wir einen leicht verwirrt dreinschauenden Pumuckl mit Pinsel in der Hand, sich im Spiegel betrachtend; im Hintergrund an der Wand hängt das inzwischen ikonische Bild *The Breakup* (2011) der amerikanischen Malerin Nicole Eisenman (geb. 1965), auf dem man eine menschliche Figur zutiefst versunken in ihr Handy sieht.[4] Pfister verbindet in ihrem Bild einen kritischen Humor, der einen Kommentar über unsere Gesellschaft in Bezug auf Social Media und künstlerisches Selbstbild – Joseph Beuys' (1921–1986) Diktum «Jeder Mensch ist ein Künstler» *gone wrong* – darstellt, mit einer Hommage an eine für sie wichtige zeitgenössische Referenz. Die kleinformatigen Malereien eröffnen im Ausstellungskontext eine Metaebene zu aktuellen Malereidiskursen. In dem Werk *Wo stehst du mit deiner*

Kunst, Kolleg?* (2023; S. 64–65) malt der kleine Maulwurf akribisch eine Birne «realistisch» ab, während im Hintergrund seiner Höhle abstrakte, kubistische und Gemälde anderer Stilrichtungen hängen. Am unteren Bildrand ist der Titel der Arbeit zu lesen. So lässt sich diese Malerei nicht nur als selbstkritischer und humorvoller Kommentar verstehen, sondern auch als Reflexion auf die Malereigeschichte mit ihren Regelwerken sowie ihren In- und Exklusionsmechanismen – der Titel selbst ist eine Referenz und kritische Aktualisierung von Jörg Immendorffs (1945–2007) Bild *Wo stehst du mit deiner Kunst, Kollege?* (1973).

Das künstlerische Werk Pfisters steht in der malerischen Tradition von Maria Lassnig (1919–2014), Nicole Eisenman, Bod Mellor (geb. 1970), Lucy Stein (geb. 1979) und anderen, die sich in ihrem Werk bewusst über malerische Konventionen hinwegsetzen. Eleganz, technische Perfektion und harmonische Kompositionen weichen einer offenen Bildsprache, die zwischen Groteskem und humorvoller Parodie changiert – oder wie bereits Lassnig in ihrem Tagebuch festhielt: «Die Bilder sollen lieber penetrant als elegant sein.»

Diese malerischen Sprachen, die sich durch «expressive Hysterie» auszeichnen, erlauben es den Künstler:innen, durch formale und inhaltliche Regelverletzungen gegenüber dem tradierten Malereiverständnis ein ebenso persönliches wie kulturelles Unbehagen auszudrücken, und sich aber auch immer wieder zu erneuern. In ihrer Studie *Das verknotete Subjekt* schlägt die Kulturwissenschaftlerin Elisabeth Bronfen vor, das «Viel-Lärm-um-Nichts» – also die sich ständig neu generierenden Symptome, die das der Hysterie inhärente «Nichts» umkreisen – als flexible Selbstentwürfe zu deuten. Als solche sollen sie ernst genommen und als eine Sprache aufgefasst werden, die genau dieses persönliche und kulturelle Unbehagen zum Ausdruck bringen könne.[5] Bronfen geht dabei nicht von einem geschlechtsspezifischen Begriff der Hysterie aus, der alle Symptome als Ausdruck eines unbefriedigten weiblichen sexuellen Begehrens versteht, sondern erinnert daran, dass Sigmund Freud ursprünglich traumatische und keine sexuellen Gründe für die Hysterie ausgemacht hatte. So lässt sich diese Konversion psychischer Ängste in körperliche Symptome als Inszenierung einer kodierten Botschaft deuten. Angesichts der eigenen Veränderungen und Sterblichkeit verkünden die Hysteriker:innen die Verwundbarkeit des Symbolischen (die Fehlbarkeit des väterlichen Gesetzes und der gesellschaftlichen Bindungen), die Verwundbarkeit der Identität (die Unsicherheit der geschlechtlichen und ethnischen Bindungen sowie der Klassenzugehörigkeit) und schliesslich die Verwundbarkeit des Körpers.

Persönlich-subjektive wie auch gesellschaftliche Entwürfe der Verwundbarkeit destillieren sich in Pfisters aufdringlichen Bildern aus dem Spannungsverhältnis zwischen verschiedenen Kategorien von Ästhetik und Geschmack, die durch ihre Kombination und Gegenüberstellung die Bedeutung von Bildregimen und Konventionen der Interpretation gleichermassen reflektieren. Pfisters Figuren haftet eine Ambiguität an, zwischen Ekstase und Leere, zwischen Pose und Kontrollverlust. Ihre Figuren scheinen oft gleichzeitig Protagonist:innen und Zuschauer:innen ihrer eigenen Existenz zu sein – gefangen in Momenten der Selbstüberschätzung, des Überschwangs, der Leere ... *But they're not gonna die.*

1   Das Bild hat die Masse 315 × 668 cm und befindet sich im Musée d'Orsay, Paris.
2   Das Bild hat die Masse 195 × 257 cm und befindet sich im Palais des Beaux-Arts, Lille.
3   Siehe Petra ten-Doesschate Chu, *The Most Arrogant Man in France. Gustave Courbet and the Nineteenth-Century Media Culture*, Princeton u. a. 2007.
4   Das Bild hat die Masse 142,2 × 109,2 cm und befindet sich im Institute of Contemporary Art, University of Pennsylvania, Philadelphia.
5   Siehe Elisabeth Bronfen, *Das verknotete Subjekt. Hysterie in der Moderne*, Berlin 1998.

1   Measuring 315 by 668 centimeters, the painting is part of the collection of the Musée d'Orsay in Paris.
2   Measuring 195 by 257 centimeters, the painting is part of the collection of the Palais des Beaux-Arts in Lille.
3   See Petra ten-Doesschate Chu, *The Most Arrogant Man in France: Gustave Courbet and the Nineteenth-Century Media Culture* (Princeton and Oxford: Princeton University Press, 2007).
4   Measuring 142 by 109.2 centimeters, the painting is part of the collection of the Institute of Contemporary Art, University of Pennsylvania, Philadelphia.
5   See Elisabeth Bronfen, *The Knotted Subject: Hysteria and Its Discontents* (Princeton: Princeton University Press, 1998).

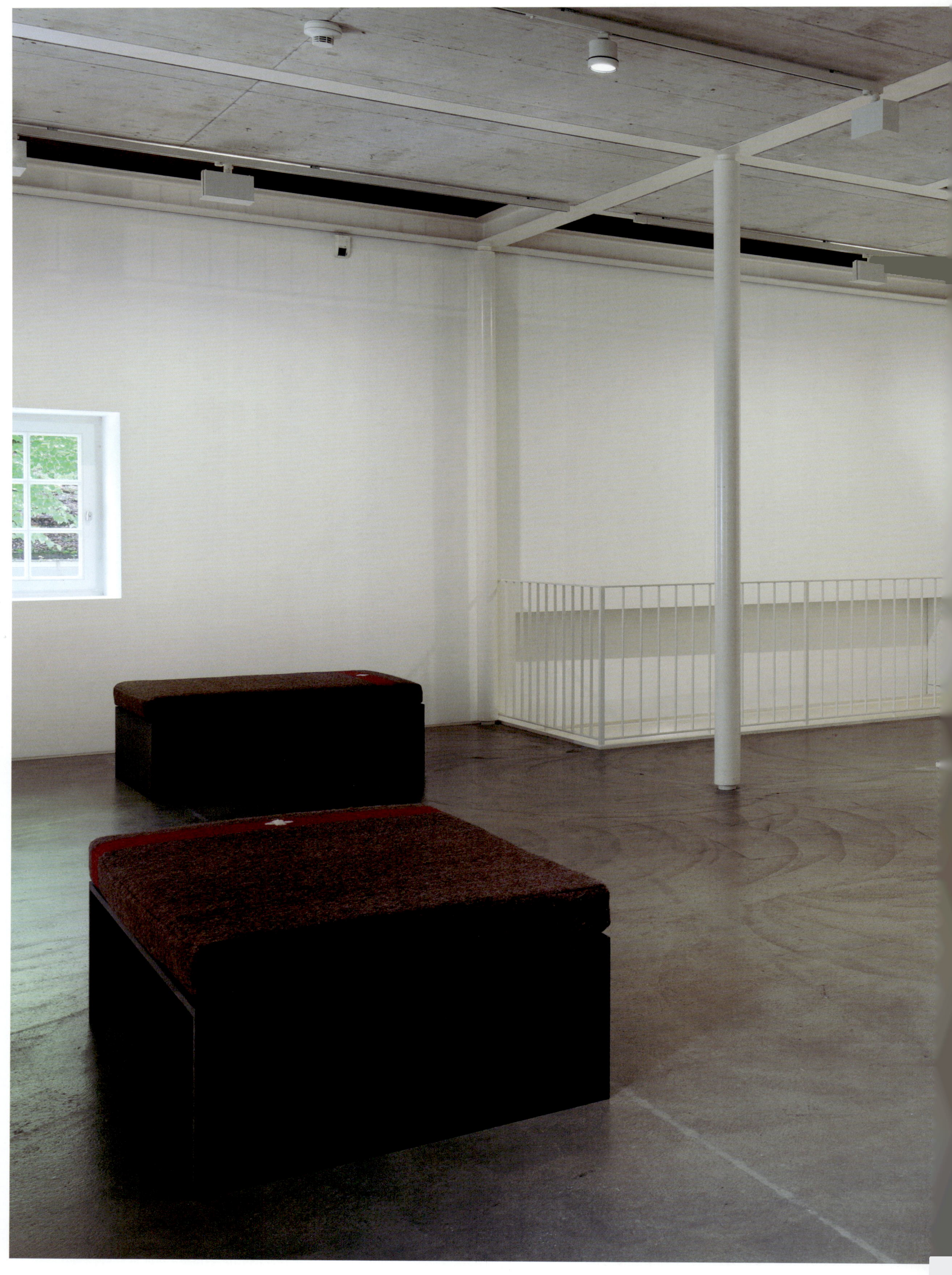

My Protagonists, 2025   Kunst Raum Riehen

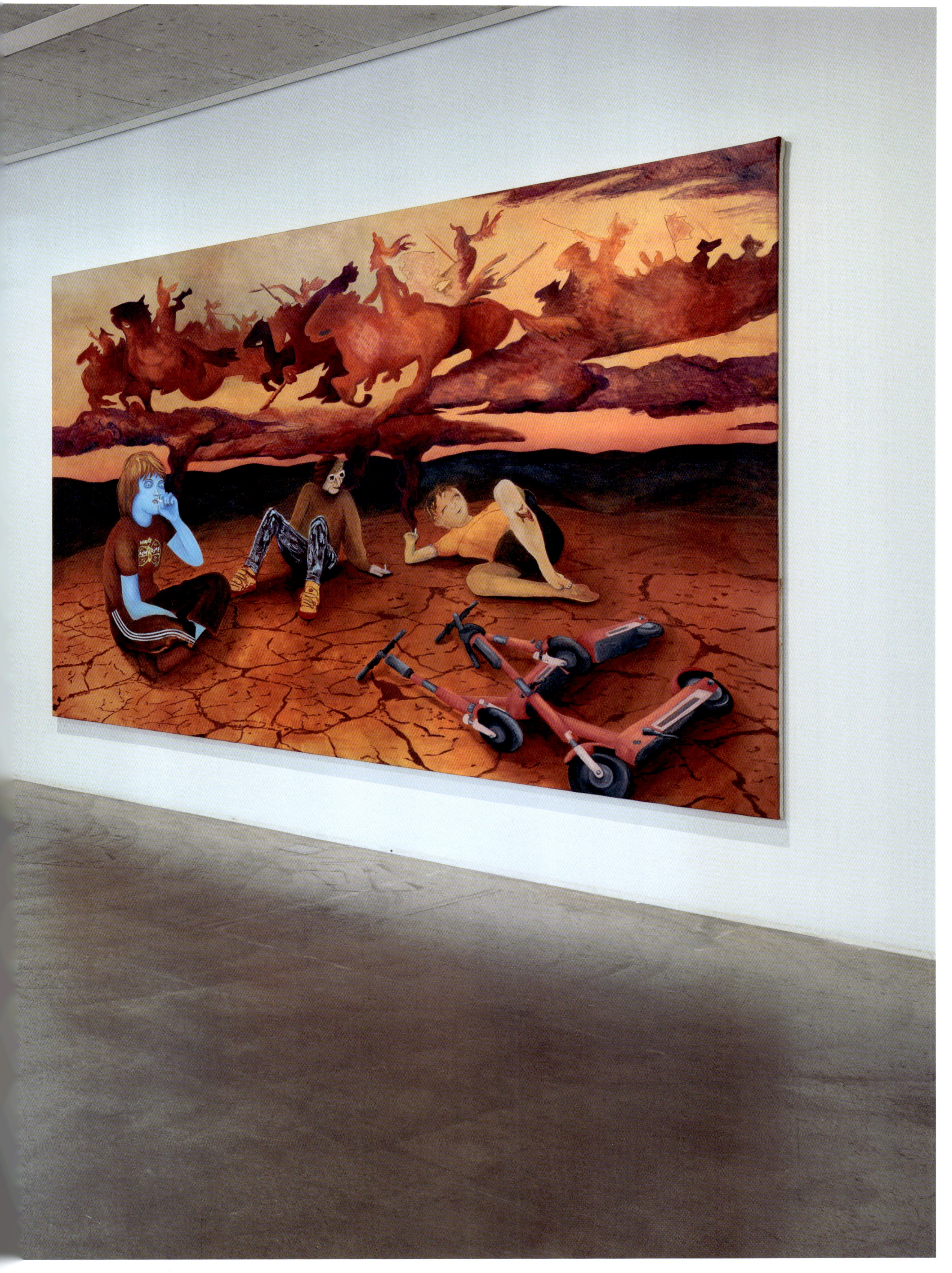

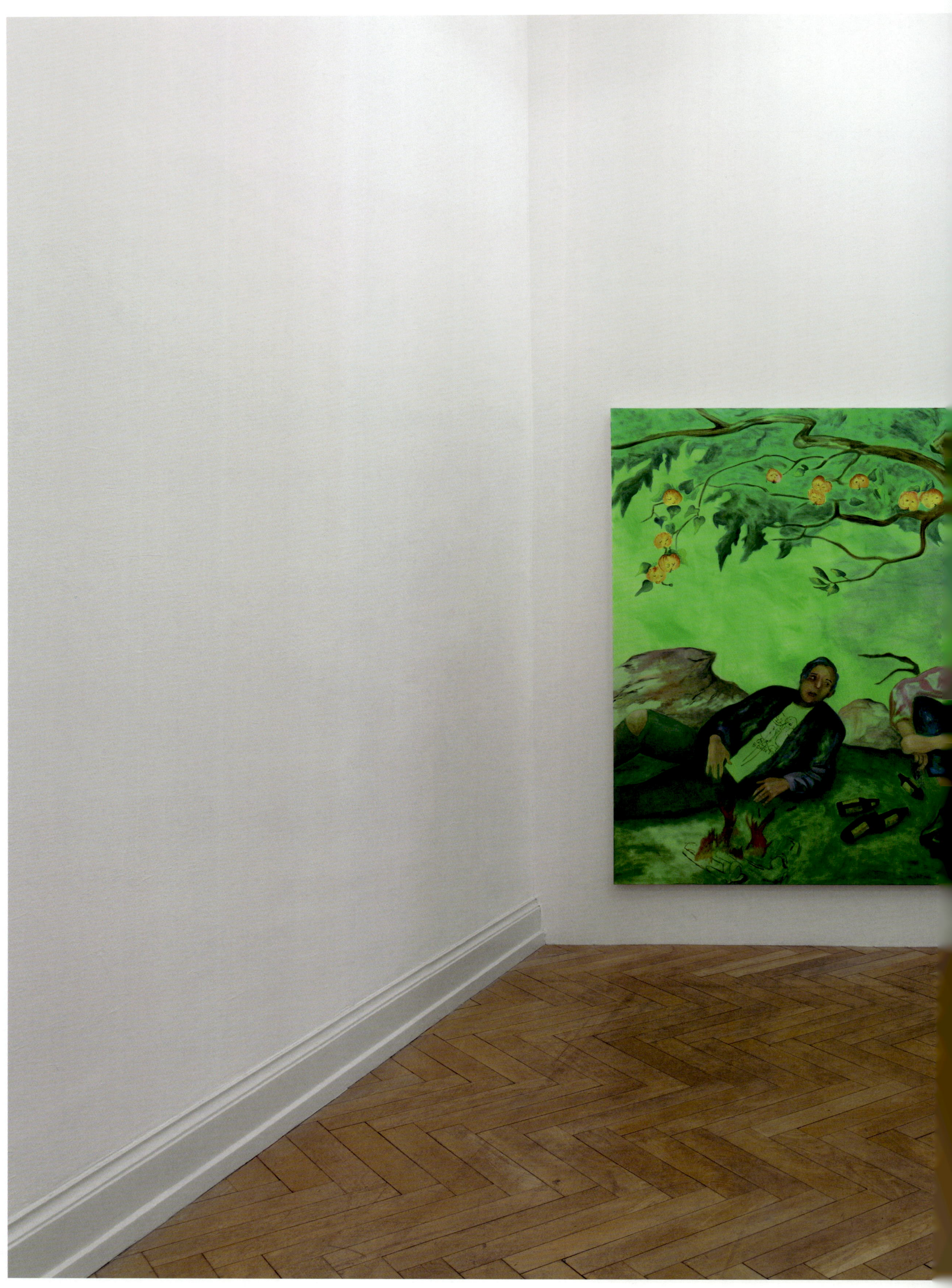

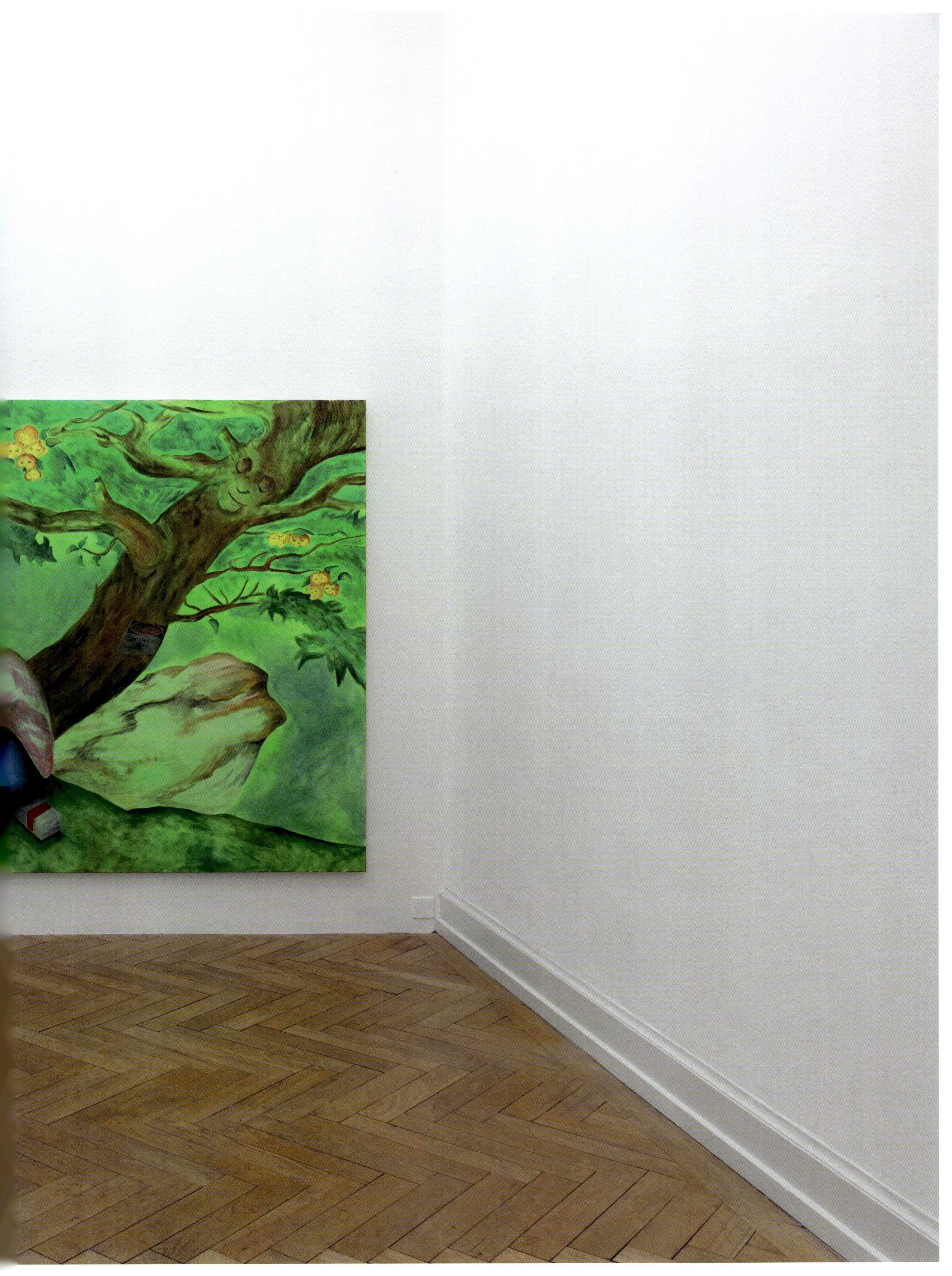

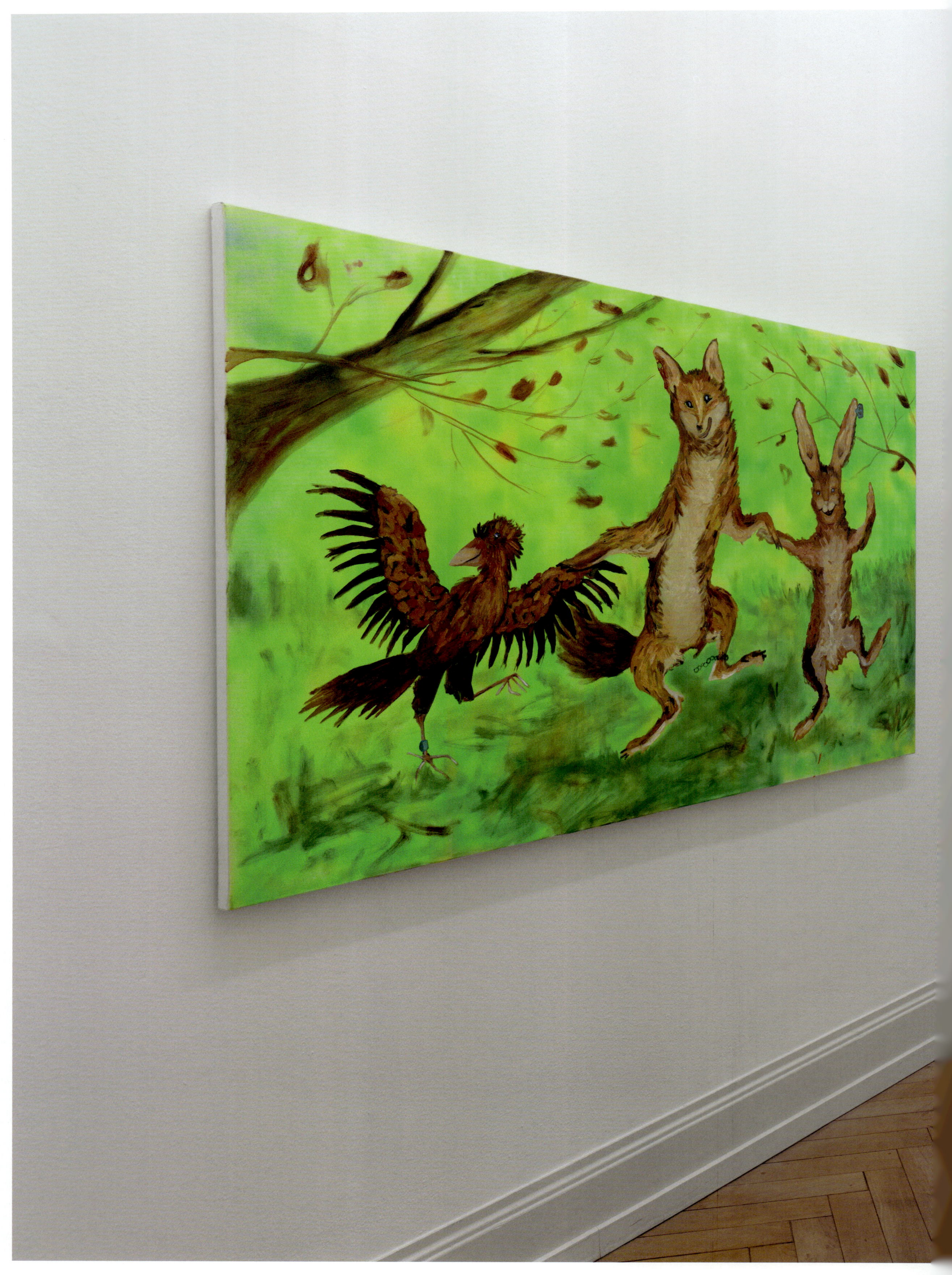

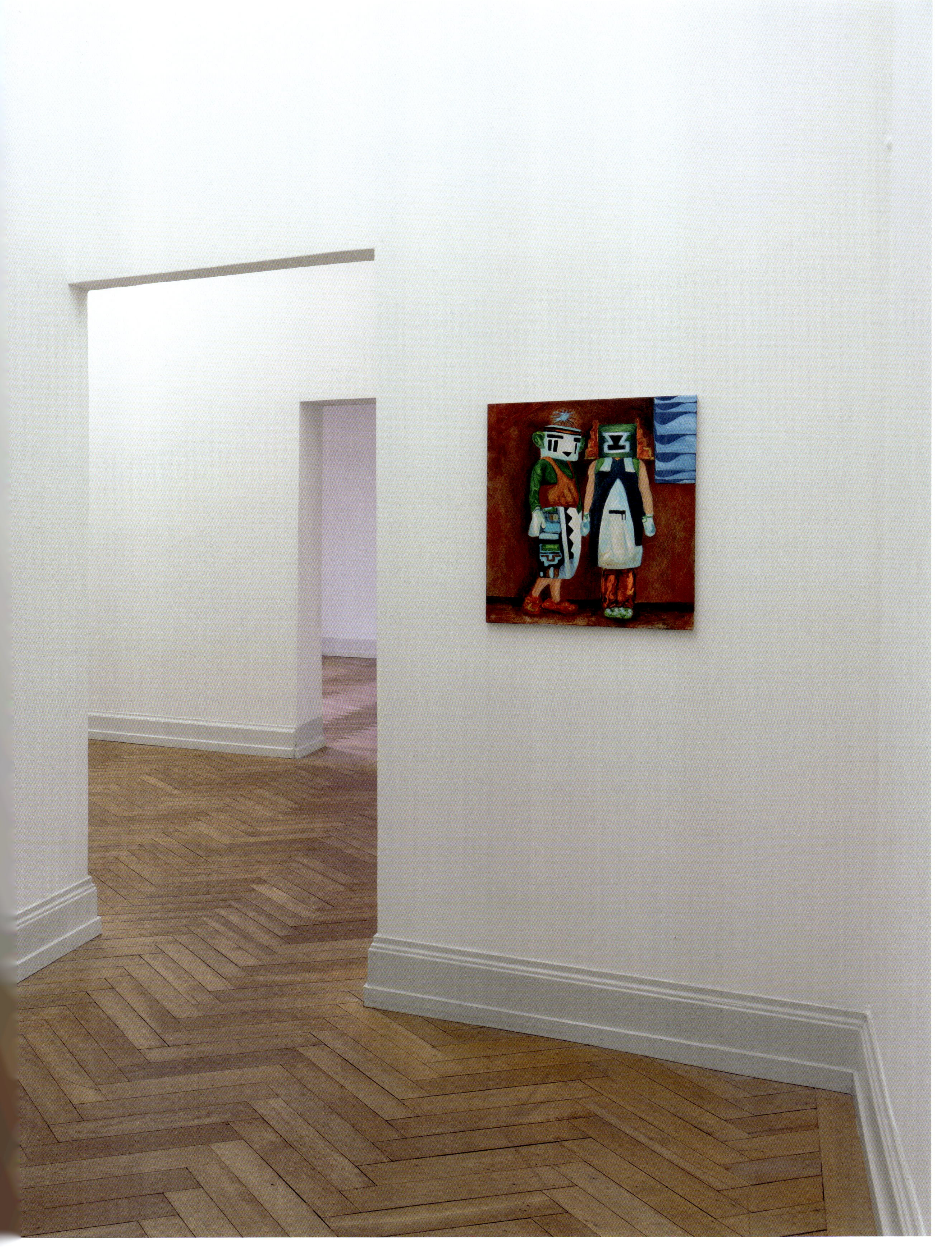

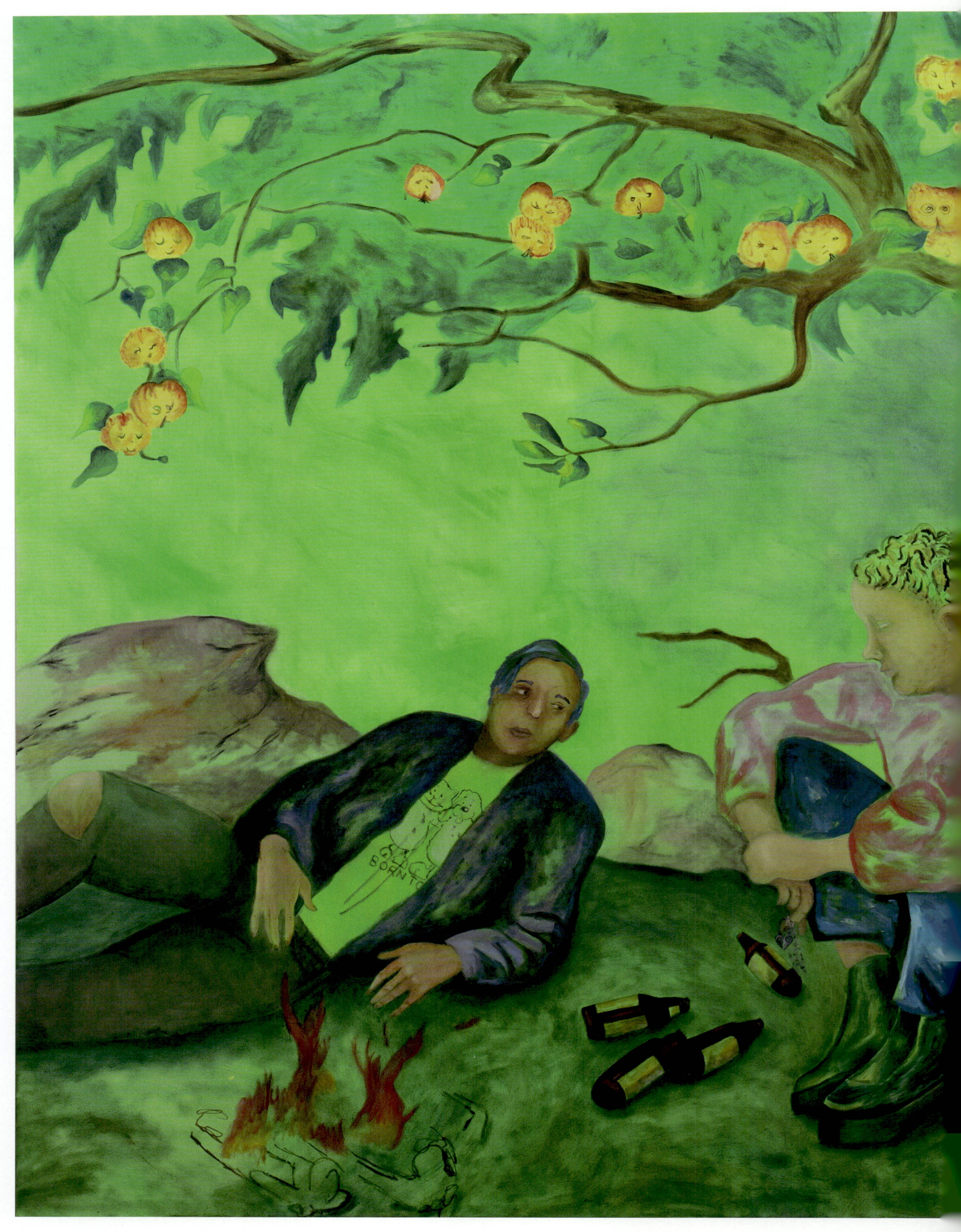

Speaking Rest, 2023   195×306 cm

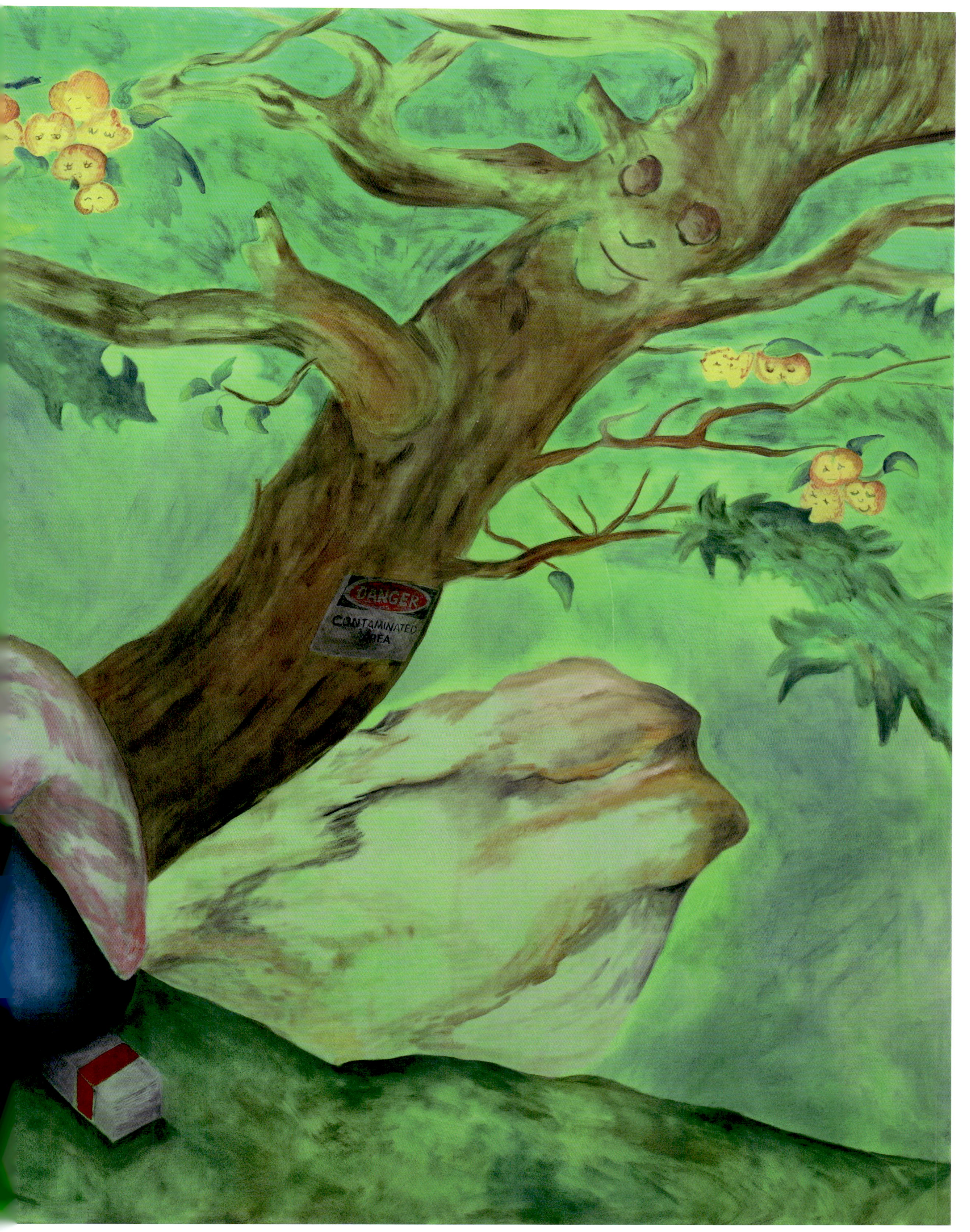

DANGER
CONTAMINATED AREA

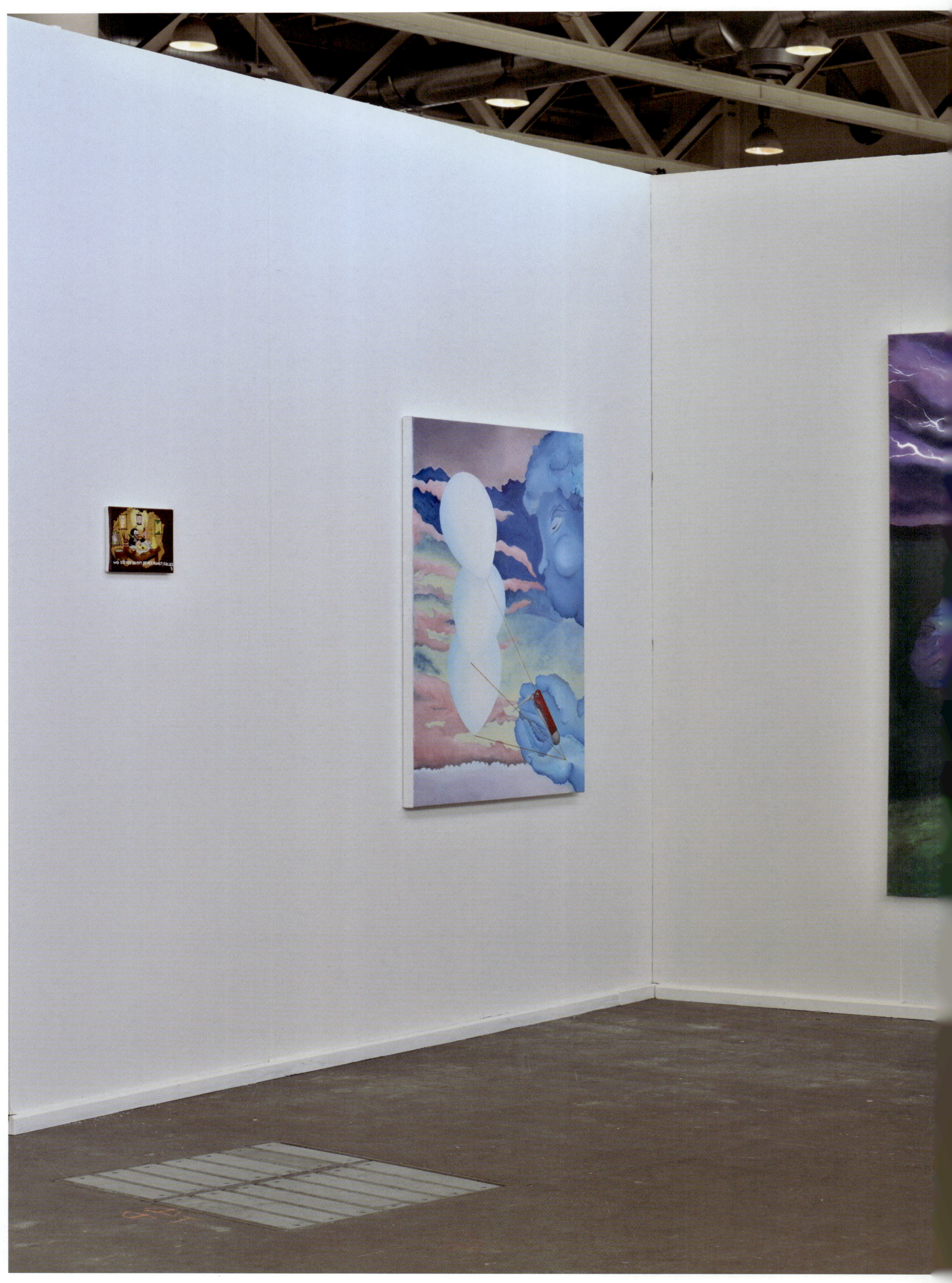

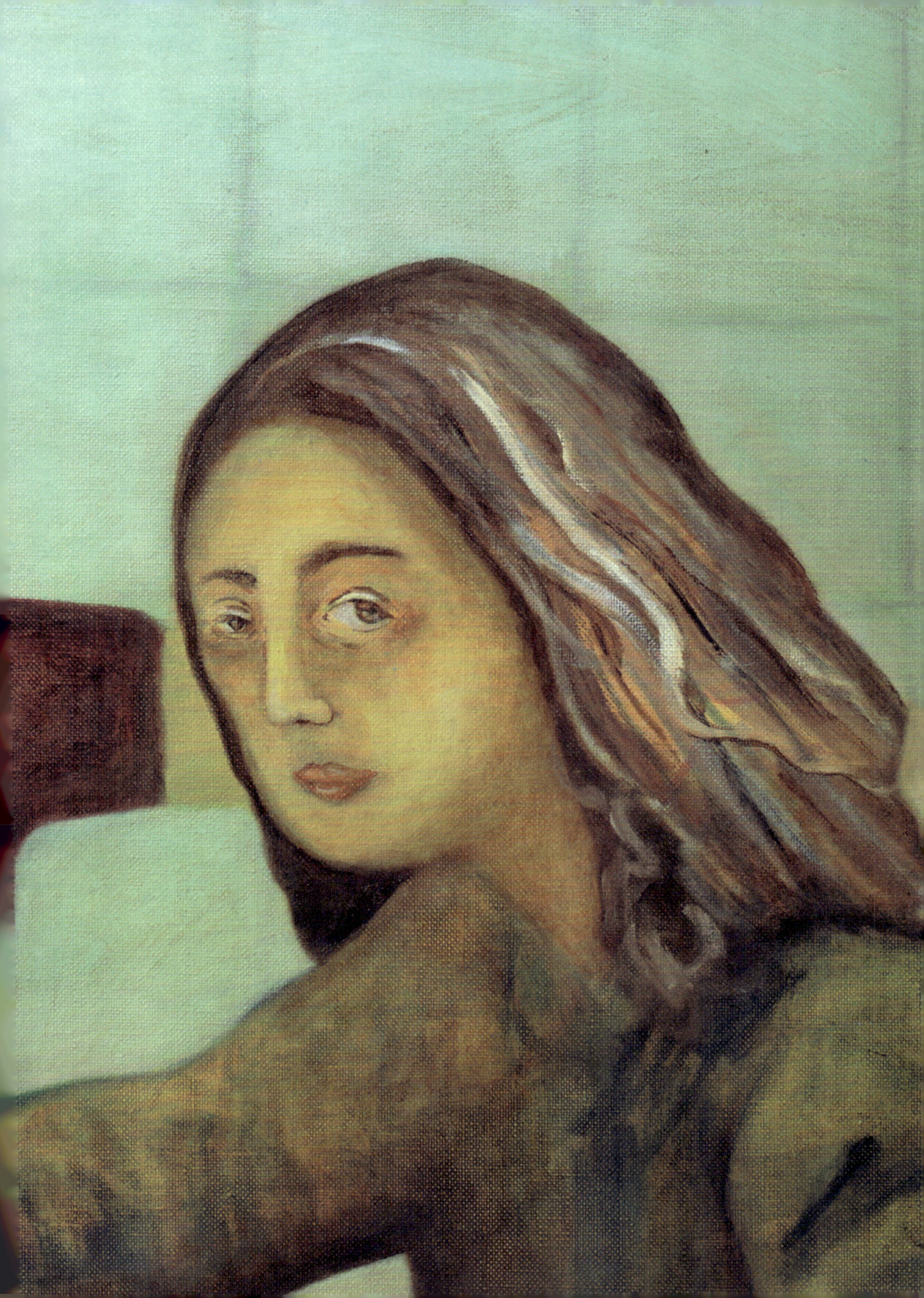

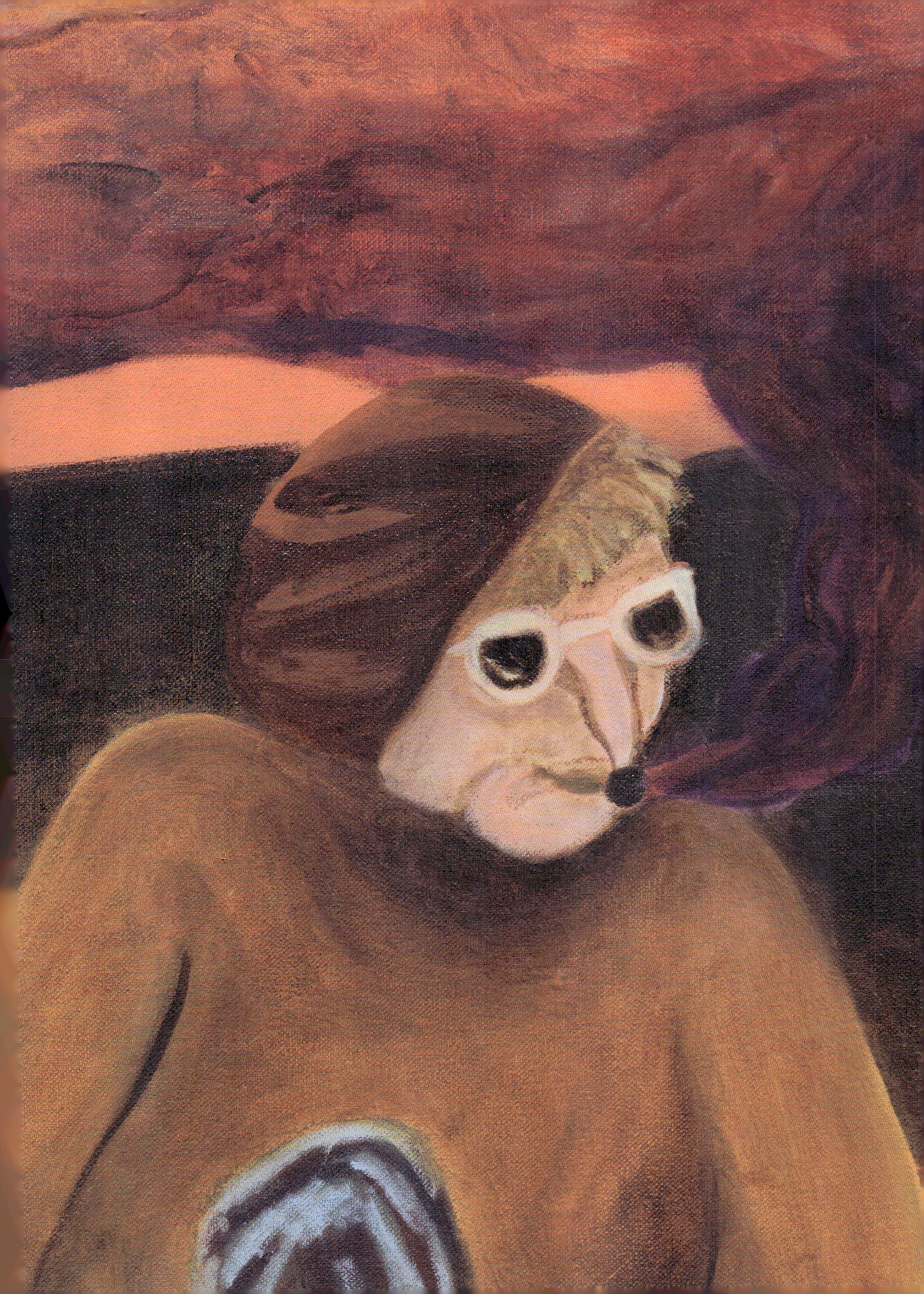

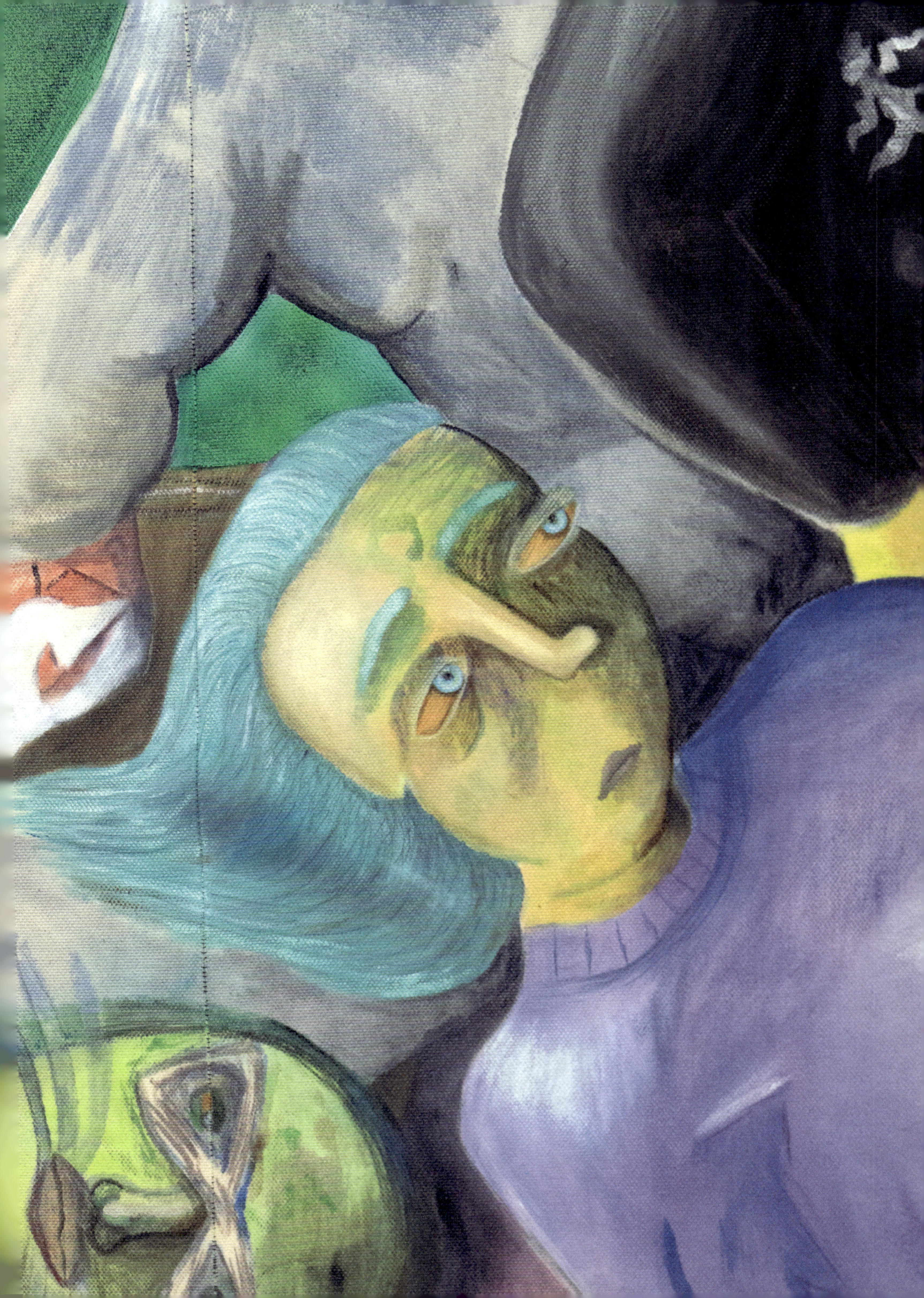

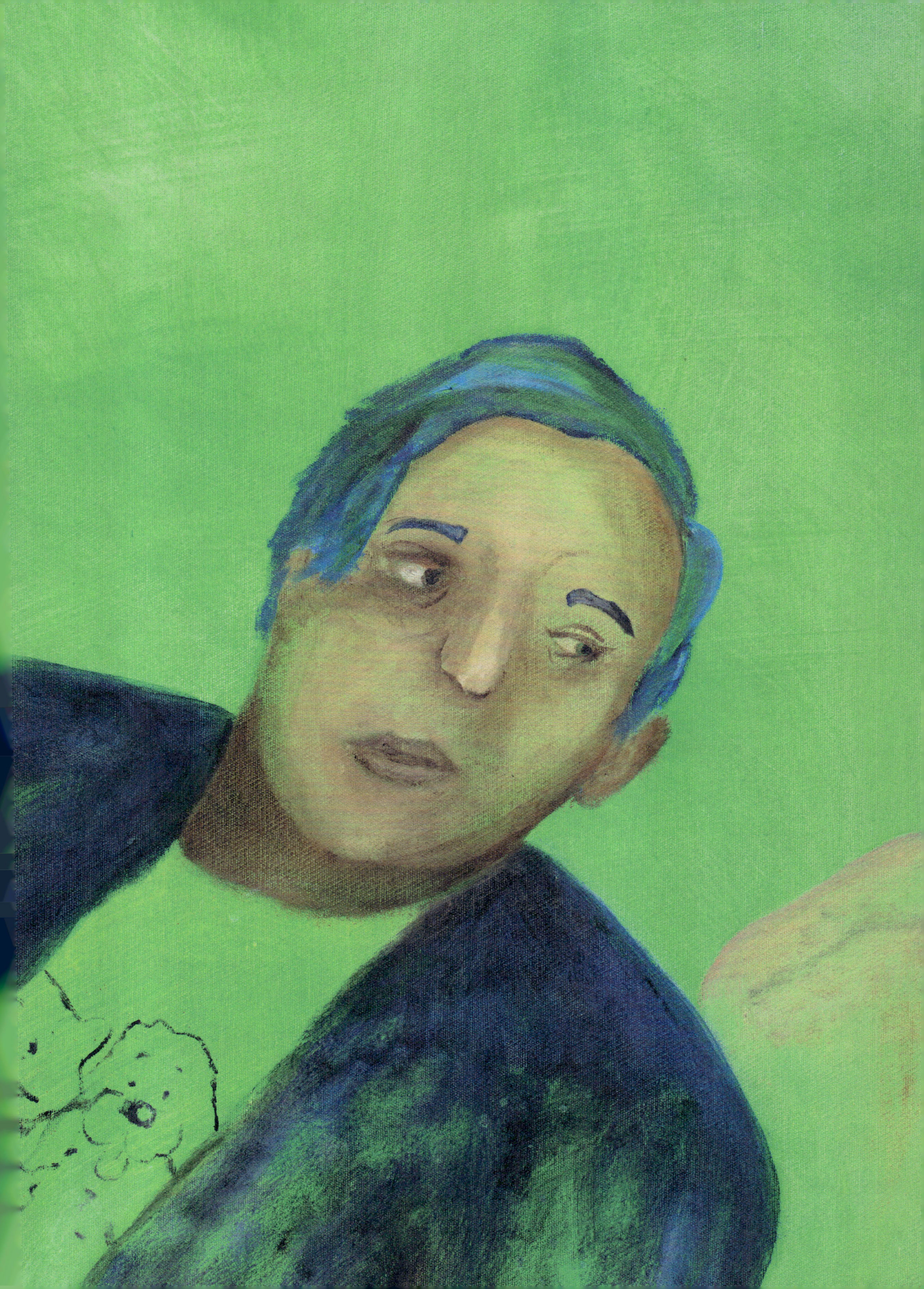

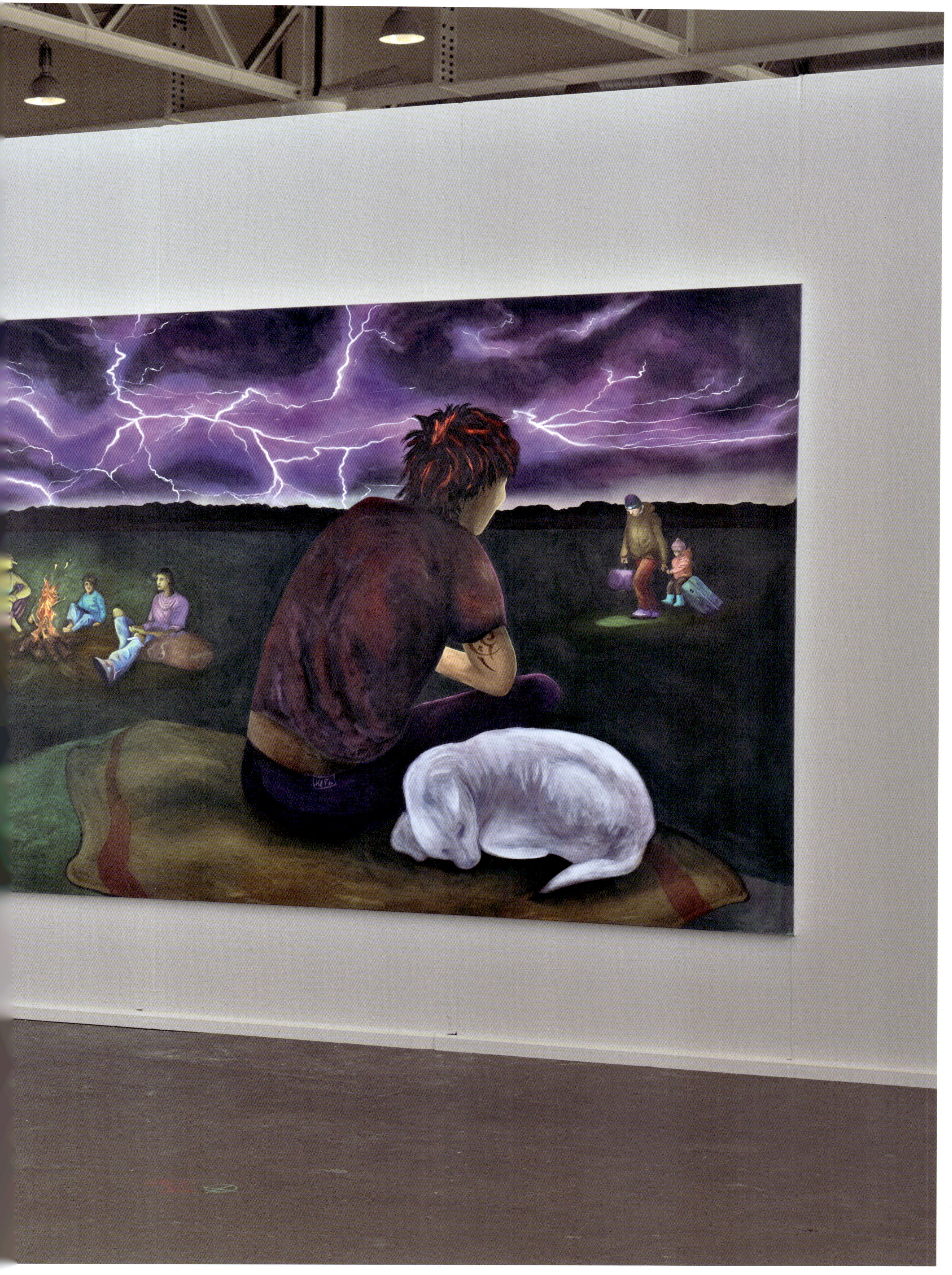

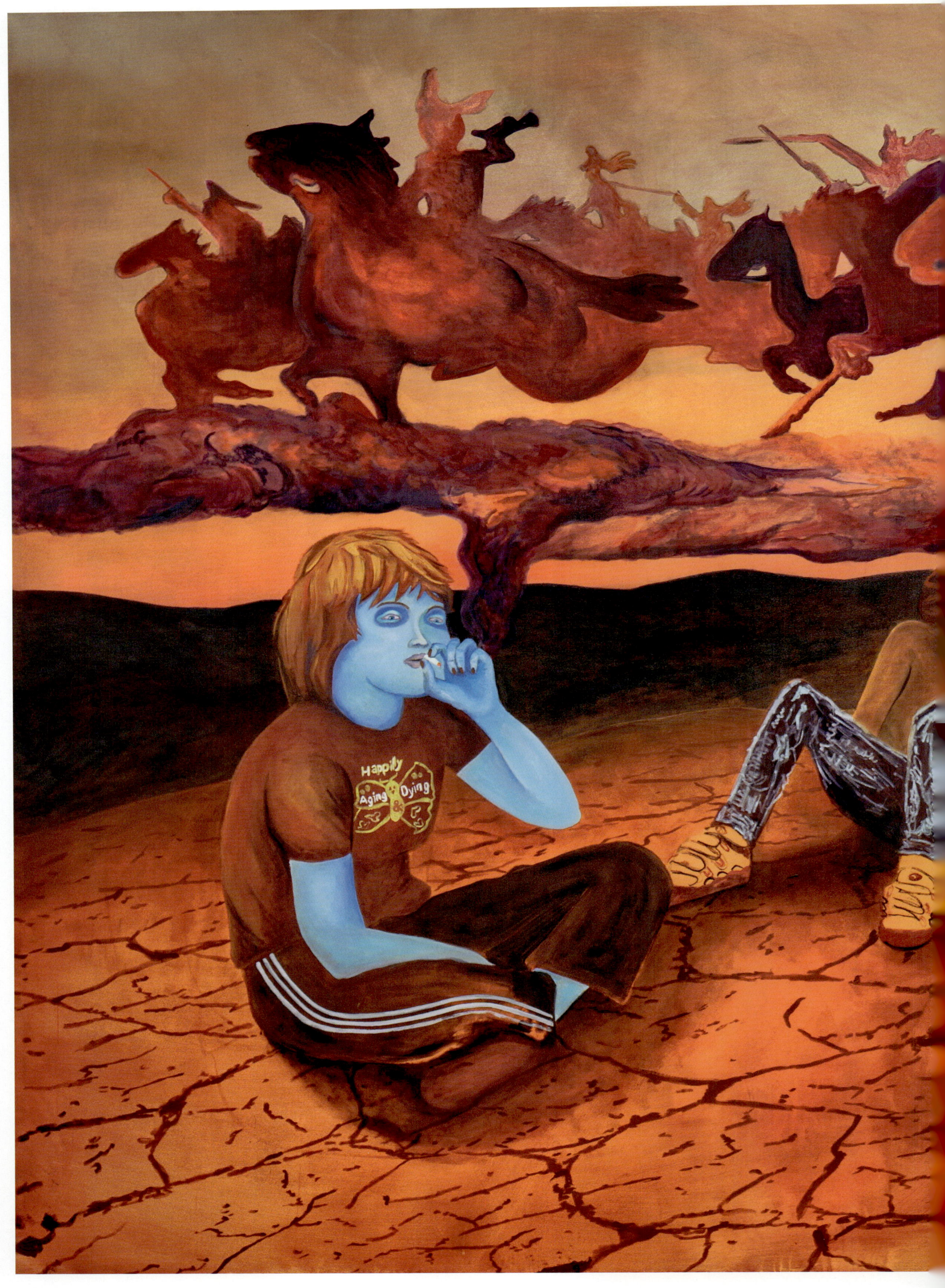

Happily Aging & Dying, 2022   210×310 cm

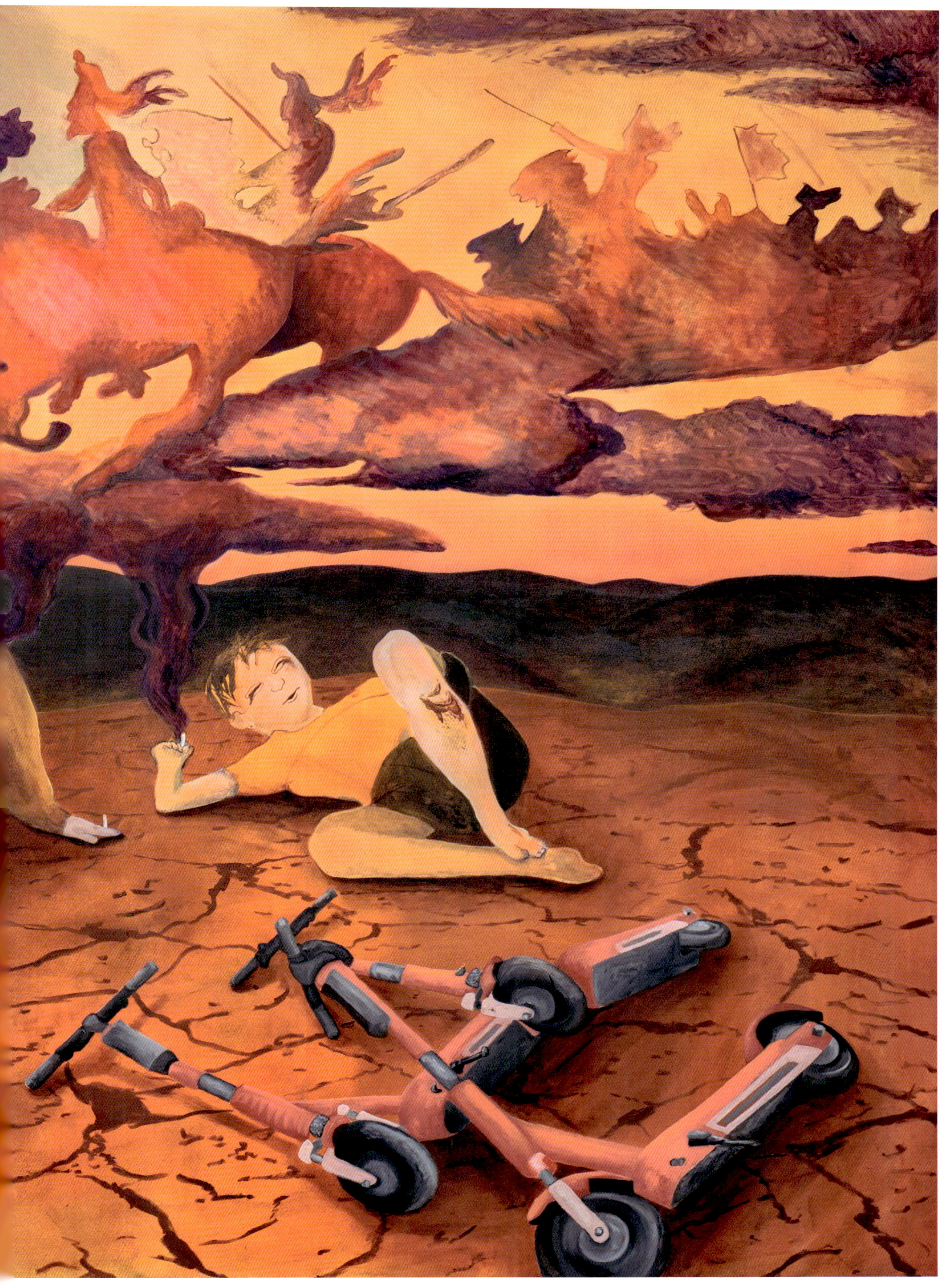

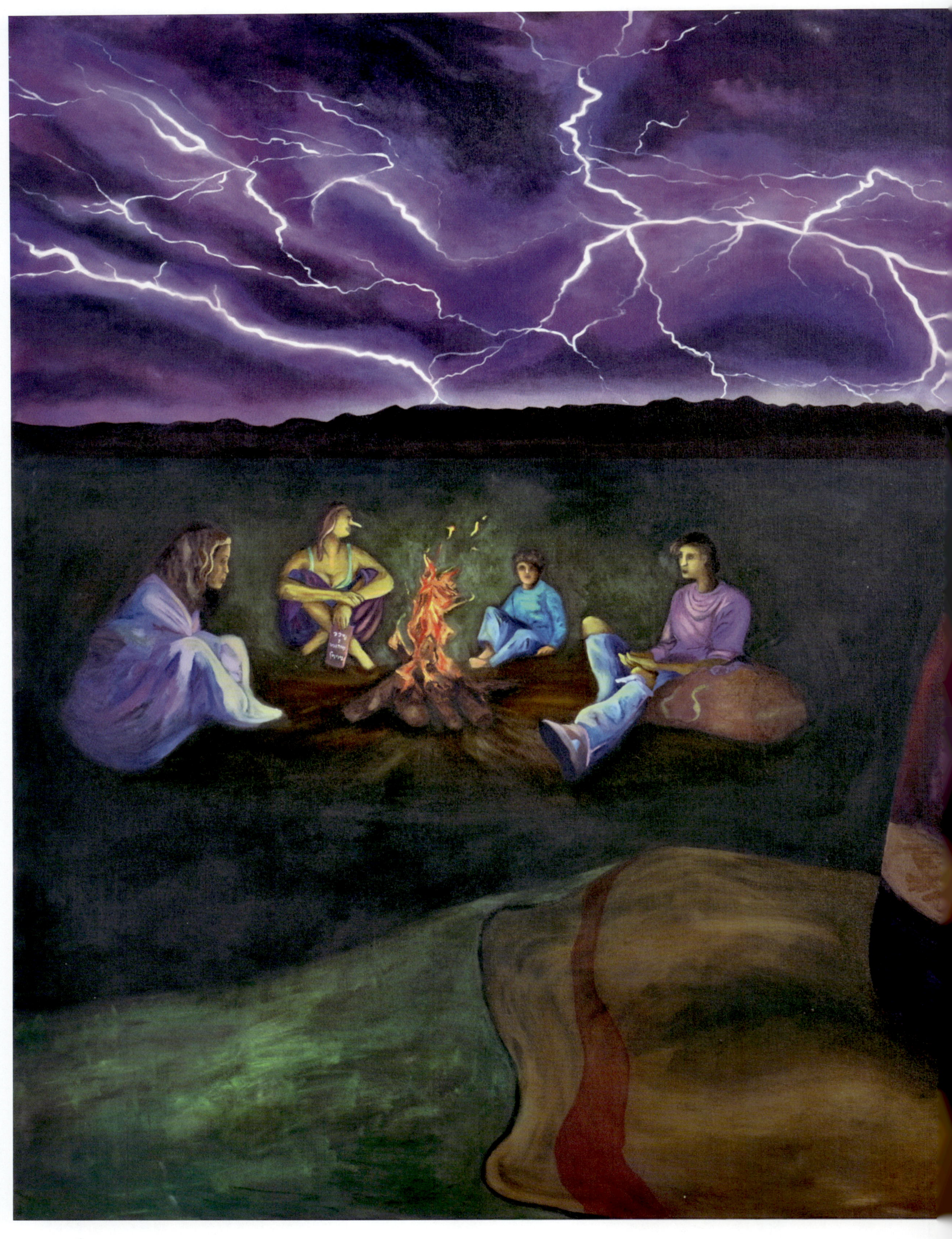

Guerra e pace (After M.O.), 2023   195×306 cm

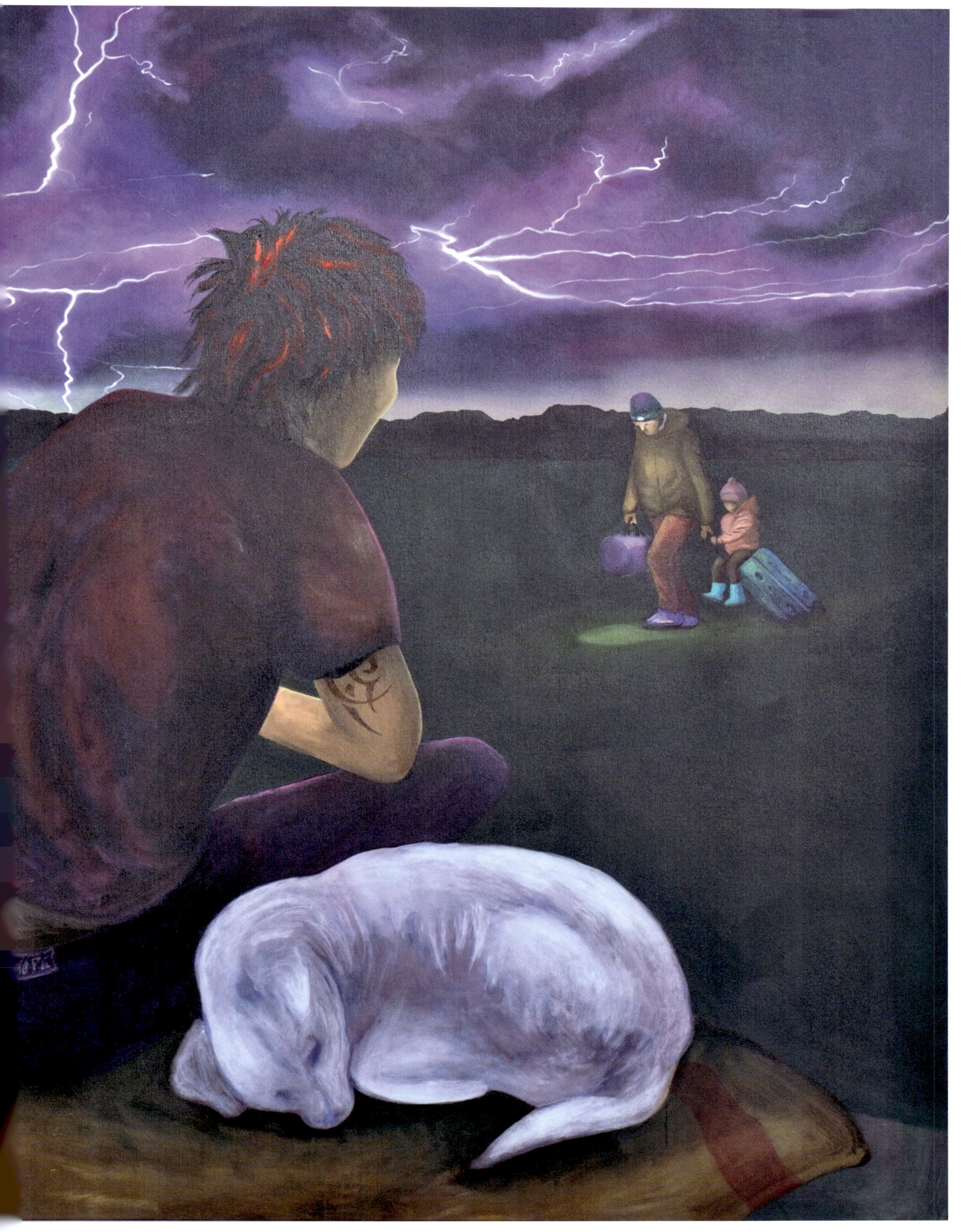

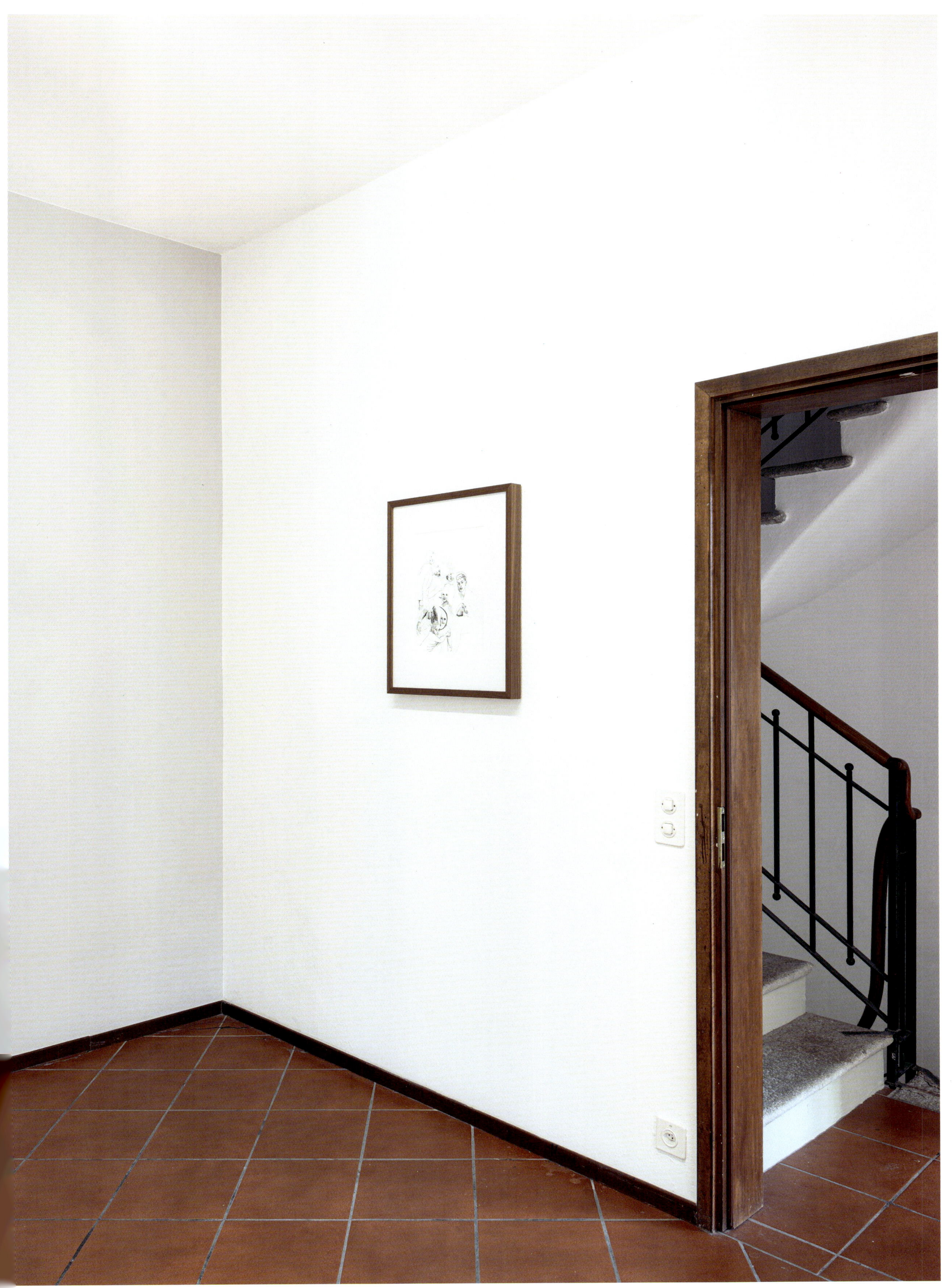

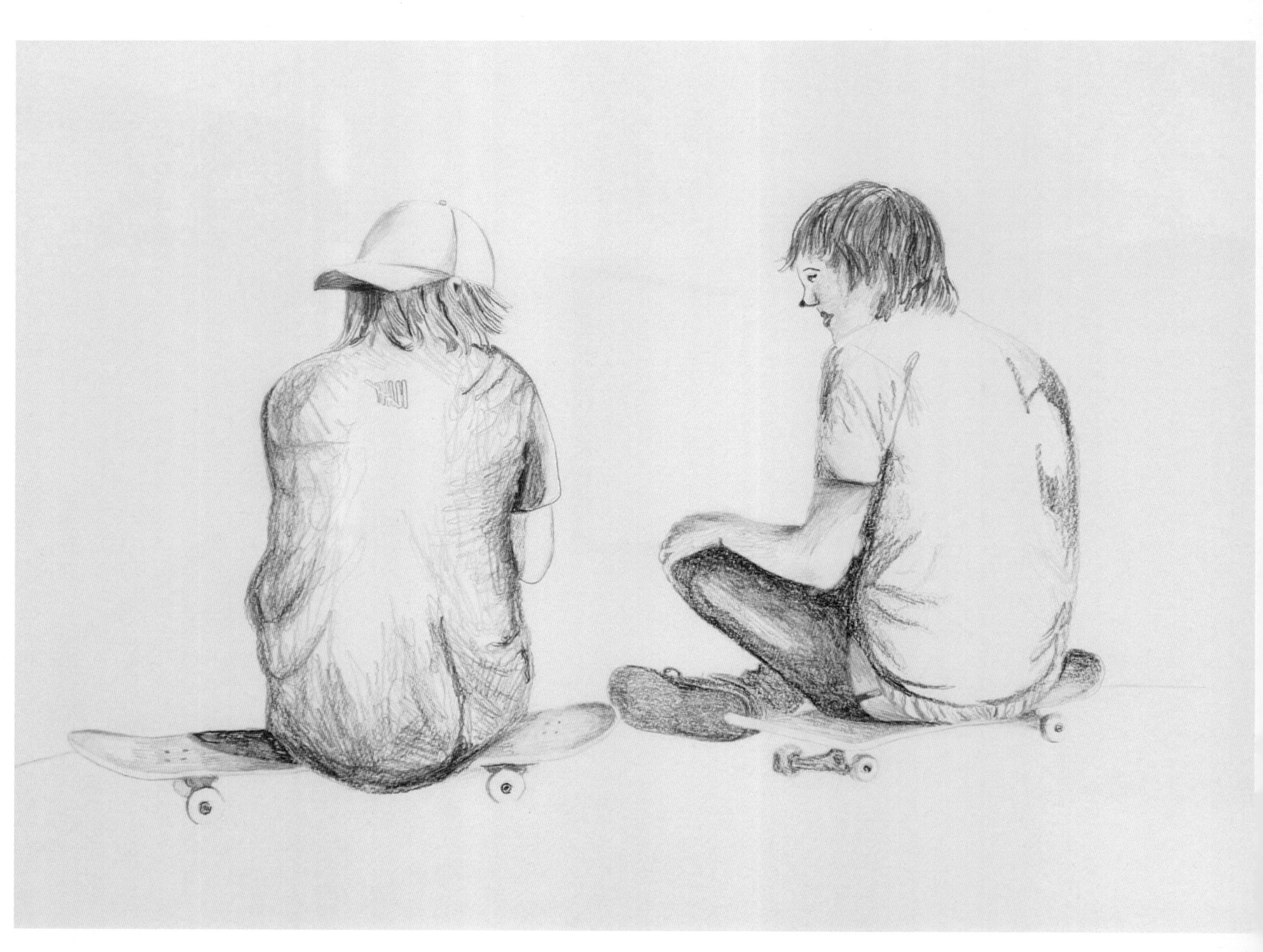

On n'est pas sérieux, quand on a dix-sept ans, 2023   29.7 × 42 cm   104

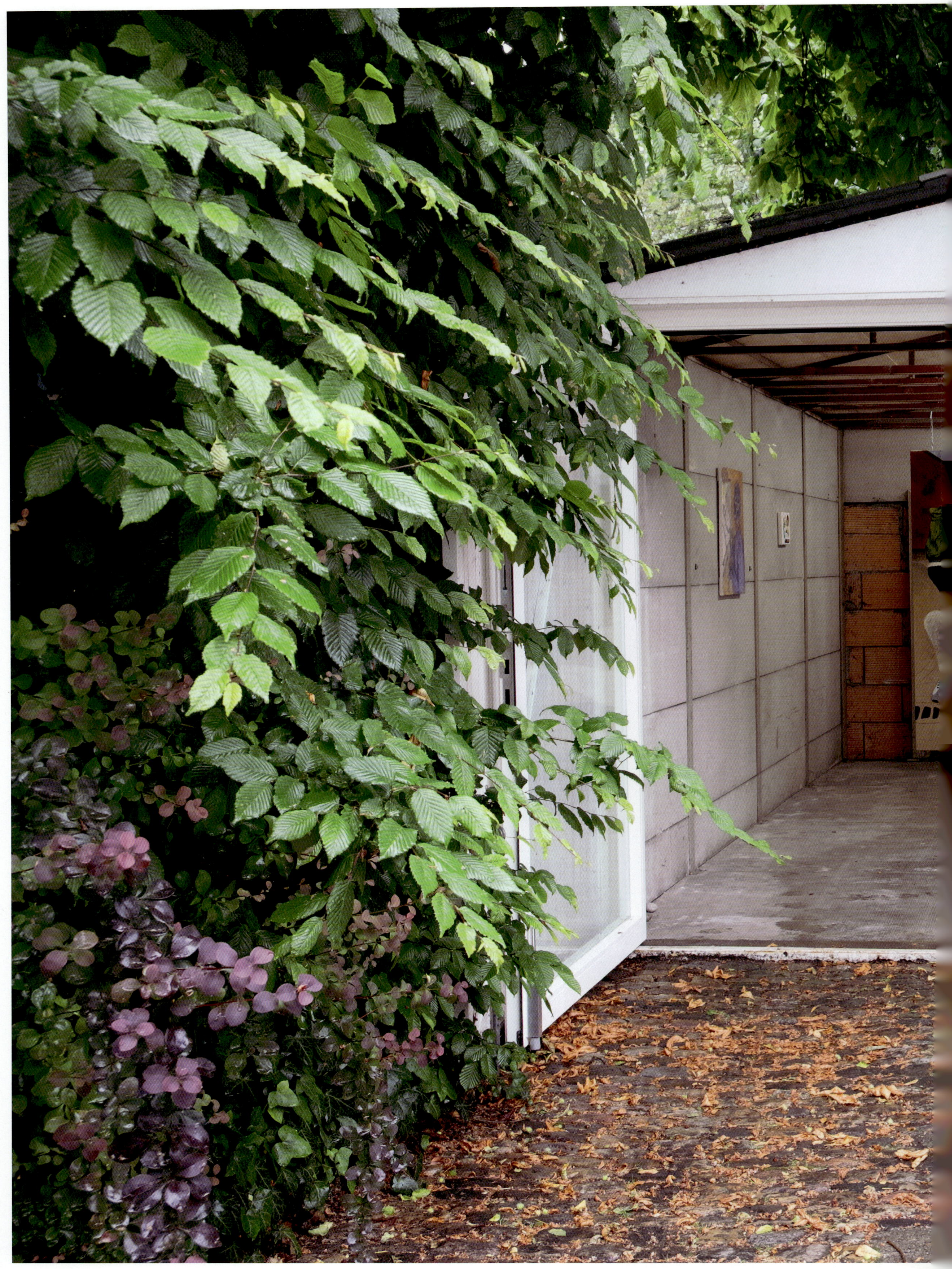

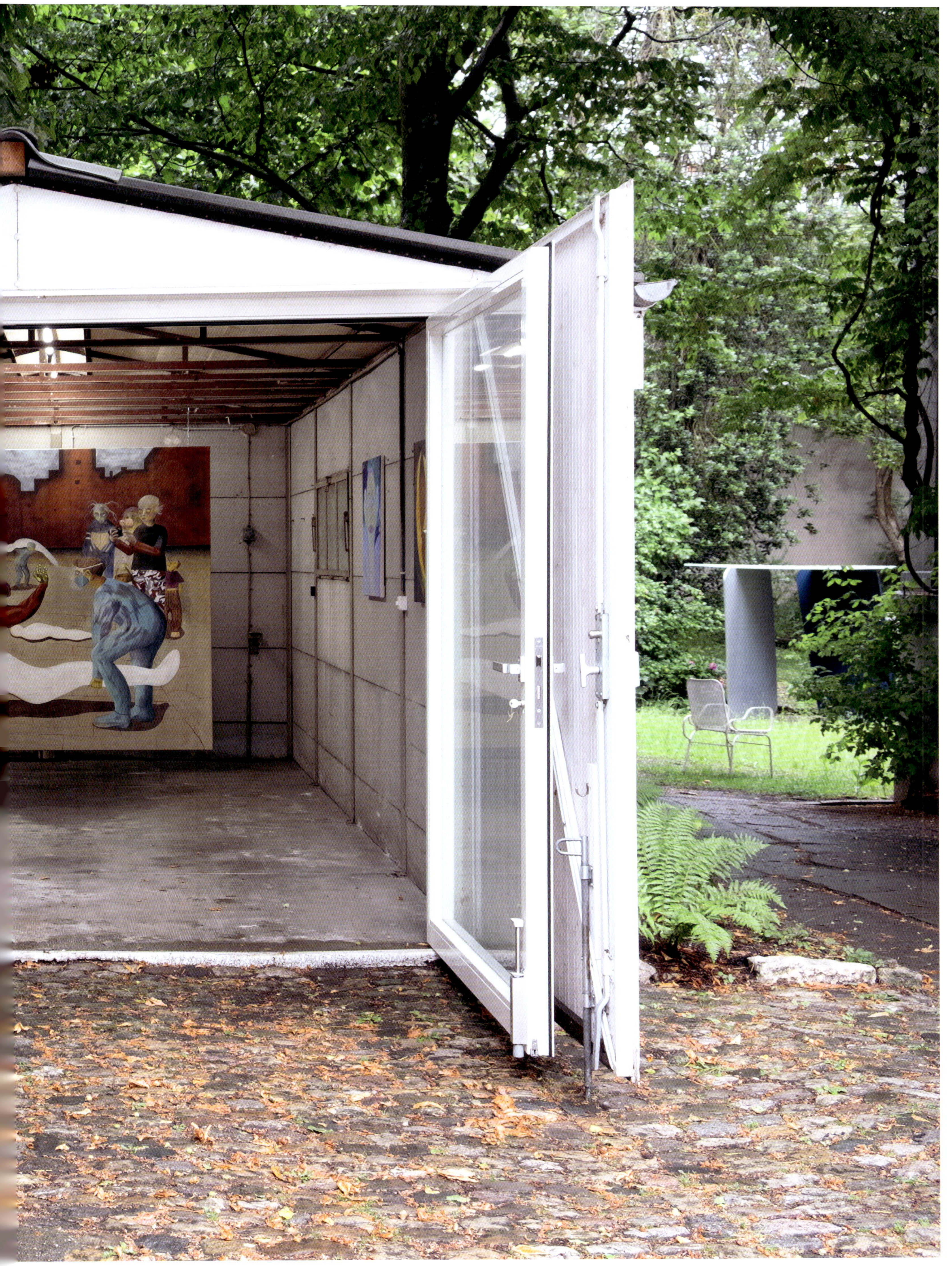

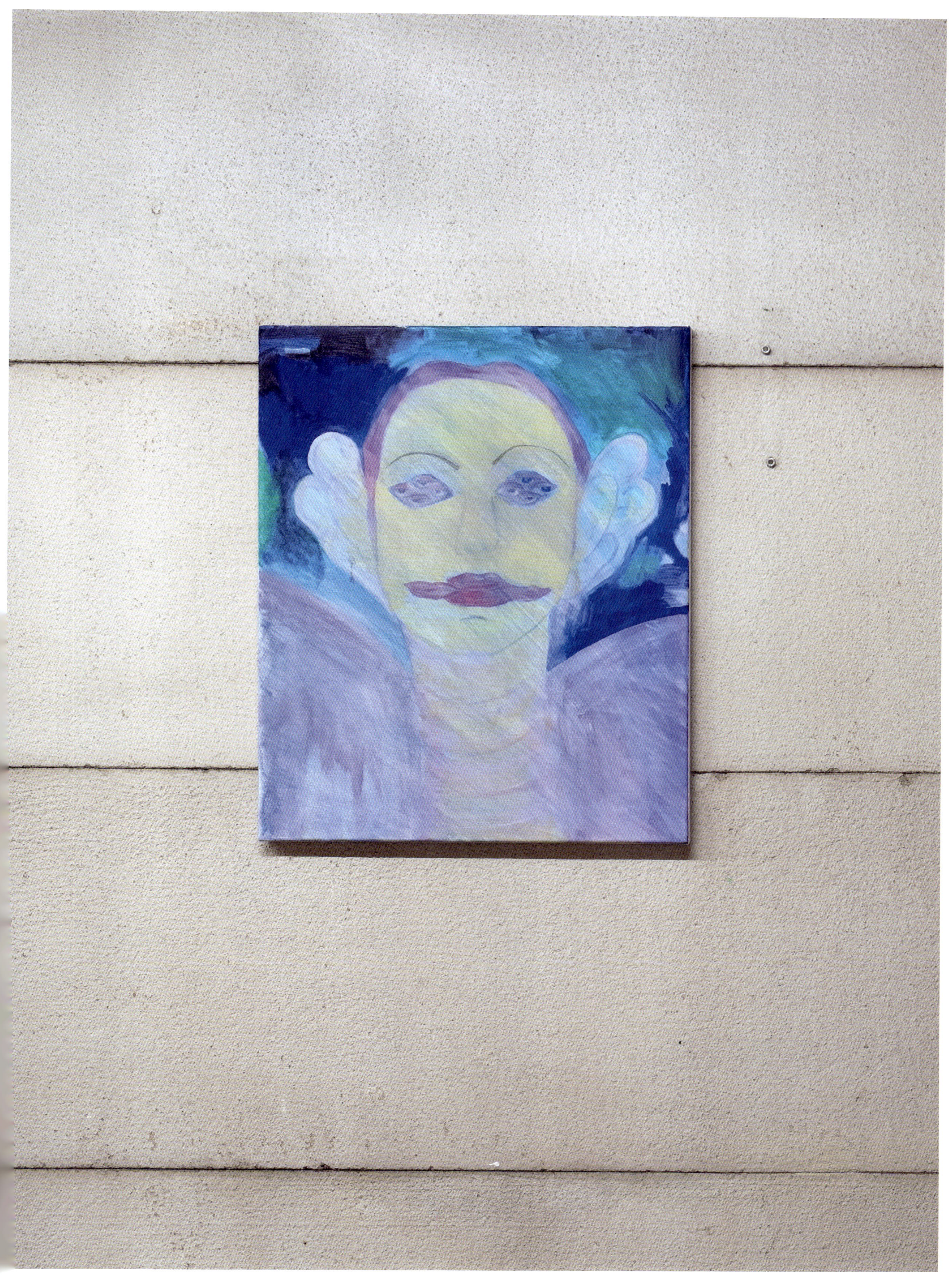

Omaggio a Marguerite Burnat-Provins, 2021   63×51 cm   109

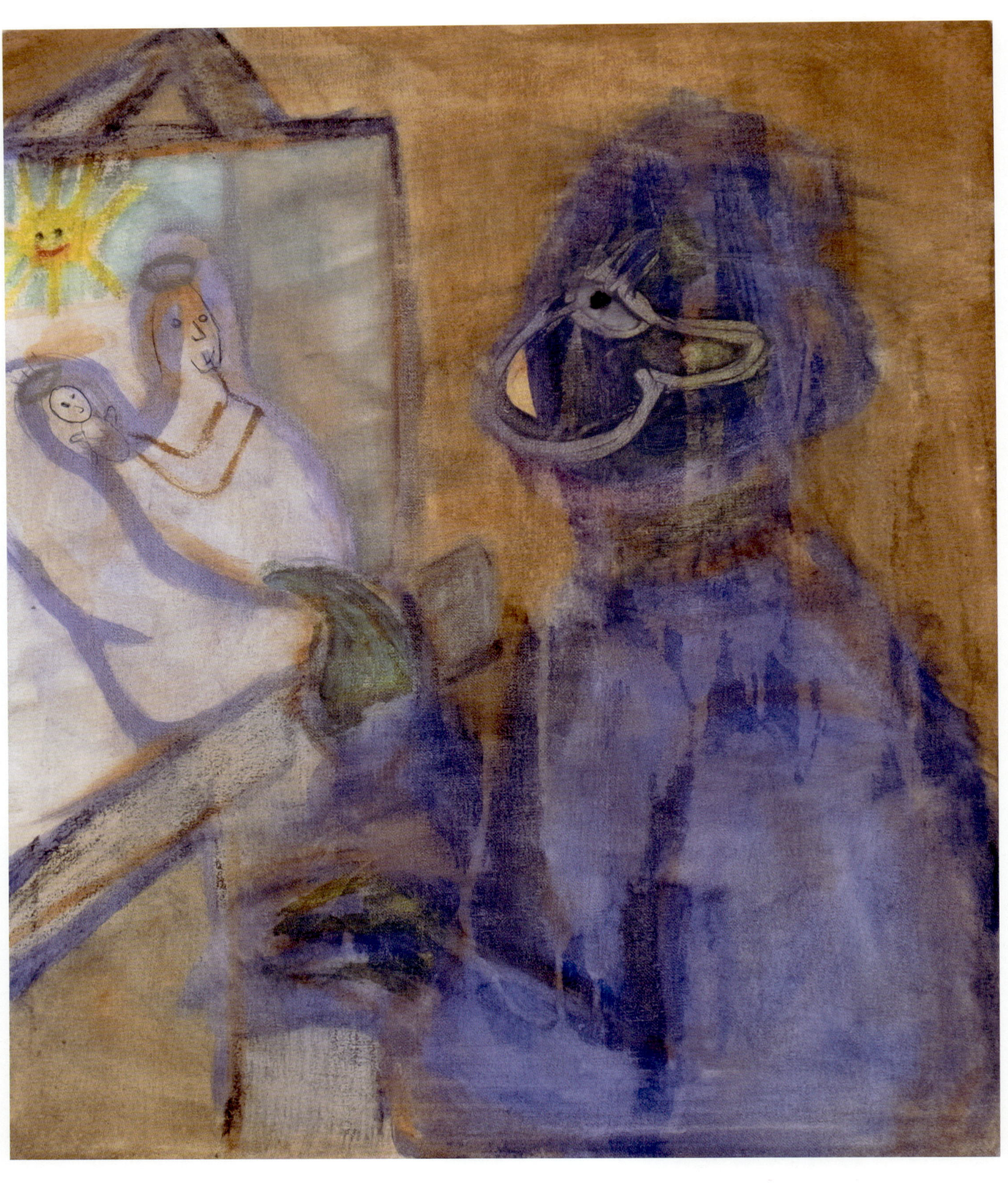

Die Malerin, 2018   59×50 cm

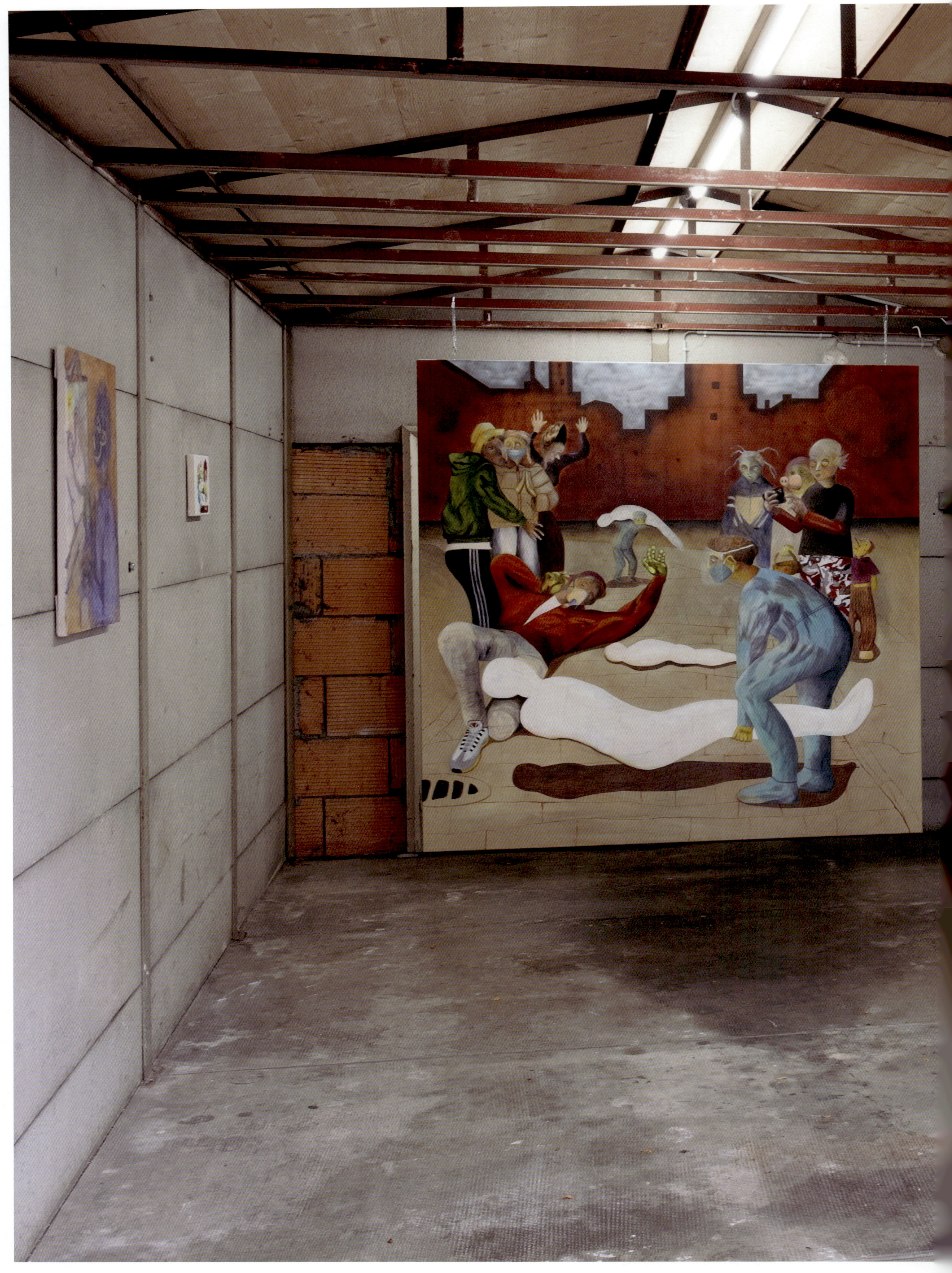

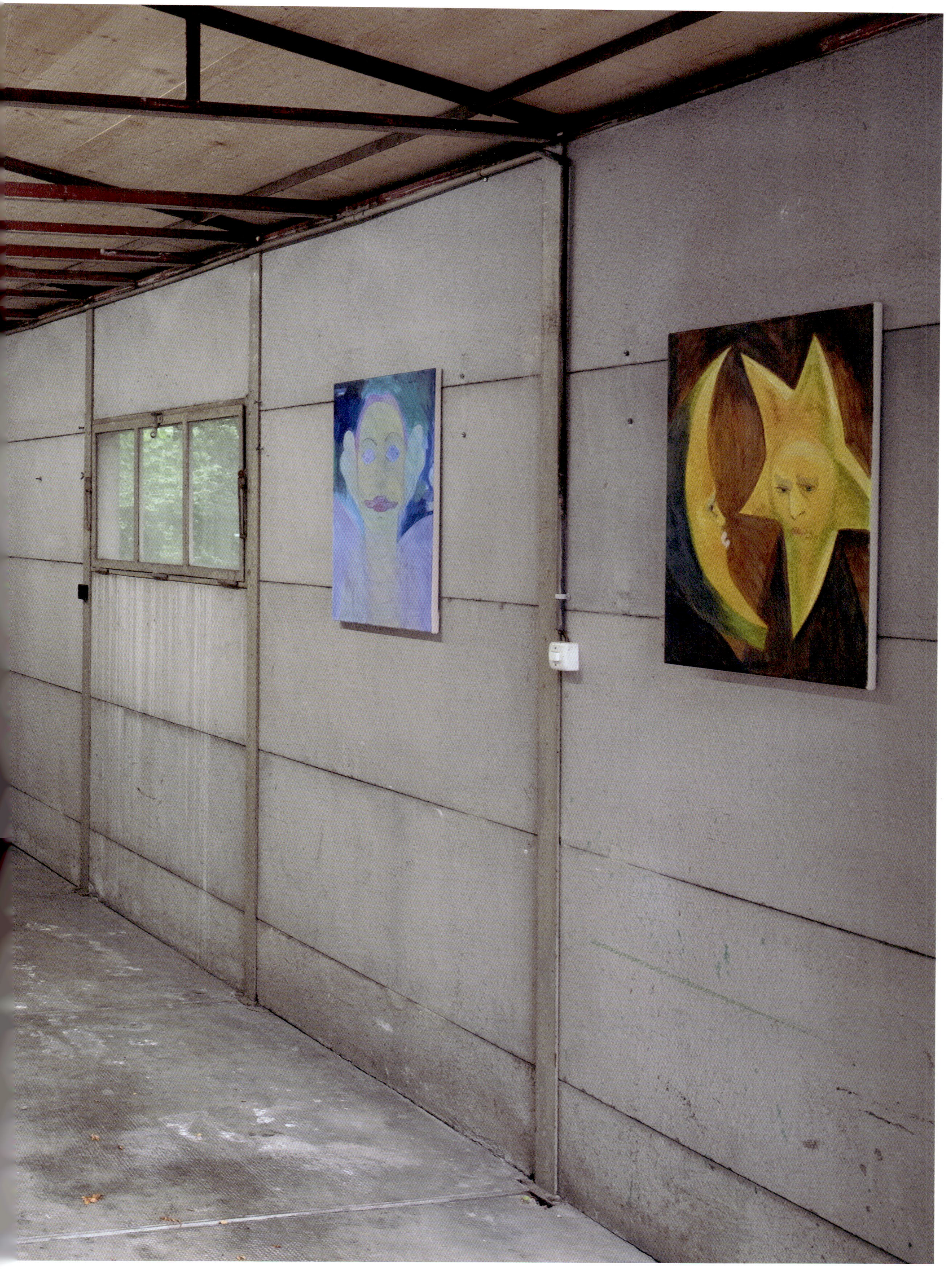

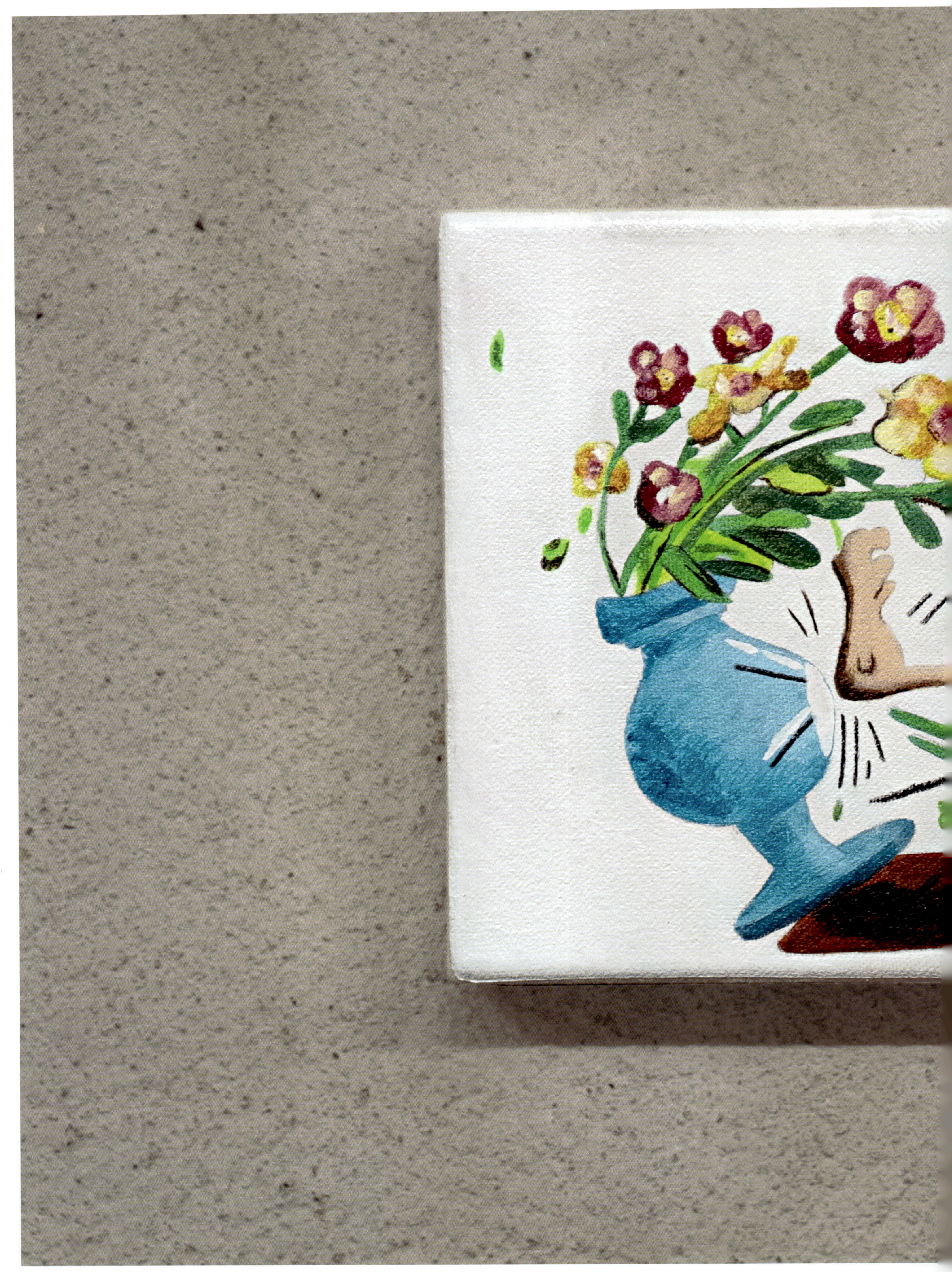

Pumuckl, 2022   18×24 cm

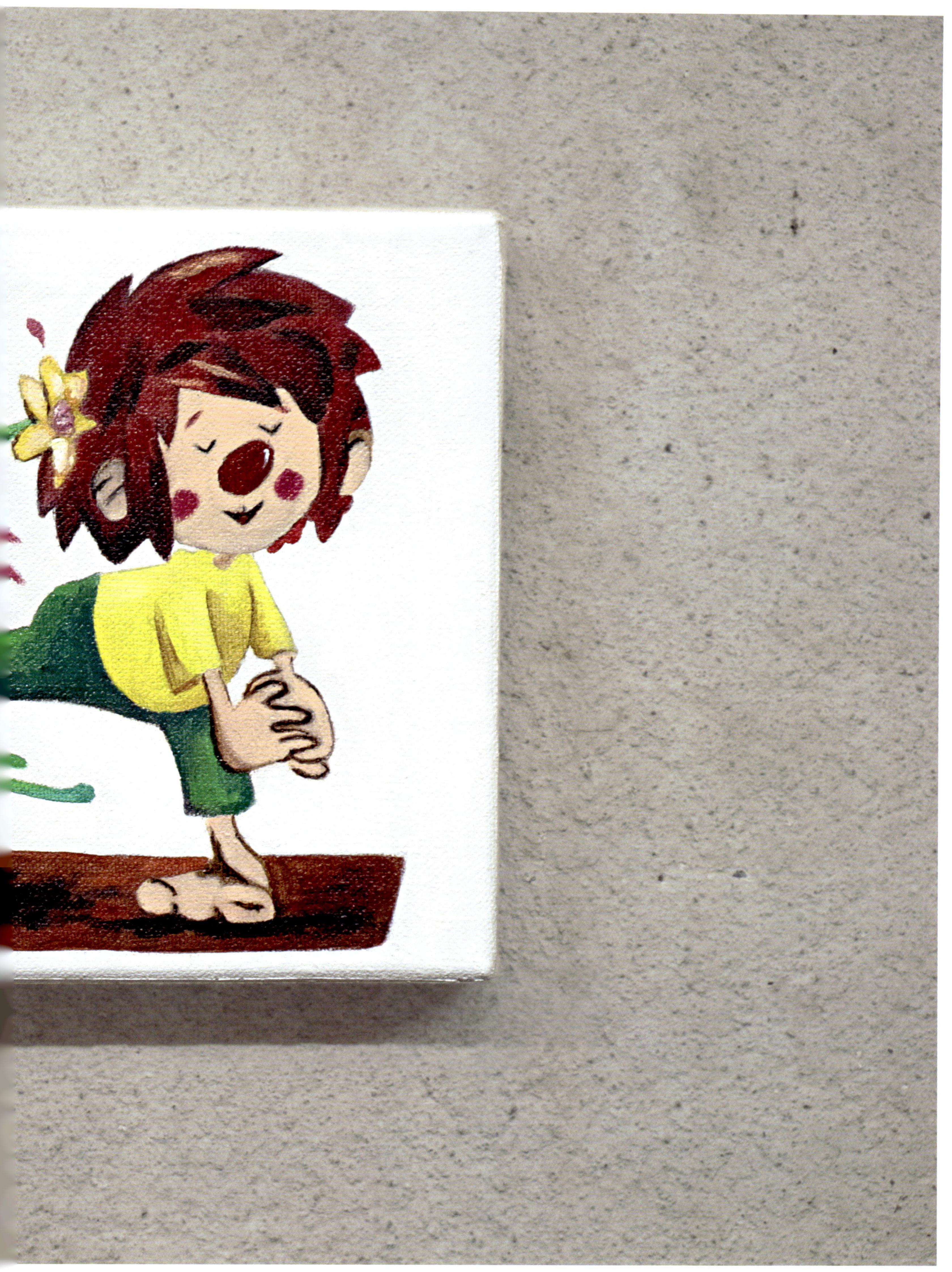

Although as children we were promised the moon, and although we grew up playfully with the idea that we would be able to achieve fulfillment in the bosom of the economic boom of our parents, it is quite challenging today to grasp this rosy future—or to even imagine it. The idea of the approaching future is inevitably shaped by the climate crisis, the collapse of capitalism without alternative systems for offsetting it, and the widespread acceptance of the dominance of the stronger ones. With this in mind, more and more broligarch techno-utopias are imposing themselves whose optimism regarding the future is given a boost in spite of—or perhaps because of—the abovementioned scenarios. The optimism is expressed with visions of human settlements on Mars and conquering the world with an army of artificial intelligence. In this megalomania, current scenarios of the future appear more as challenges requiring technical solutions from human geniuses than irreversible catastrophes. As philosopher and psychoanalyst Daniel Strassberg stated, "Reality is denied by suggesting a future that will not be able to exist because the present has already done away with it."[1]

We can either accept that the rosy future of our childhood no longer exists or forget that this promise of the future ever existed. If we choose the latter, we can continue as before and pursue the goal that at some point we will belong to those who call themselves winners in spite of the dysfunctional tendencies of the system. All we have to do is call upon the entrepreneurial self that we have learned to activate in our careers: a self that sees itself as an autonomous center of action and planning office for its own life and chalks it up as its own "defeats as individual planning deficits."[2] The failure of the earlier vision of the future does not require political answers but the assumption of self-responsibility: it is possible to learn from the present, with the goal of fortifying oneself. In this learning process, the entrepreneurial self does not take responsibility for problems that arose, but it does take responsibility for finding a solution. Instead of being related to the past, the present is oriented on the future: the self is ahead of its time, on its way with a breath of fresh air and deploys its current entrepreneurship in a speculative manner.

Philosopher Armen Avanessian and cultural scholar Suhail Malik even describe the future-oriented present as the basic structure of our era.[3] According to them, we have long been living in a boom of the future, in which the future replaces the present as the primary structuring aspect of time. Much of what we do is investment. What we do takes the future into account, that is, it happens with one foot firmly in the future. More than the meaning of the action itself, what motivates us is the possibilities that it might open for us. However, the future-oriented present does not have to be accompanied at all by an optimistic belief in the future. The entrepreneurial self would not be itself if it did not practice resilience and prepare itself for future catastrophes

so that if the hoped-for future does not arrive, it can survive that which comes in the mildest possible way. This means: if you remain pliable and are able to react in a flexible manner, you will be successful. If you are inflexible and remain confidently on course, you are in danger of suffering damage. Once you have learned to deal with disasters, you seem to have the power to act, and the catastrophe is only half as bad. The aim of empowerment in this case is not the distribution of power but overcoming the feeling of impotence. As long as we can convince ourselves to aspire at some point, all is well.

However, when the enthusiasm of crisis management is exhausted and hesitation sets in on the racetrack, it becomes possible to view the catastrophes as such. If we compare the present with what was once promised to us as the future, and then look into the future from this point, that is when a sort of "future nostalgia" sets in, as cultural scholar Maximilian Jablonowski outlines.[4] This sort of future nostalgia does not come about through the absence of (alternative) utopias, but through the loss of "future shocks," as cultural scholar Marc Fisher describes: the loss of a feeling of disruptive futurity that is triggered by something that seems so new it cannot be categorized in existing patterns of understanding.[5] It is such promising, condensed avant-garde moments of shock that fail to materialize when the already failed promises of the future begin to repeat themselves and there is already a sense of disappointment about the proposed future. This is the moment in which the loss of the future visions becomes clear, although the loss has not yet been mourned.

According to the psychoanalyst Sigmund Freud, melancholy means the abnormal inability to mourn a loss.[6] Loss that is unmourned remains latently present as a melancholy gap that only can be healed by a true process of mourning. Yet with or without Freudian pathologization: anticipated disappointment from repeated promises and the admittance of loss of those visions of the future that were forgotten on the racetrack of one's own biography need to be examined more thoroughly. Instead of mourning loss and replacing it with a new "object of desire"—as Freud describes the process of healing—it needs to be asked which losses need to be mourned and which need to be revived. Which nearly forgotten hopes are to be remembered, which ideals are to be buried? This is less about differentiating between healthy and sick forms of dealing with loss than about the deliberate selection between remembering again and wanting to forget. This task cannot be approached as an entrepreneurial self but requires a completely different state of mind and body.

In order not to suffer a heat stroke in an overheated world, staying cool or practicing self-cooling can prove helpful. Whether it is done with sunglasses, Jump 'n' Run, wellness or drugs, binge-watching series about emigration, encounters with animals,

techno raves, yoga retreats, memes about getting up, nature excursions, or watching late-night shows: cooling the mind can be done in very different ways. In order not to lapse into a fundamental indifference about the great variety of cooling available but to achieve the desired state of mind and body, to dedicate oneself to the mindful selection of remembering and forgetting, there is also the possibility of warming oneself in places and on a small scale. It is a matter of persevering and lingering, trusting one another, creating proximity, being cute, establishing a new definition of love, and sharing current feelings (through emojis). Around the fire pit of e-scooters, you can simultaneously warm yourself and cool off from the rest of the world.

At this melting point of states of being, a temporary, fragile space might develop in which past ideas are mourned together and unclaimed desires are revived. The melancholy that we bear together can then serve as fertile ground for temporarily giving up the leap into the future and making longings that were forgotten present again. Only then can a vague feeling of futurity be developed that is expressed less through "future shocks" than in emotional awareness for visions of living together: "future nostalgia." This makes melancholy and coolness the right resources for not forgetting what seems to have been lost. Melancholy allows things that were formerly important to continue slumbering so that at some point they can be collectively reformulated with a cool head and body.

In this conflation of feelings, thoughts, persons, and surroundings we turn our backs to a very specific conception of being human: the rational, autonomous, consistent, and self-reflective subject that understands itself and elevates the world surrounding it to an idea. It is a construct of modernism that needs to be done away with, a concept of subject that is based on the ideals of the Enlightenment and was linked with neoliberal ideals of a productive society: we are responsible for our own destiny and earn our happiness individually and independently. Bumming around together as a cyborg may, however, be revealed as resilience, in which resistance does not represent a new act of heroic self-assertion but rather a loss of function and a failure within a rotten system. It is Haraway's cyborg[7]: instead of engaging in star wars, it would represent a social and physical reality in which no one fears proximity to other people, animals, machines, and environments. Categories would be rejected, dichotomies blurred, and gender and origin dissolved. It would be a dismantled, reassembled, collective, and individual self, a "friendly self" without a common language that nevertheless phrases things collectively. Perhaps it is this cyborg that in the current storm of wildfires, ideological hardening, and the return of imperialism will be able to evade temporal directionality and imagine a viable path into the future by processually linking present and past.

Melancholie und Coolness. Ressourcen zur Bildung von Zukunft
Valerie Keller

Obwohl uns Kindern das Blaue vom Himmel versprochen wurde, obwohl wir spielend heranwuchsen mit der Idee, uns im Schosse des elterlichen Wirtschaftsaufschwungs später selbst zu verwirklichen, bereitet es uns heute grösste Mühe, diese rosige Zukunft zu ergreifen, oder gar zu imaginieren. Die Vorstellung einer nahenden Zukunft ist unweigerlich geprägt von der Klimakatastrophe, dem Kollaps des Kapitalismus ohne alternative Auffangsysteme und der breiten Akzeptanz von der Dominanz des Stärkeren. Vor diesem Hintergrund drängen sich vermehrt broligarchische Tech-Utopien auf, deren Zukunftsoptimismus trotz oder gerade wegen der genannten Szenarien Aufwind erhält. Er drückt sich in Visionen aus, den Mars zu besiedeln und mit einer Armee aus künstlichen Intelligenzen die Welt zu erobern. Gegenwärtige Zukunftsszenarien erscheinen in diesem Grössenwahn weniger als irreversible Katastrophen denn als Herausforderungen, für die es technischer Lösungen von genialen Menschen bedarf. Mit dem Philosophen und Psychoanalytiker Daniel Strassberg ausgedrückt: «Die Realität wird verleugnet, indem eine Zukunft suggeriert wird, die es nicht mehr geben wird, weil die Gegenwart sie schon abgeschafft hat.»[1]

Entweder können wir akzeptieren, dass es die rosige Zukunft unserer Kindheit nicht mehr gibt, oder wir können vergessen, dass es dieses Zukunftsversprechen überhaupt einmal gab. Wählen wir Letzteres, können wir fortfahren wie bisher und das Ziel verfolgen, irgendwann zu denen zu gehören, die sich trotz dysfunktionaler Tendenzen Gewinner:innen des Systems nennen. Dazu müssten wir nur das unternehmerische Selbst aufrufen, das wir in unserer Laufbahn zu aktivieren gelernt haben: ein Selbst, das sich als autonomes Handlungszentrum und Planungsbüro des eigenen Lebens versteht, und die eigenen «Niederlagen als individuelle Planungsdefizite»[2] verbucht. Das Nichteintreffen von einstmaligen Zukunftsvorstellungen erfordert dann keine politischen Antworten, sondern die Übernahme von Eigenverantwortung: Gelernt wird aus der Gegenwart und mit dem Ziel, sich selbst zu stärken. Das unternehmerische Selbst übernimmt in diesem Lernprozess also nicht die Verantwortung für entstandene Probleme, sondern die Verantwortung dafür, eine Lösung zu finden. Die Gegenwart wird nicht auf die Vergangenheit bezogen, sondern nach der Zukunft ausgerichtet: Das Selbst ist seiner Zeit stets voraus, mit Zukunftswind unterwegs und entfaltet sein gegenwärtiges Unternehmertum in spekulativer Weise.

Der Philosoph Armen Avanessian und der Kulturwissenschaftler Suhail Malik beschreiben die zukunftsorientierte Gegenwart sogar als grundlegende Struktur unserer Zeit.[3] Ihnen zufolge leben wir längst in einer Konjunktur der Zukunft, in der die Zukunft die Gegenwart als den primär strukturierenden Aspekt von Zeit ersetzt hat. Vieles von dem, was wir tun, ist Investition. Was wir tun, geschieht mit dem Blick in die Zukunft, ist mit einem Bein schon in ihr drin. Was uns dazu motiviert, ist weniger der Sinn der Handlungen selbst als die Möglichkeiten, die sie uns eröffnen könnten. Die zukunftsorientierte Gegenwart muss jedoch keinesfalls mit einem optimistischen Glauben an die Zukunft einhergehen. Das unternehmerische Selbst wäre nicht es selbst, würde es sich nicht in Resilienz üben und sich auf zukünftige Katastrophen vorbereiten, um – sollte die erhoffte Zukunft nicht eintreffen – das Kommende möglichst glimpflich zu überstehen. Es gilt: Erfolgreich wird, wer biegbar bleibt und flexibel auf Anforderungen reagieren kann. Wer starr und überzeugt auf Kurs bleibt, läuft Gefahr, Schäden zu erleiden. Ist erst erlernt, mit Katastrophen umzugehen, scheint auch die Handlungsmacht gegeben und die Katastrophe nur halb so wild zu sein. Empowerment zielt in diesem Fall nicht auf die Umverteilung von Macht, sondern darauf, das Gefühl von Ohnmacht zu überwinden. Solange wir uns selbst überzeugen, irgendwann aufzustreben, ist alles gut.

Wenn sich aber der Enthusiasmus der Krisenbewältigung erschöpft und sich ein Zögern auf der Rennbahn einstellt, dann wird es möglich, die Katastrophen als solche zu betrachten. Vergleichen wir die Gegenwart mit dem, was uns einst als Zukunft versprochen wurde, und blicken davon ausgehend in die Zukunft: Dann kann sich im Sinn des Kulturwissenschaftlers Maximilian Jablonowski eine Art «Future Nostalgia» einstellen.[4] Diese Art von Zukunftsnostalgie entstehe nicht etwa durch das Ausbleiben von (alternativen) Utopien, sondern durch den Verlust von «Future Shocks», wie ihn Fachkollege Marc Fisher beschreibt: der Verlust von einem Gefühl disruptiver Zukünftigkeit, ausgelöst durch etwas, was sich derart neu anfühlt, dass es nicht in bisherige Verstehensmuster eingeordnet werden könne.[5] Es sind diese verheissungsvollen, avantgardistisch verdichteten Schockmomente, die ausbleiben, wenn sich bereits gescheiterte Zukunftsversprechen zu wiederholen beginnen und die Enttäuschung über die skizzierte Zukunft bereits vorgefühlt wird. Es ist der Moment, in dem der Verlust an Zukunftsvisionen deutlich wird, dieser Verlust aber noch nicht betrauert wurde.

Nach dem Psychoanalytiker Sigmund Freud bedeutet Melancholie die krankhafte Unfähigkeit, einen Verlust zu betrauern.[6] Das unbetrauert Verlorene bleibe latent als melancholische Lücke präsent, die nur durch einen richtigen Trauerprozess geheilt werden könne. Doch ob mit oder ohne freudianische Pathologisierung: Antizipierte Enttäuschung aus sich wiederholenden Versprechungen und das Eingeständnis des Verlusts all jener Zukunftsvisionen, die auf der Rennstrecke der eigenen Biografien vergessen gingen, bedürfen einer intensiven Zuwendung. Anstatt den Verlust zu betrauern und ihn mit einem neuen «Objekt der Begierde» zu ersetzen, wie Freud den Genesungsprozess beschreibt, muss die Frage gestellt werden, welche Verluste denn überhaupt betrauert und welche wiederbelebt werden wollen. Welche fast vergessenen Hoffnungen sollen erinnert, welche Ideale begraben werden? Dabei ginge es weniger um die Unterscheidung zwischen gesunden und kranken Formen der Verlustbewältigung denn um die bewusste Selektion zwischen Wieder-Erinnern und Vergessen-Wollen. Diese Aufgabe lässt sich nicht als unternehmerisches Selbst angehen, sondern bedarf eines ganz anderen Geistes- und Körperzustands.

Um in einer überhitzten Welt nicht dem Hitzschlag zu erliegen, kann sich die Coolness beziehungsweise die Praxis der Selbstkühlung gegenüber aufreibenden Umständen als hilfreich erweisen. Ob mit Sonnenbrille, Jump 'n' Run, Wellness oder Drogen, dem Bingewatching von Serien übers Auswandern, Begegnungen mit Tieren, Techno-Raves, Yoga-Retreat, Memes zum Aufstehen, Ausflügen in die Natur oder dem Verfolgen von Late-Night-Shows: Die Kühlung der Gemüter kann auf sehr unterschiedliche Weise erfolgen. Um im Grossaufgebot der Kühlung keiner grundsätzlichen Gleichgültigkeit zu verfallen, sondern den erwünschten Geistes- und Köperzustand zu erreichen, um sich darin der bewussten Selektion von Erinnern und Vergessen zu widmen, besteht auch die Möglichkeit, sich punktuell und im Kleinen zu erwärmen. Es geht darum, gemeinsam zu verharren und zu verweilen, aufeinander zu vertrauen, Nähe herzustellen, Cuteness zu kommunizieren, Liebe neu zu definieren und gegenwärtige Gefühle (durch Emojis) zu teilen. Um die Feuerstelle aus E-Scootern herum kann man sich gleichzeitig wärmen und gegen den Rest der Welt kühlen.

An diesem Schmelzpunkt der Seinszustände mag vielleicht ein vorübergehender, fragiler Raum entstehen, in dem vergangene Ideen gemeinsam betrauert und nicht eingelöste Wünsche wiederbelebt werden. Die gemeinsam getragene Melancholie kann dann als fruchtbarer Boden dienen, um den Hechtsprung in die Zukunft vorerst aufzugeben und in Vergessenheit geratene Sehnsüchte gegenwärtig zu machen. Erst damit kann ein vages Gefühl von Zukünftigkeit entwickelt werden, das sich weniger durch «Future Shocks» denn durch ein emotionales Bewusstsein für Visionen des Zusammenlebens ausdrückt: «Future Nostalgia». Melancholie und Coolness werden damit zu wichtigen Ressourcen, um nicht zu vergessen, was verloren gegangen zu sein scheint. Die Melancholie lässt weiterschlummern, was einmal wichtig war, um irgendwann mit kühlem Kopf und Körper gemeinsam neu formuliert zu werden.

In dieser Verschmelzung von Gefühlen, Gedanken, Personen und Umgebungen kehren wir uns ab von einer ganz bestimmten Vorstellung vom Menschsein: dem rationalen, autonomen, konsistenten und selbstreflexiven Subjekt, das sich selbst erkennt und die Welt um sich herum zur Idee erhebt. Es ist ein Konstrukt der Moderne, das es zu verabschieden gilt, ein auf Idealen der Aufklärung basierender Subjektbegriff, der mit neoliberalen Idealen einer produktiven Gesellschaft verbunden wurde: Selbstverantwortlich haben wir unser Schicksal in der Hand und verdienen unser Glück individuell und selbstständig.

Gemeinsames Gammeln als Cyborg mag sich demgegenüber als Widerstandskraft entpuppen, bei der der Widerstand keinen erneuten Akt heldenhafter Selbstbehauptung darstellt, sondern eher eine Funktionsuntauglichkeit und ein Versagen innerhalb eines faulen Systems. Es ist ein Haraway'scher Cyborg:[7] Er führe nicht den Krieg der Sterne, sondern stelle eine soziale und körperliche Wirklichkeit dar, in der niemand die Nähe zu anderen Menschen, Tieren, Maschinen und Umgebungen fürchte. Kategorien würden abgelehnt, Dichotomien verwischt und damit auch Geschlecht und Herkunft aufgelöst. Es sei ein zerlegtes, neu zusammengesetztes, kollektives und individuelles Selbst, ein *friendly self* ohne gemeinsame Sprache, das doch gemeinsam formuliere. Vielleicht ist es genau dieser Cyborg, der es im gegenwärtigen Sturm aus Waldbränden, ideologischen Verhärtungen und der Rückkehr des Imperialismus vermag, sich einer zeitlichen Gerichtetheit zu entziehen und in der prozessualen Verbindung von Gegenwart und Vergangenheit einen gangbaren Weg in die Zukunft zu imaginieren.

1   Daniel Strassberg, «Die Unfähigkeit zu trauern», in: *Republik*, 11.2.2025, https://www.republik.ch/2025/02/11/strassberg-die-unfaehigkeit-zu-trauern, abgerufen am 10.3.2025.
2   Ulrich Bröckling, *Das unternehmerische Selbst. Soziologie einer Subjektivierungsform*, Frankfurt am Main 2007.
3   Armen Avanessian und Suhail Malik (Hrsg.), *The Time Complex. Post-Contemporary*, Miami 2016.
4   Maximilian Jablonowski, «Zurück zur guten, neuen Zeit? Future Nostalgia», in: *For* 1 (2023), S. 30–37, https://for-space.ch/static/31d9d2039a5b26c3051a61c02ae29723/For_DRDN_No.1.pdf, abgerufen am 10.3.2025.
5   Marc Fisher, *Ghosts of My Life. Writings on Depression, Hauntology and Lost Futures*, Winchester 2014.
6   Sigmund Freud, «Trauer und Melancholie» [1915], in: ders., *Gesammelte Werke. Chronologisch geordnet*, Bd. 10: *Werke aus Jahren 1913–1917*, London 1949, S. 427–446.
7   Die Naturwissenschaftshistorikerin und Feministin Donna Haraway lieferte in den 1980er-Jahren in ihrem berühmten, von Ironie gezeichneten Essay «A Cyborg Manifesto» eine Neuinterpretation der Figur des Cyborgs: Als Mischwesen stellt es der Dystopie eines nach Besitz und Macht strebenden Kriegs der Sterne eine Utopie gegenüber, in der dichotome Denkmuster durchkreuzt und Herrschaftsverhältnisse untergraben werden. Siehe Donna J. Haraway, «Manifesto for Cyborgs: Science, Technology, and Socialist Feminism in the 1980s», in: *Socialist Review* 80 (1985), S. 65–107.

1   Daniel Strassberg, "Die Unfähigkeit zu trauern," *Republik* (February 11, 2025), https://www.republik.ch/2025/02/11/strassberg-die-unfaehigkeit-zu-trauern (accessed on March 10, 2025).
2   Ulrich Bröckling, *Das unternehmerische Selbst: Soziologie einer Subjektivierungsform* (Frankfurt am Main: Suhrkamp, 2007).
3   Armen Avanessian and Suhail Malik, eds., *The Time Complex: Post-Contemporary* (Miami: Name Publications, 2016).
4   Maximilian Jablonowski, "Zurück zur guten, neuen Zeit? Future Nostalgia," *For* 1 (2023): 30–37, https://for-space.ch/static/31d9d2039a5b26c3051a61c02ae29723/For_DRDN_No.1.pdf (accessed on March 10, 2025).
5   Marc Fisher, *Ghosts of My Life: Writings on Depression, Hauntology and Lost Futures* (Winchester: Zero Books, 2014).
6   Sigmund Freud, "Mourning and Melancholia" [1915], in *The Standard Edition of the Complete Psychological Works of Sigmund Freud*, vol. 14 (London: Hogarth Press and the Institute of Psychoanalysis, 1955), 243–58.
7   In the 1980s natural scientist and feminist Donna Haraway published her famous, ironic essay "A Cyborg Manifesto," a new interpretation of the figure of the cyborg: as a hybrid being, it contrasts the dystopia of a star wars striving for possession and power with the utopia in which dichotomic thought patterns are thwarted and power relations are undermined. See Donna J. Haraway, "Manifesto for Cyborgs: Science, Technology, and Socialist Feminism in the 1980s," *Socialist Review* 80 (1985): 65–107.

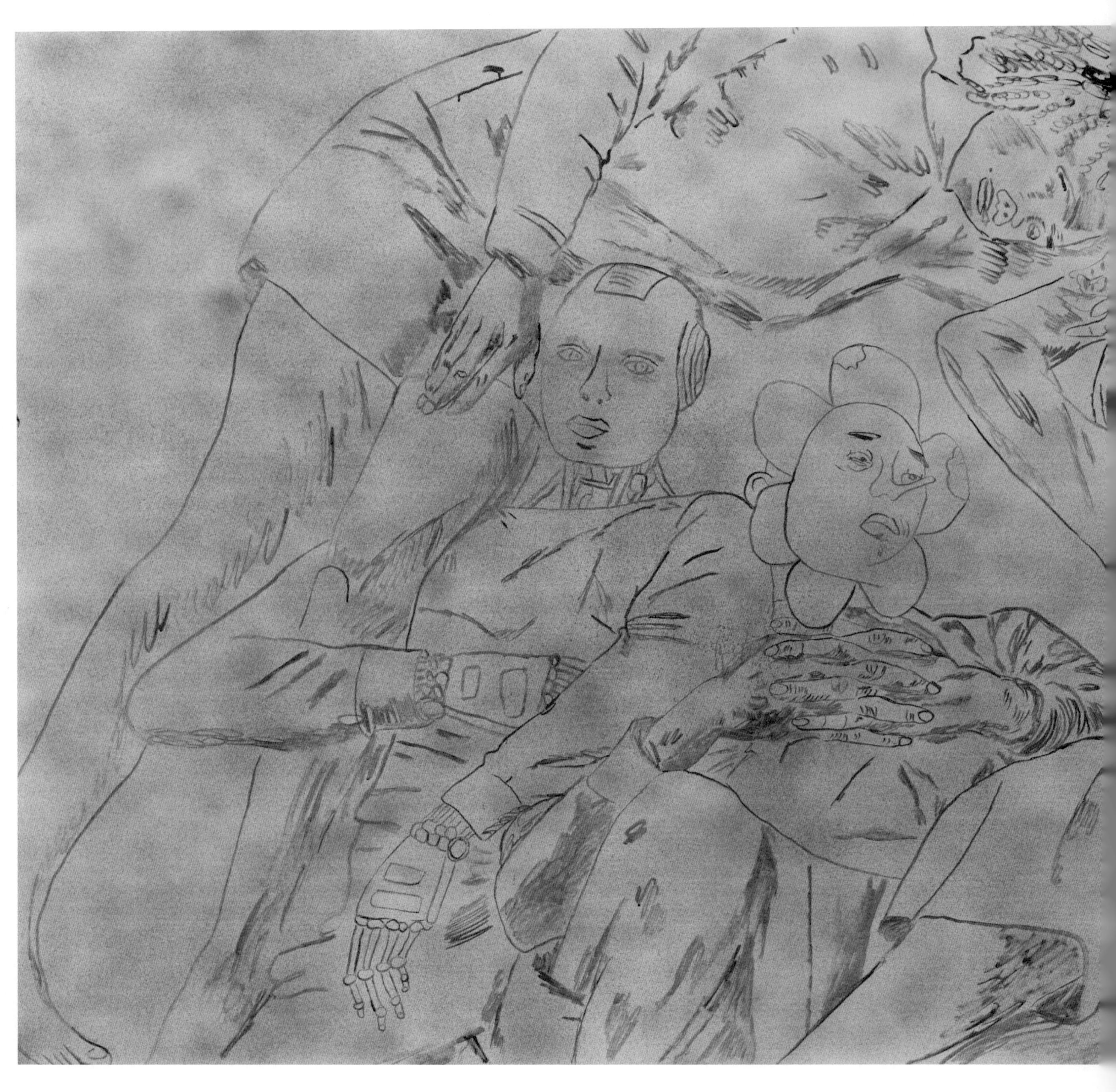

Blue, 2022   150×320 cm

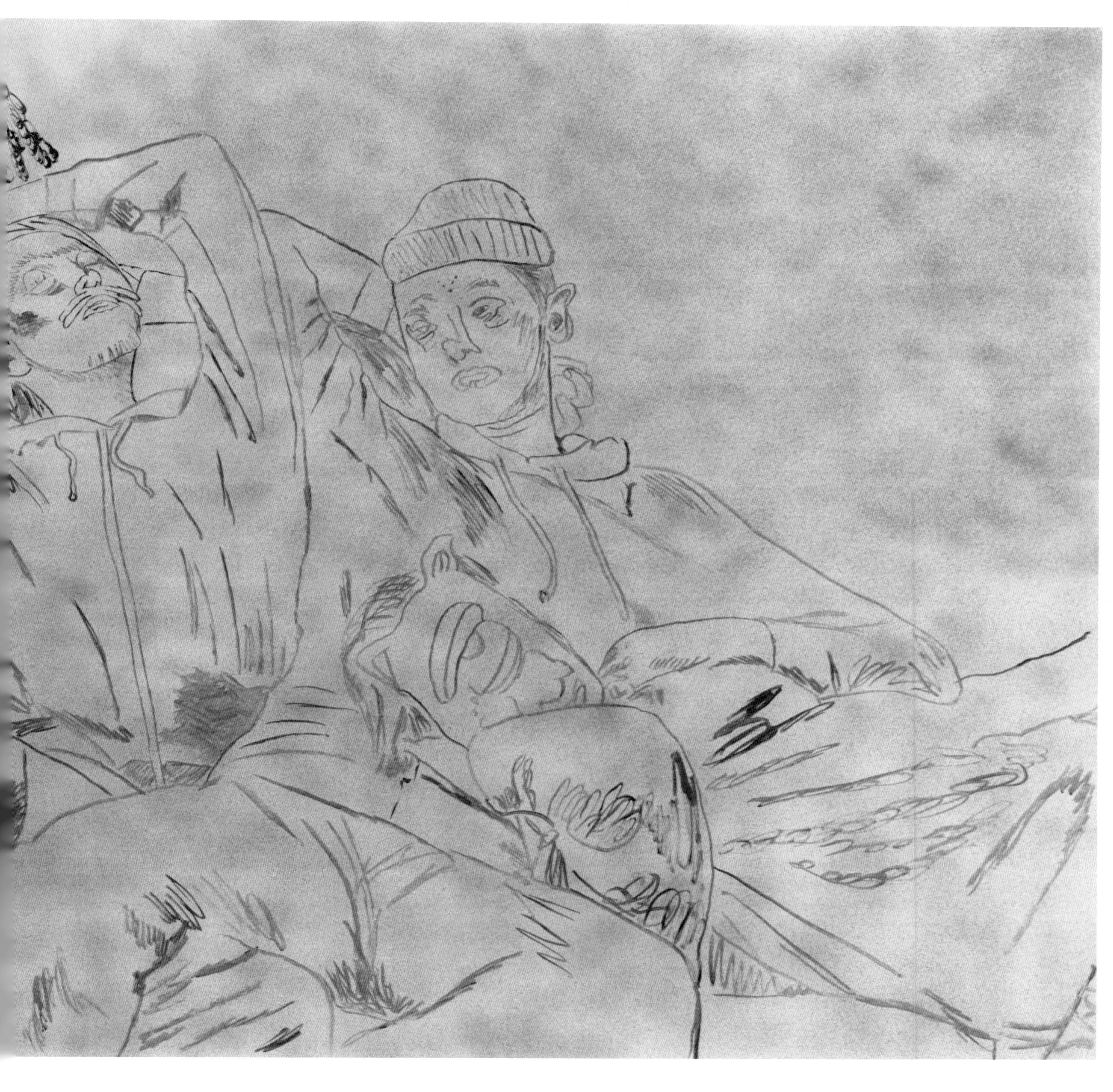

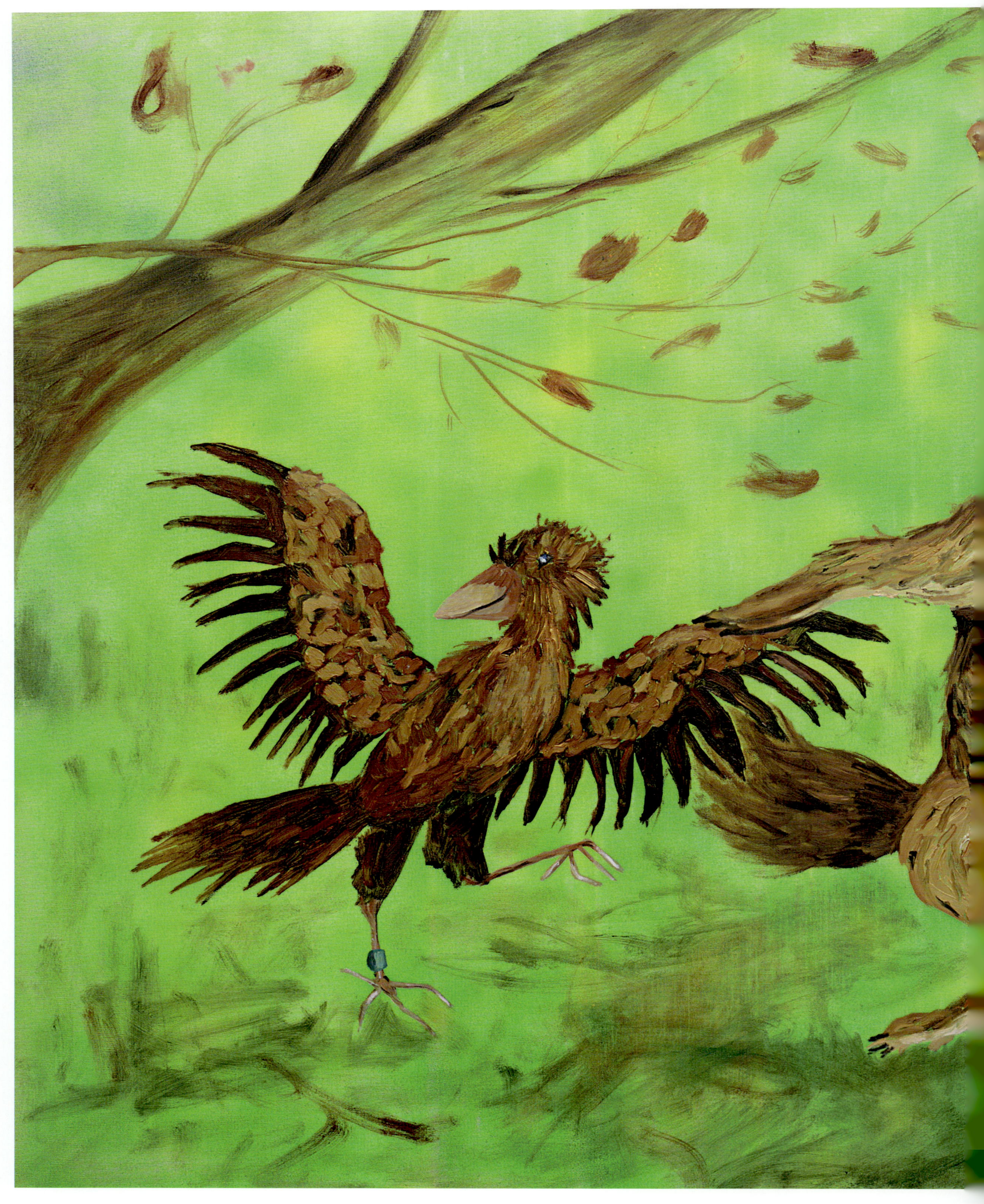

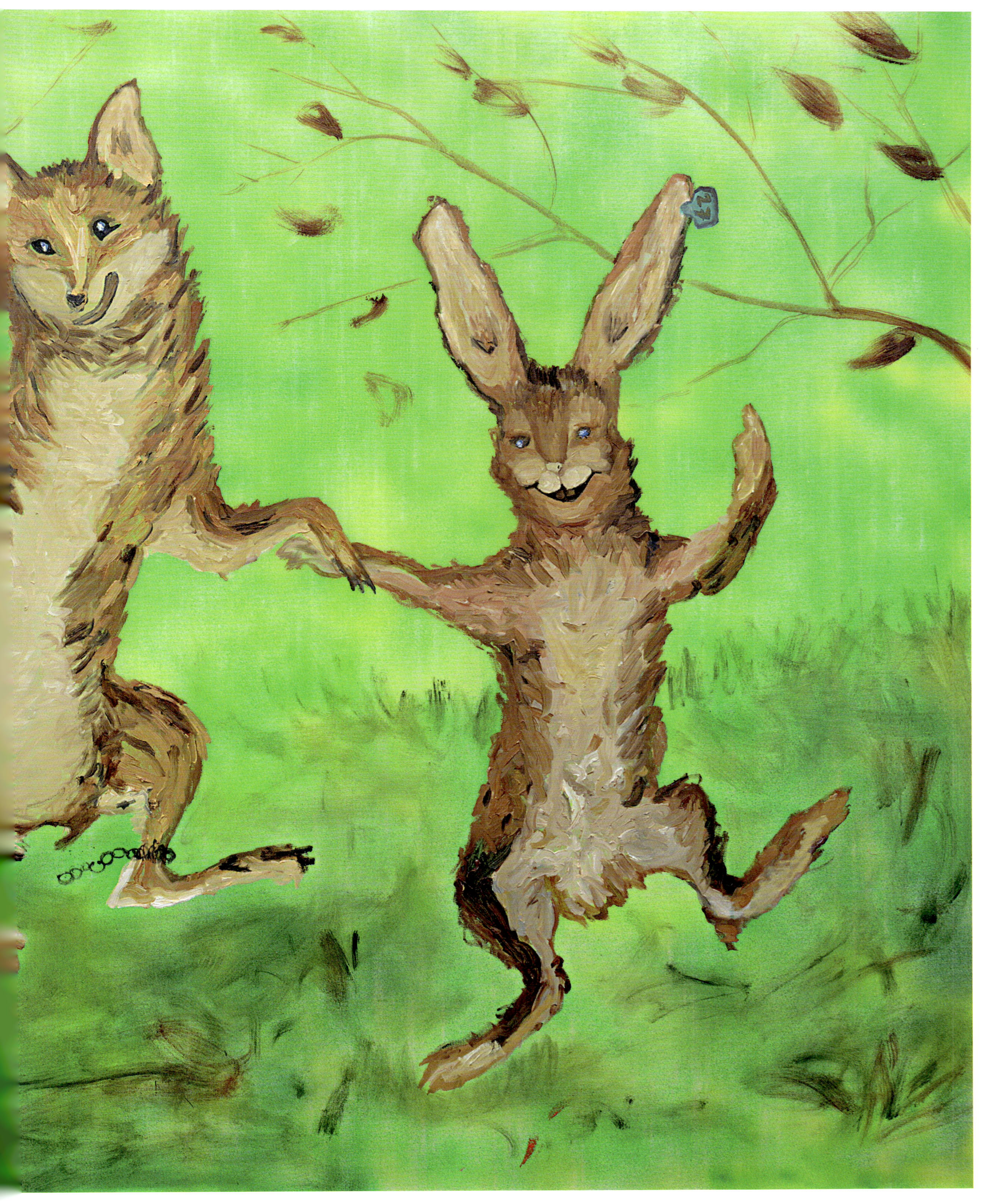

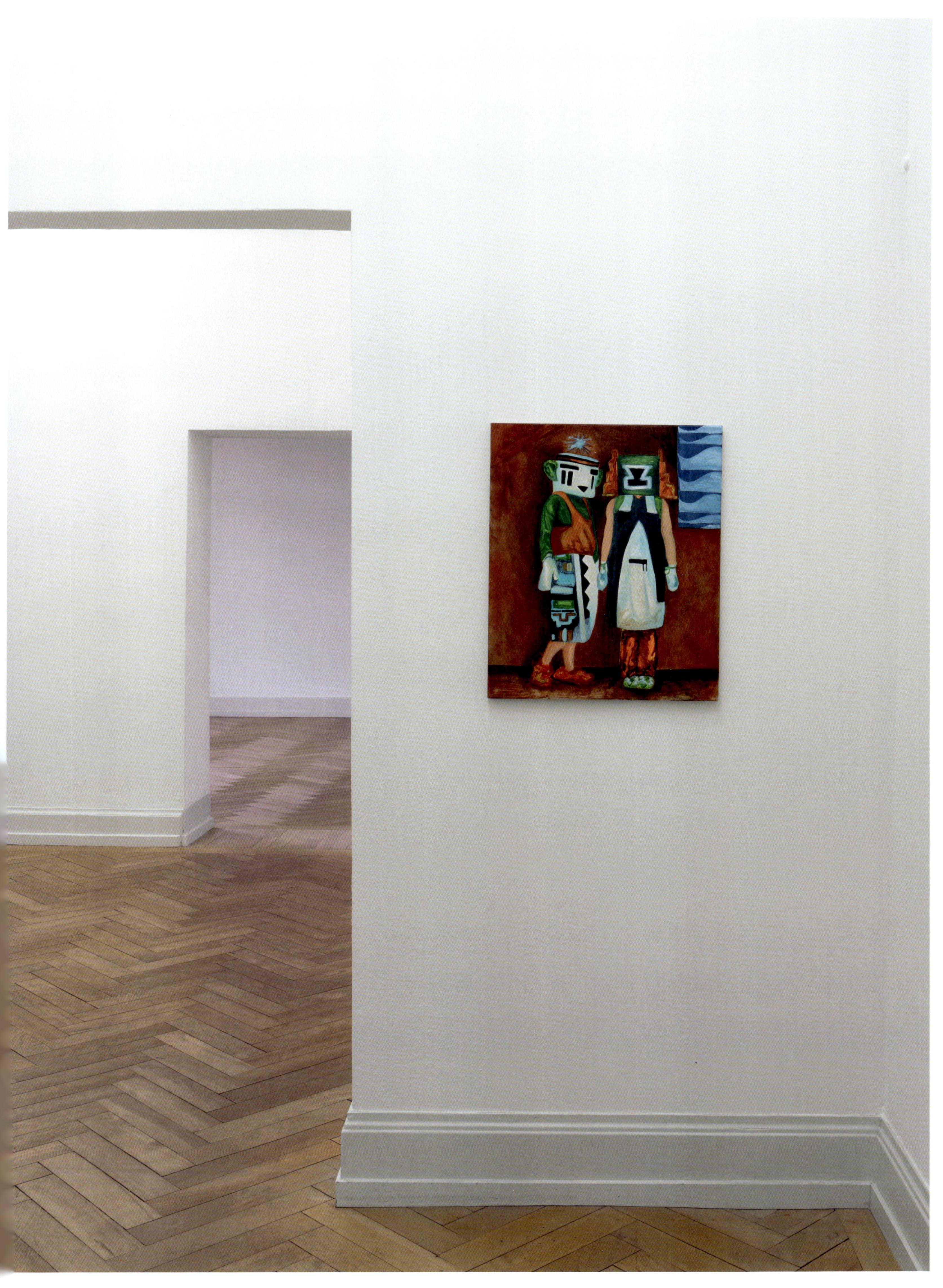

Omaggio a Sophie Taeuber-Arp, 2022   63×51 cm

Spleen, 2022   18×24 cm

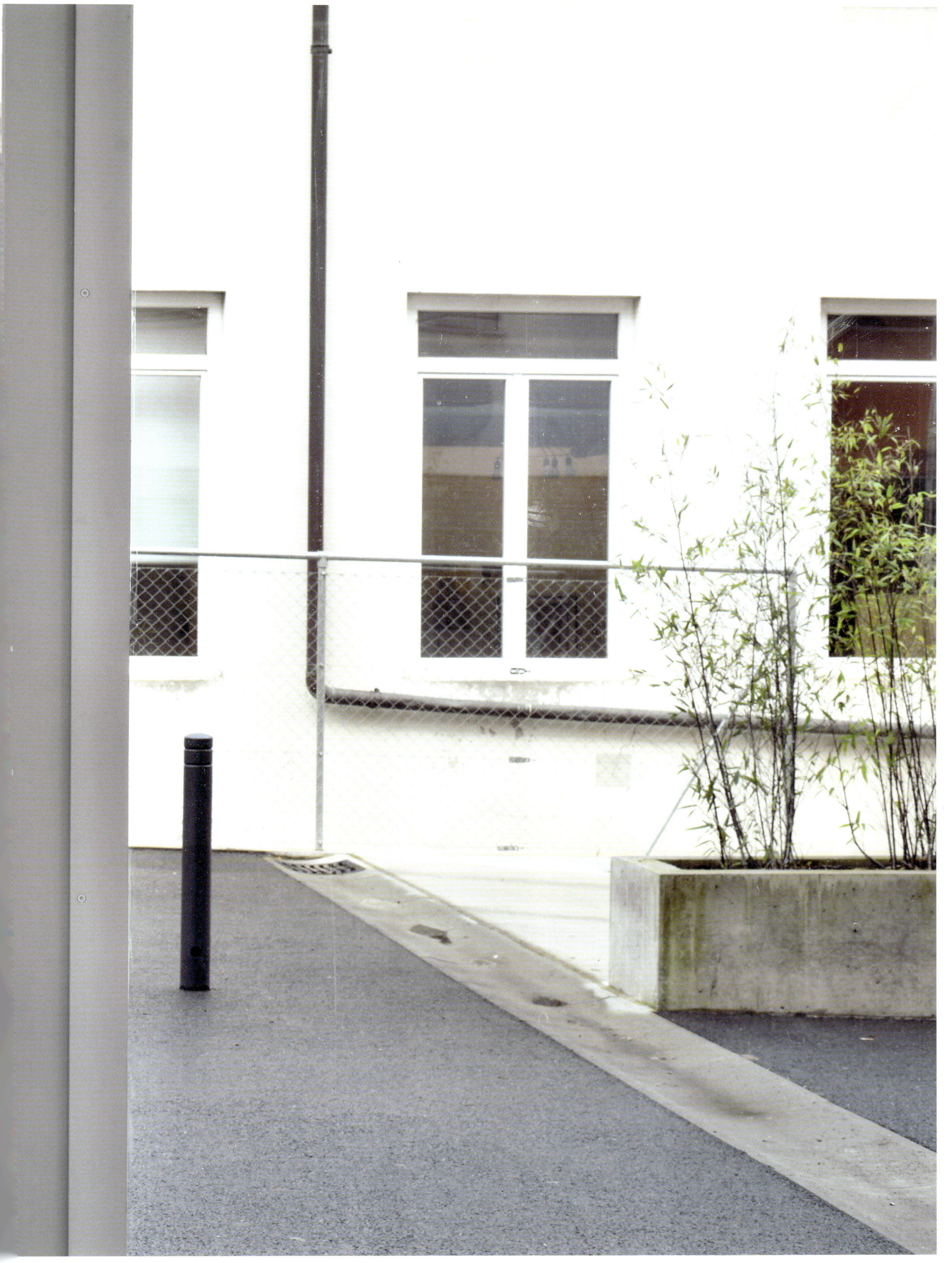

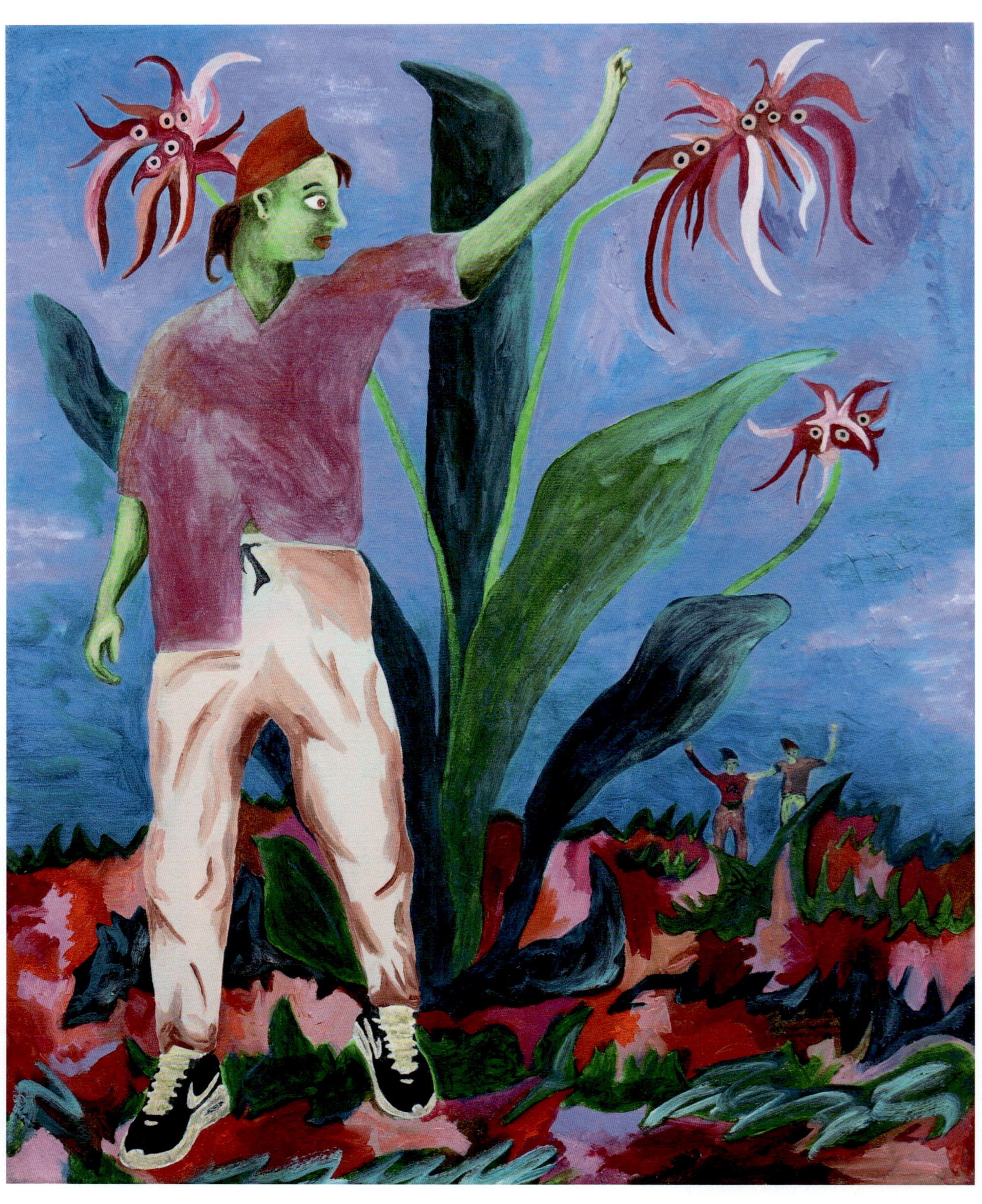

You Are So Brave and Quiet That I Forget You Are Suffering, 2022
63×51 cm

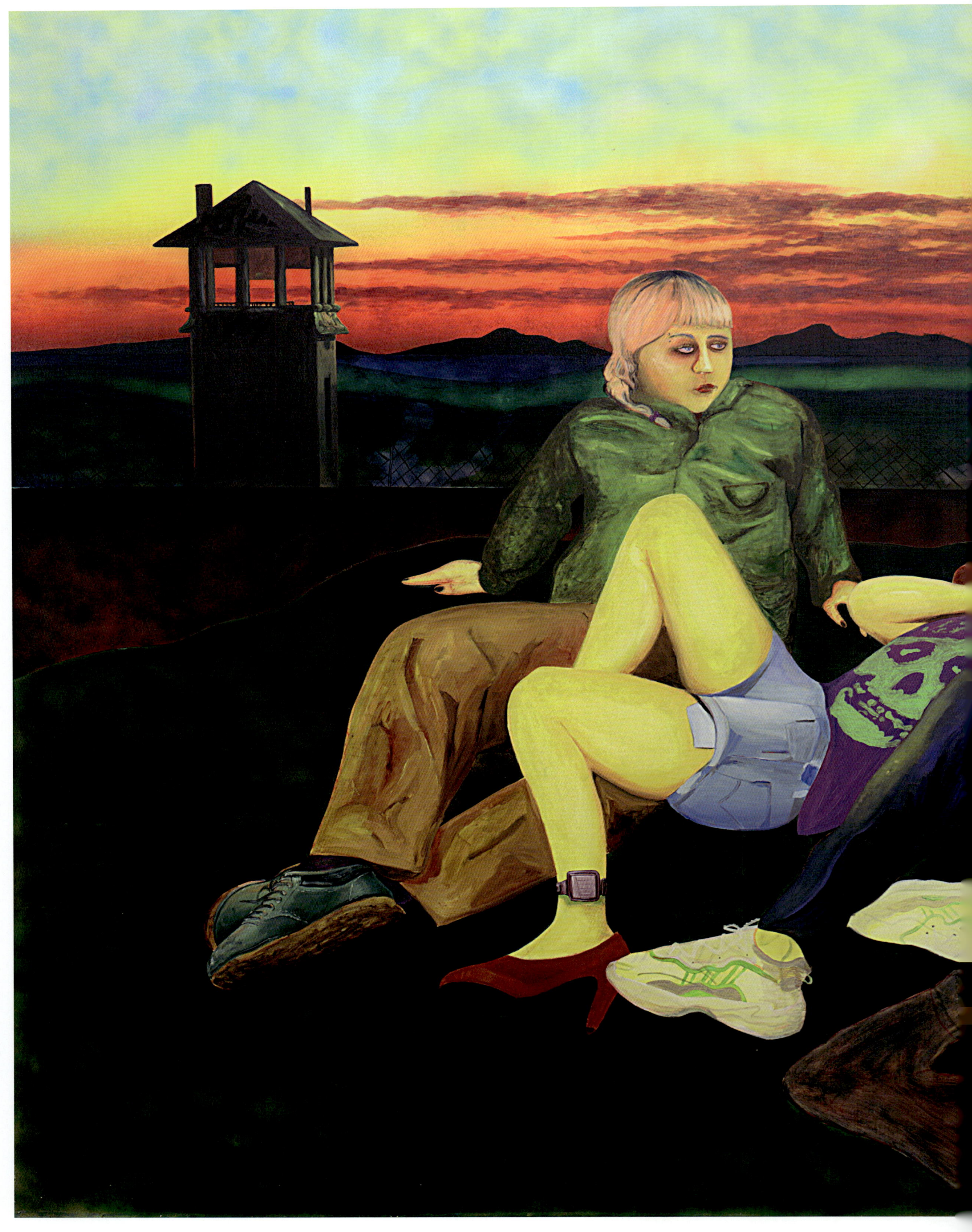

Border Sunset, 2022   195×306 cm

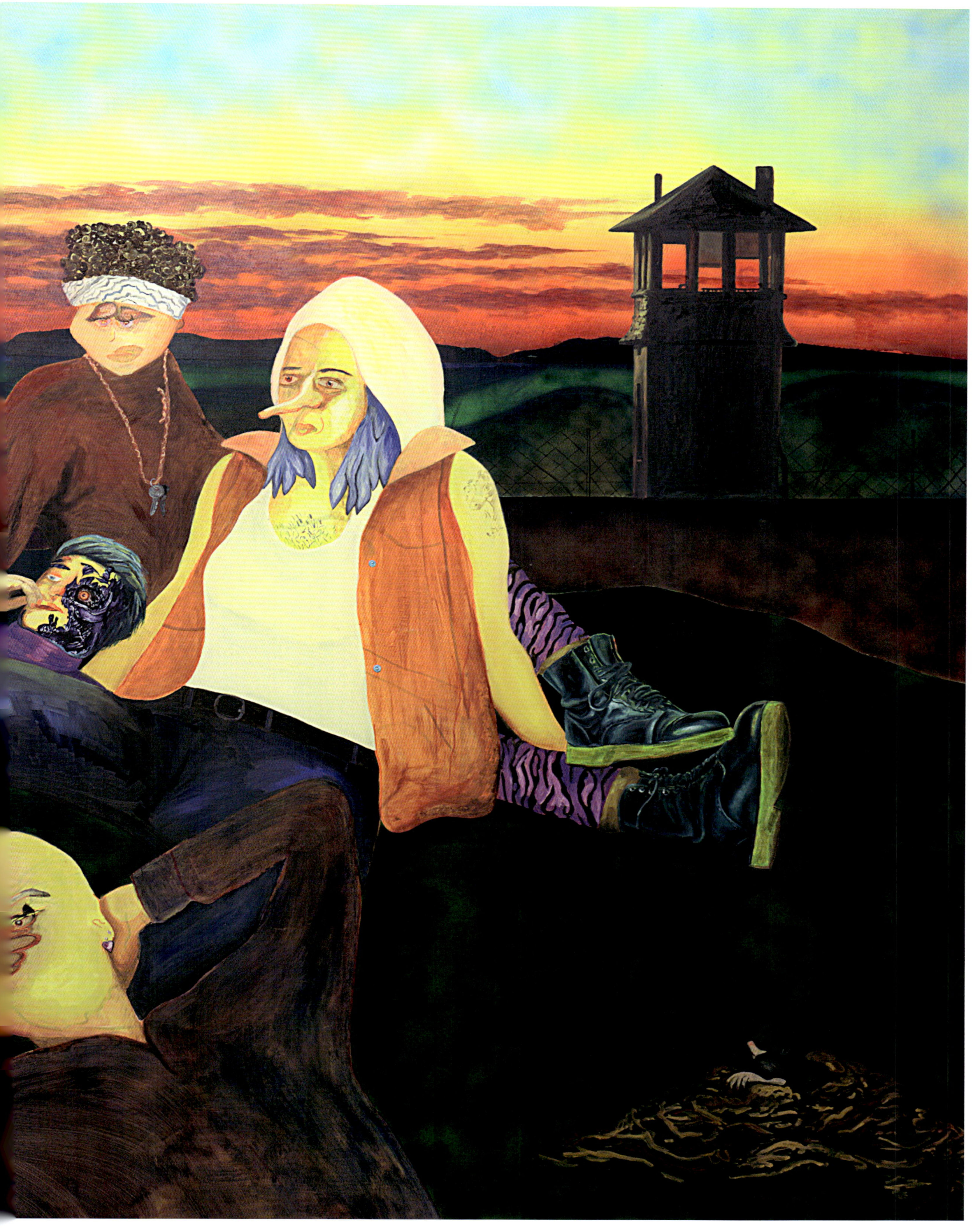

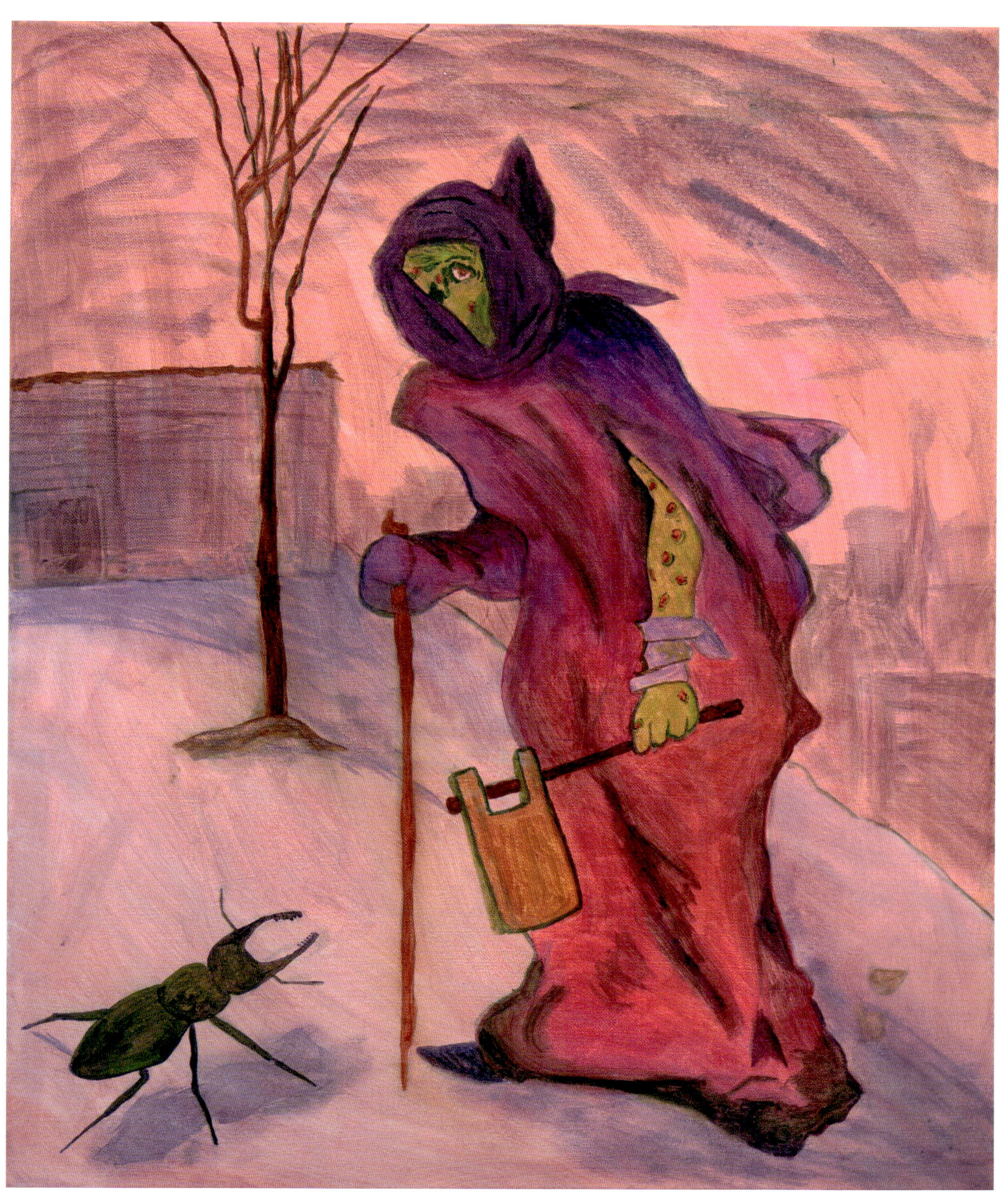

Everyone Needs a Friend, 2021   63×51 cm   133

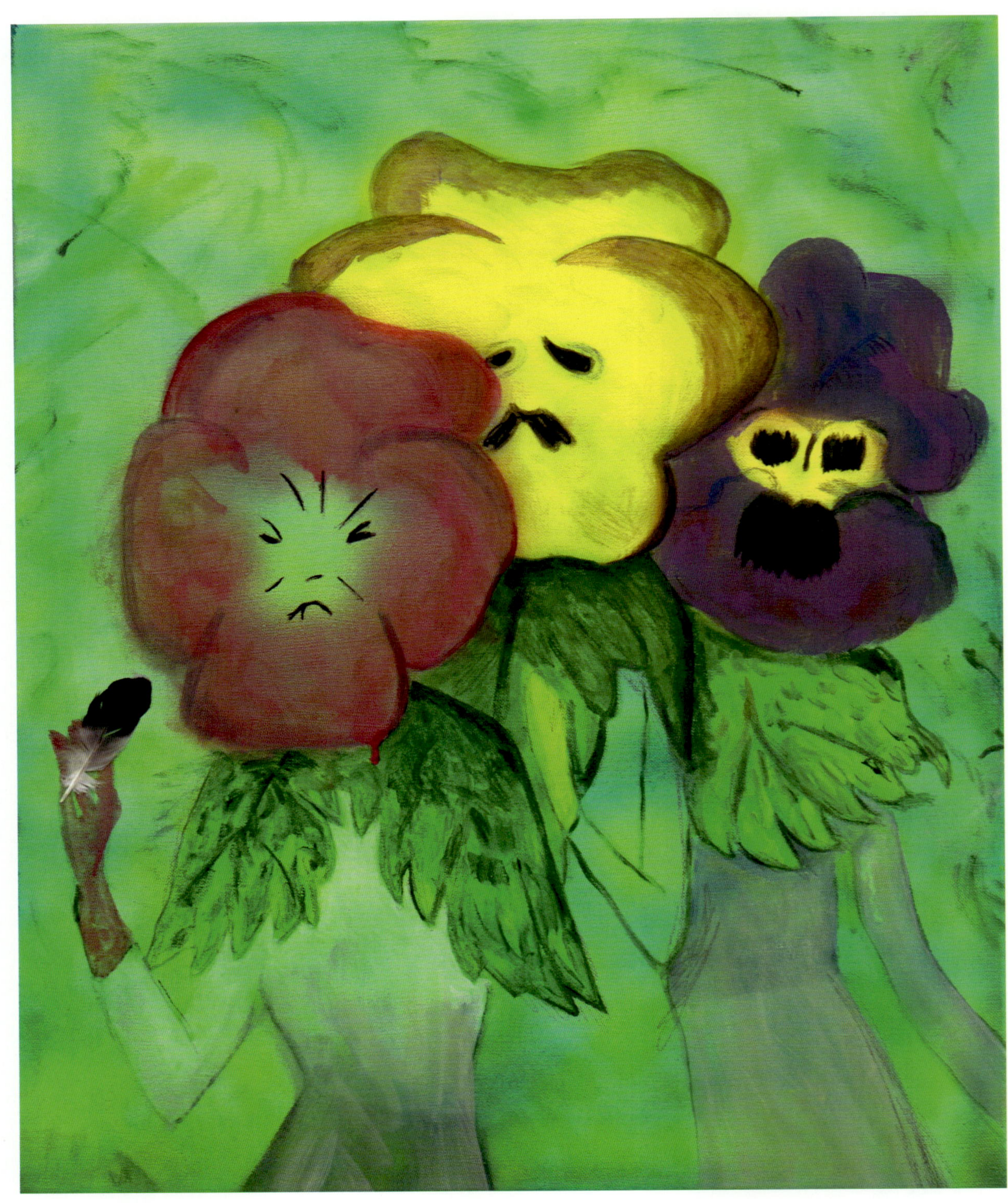

Untitled, 2021   63×51 cm

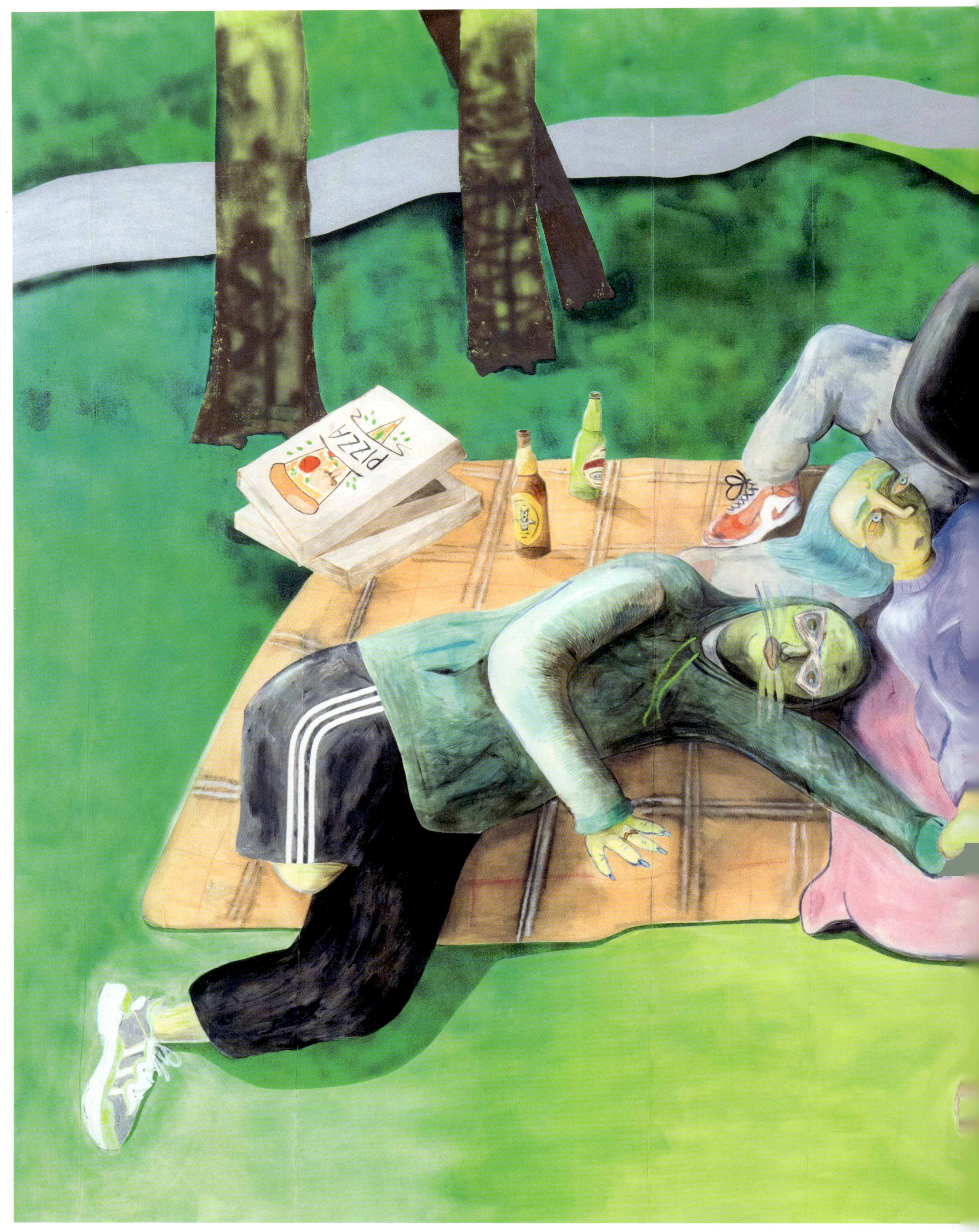

Colazione sull'erba, 2021 210×333 cm

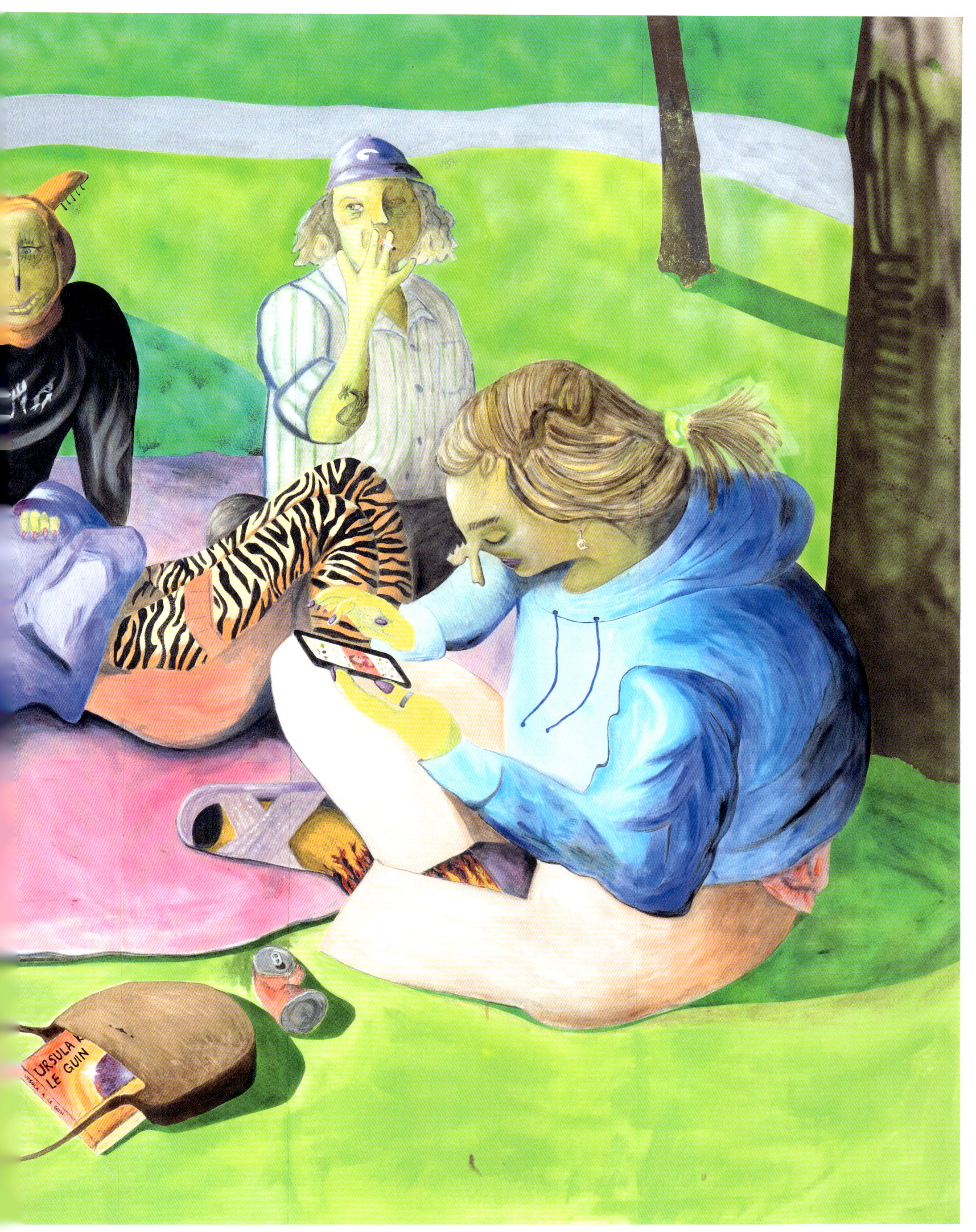
URSULA K.
LE GUIN

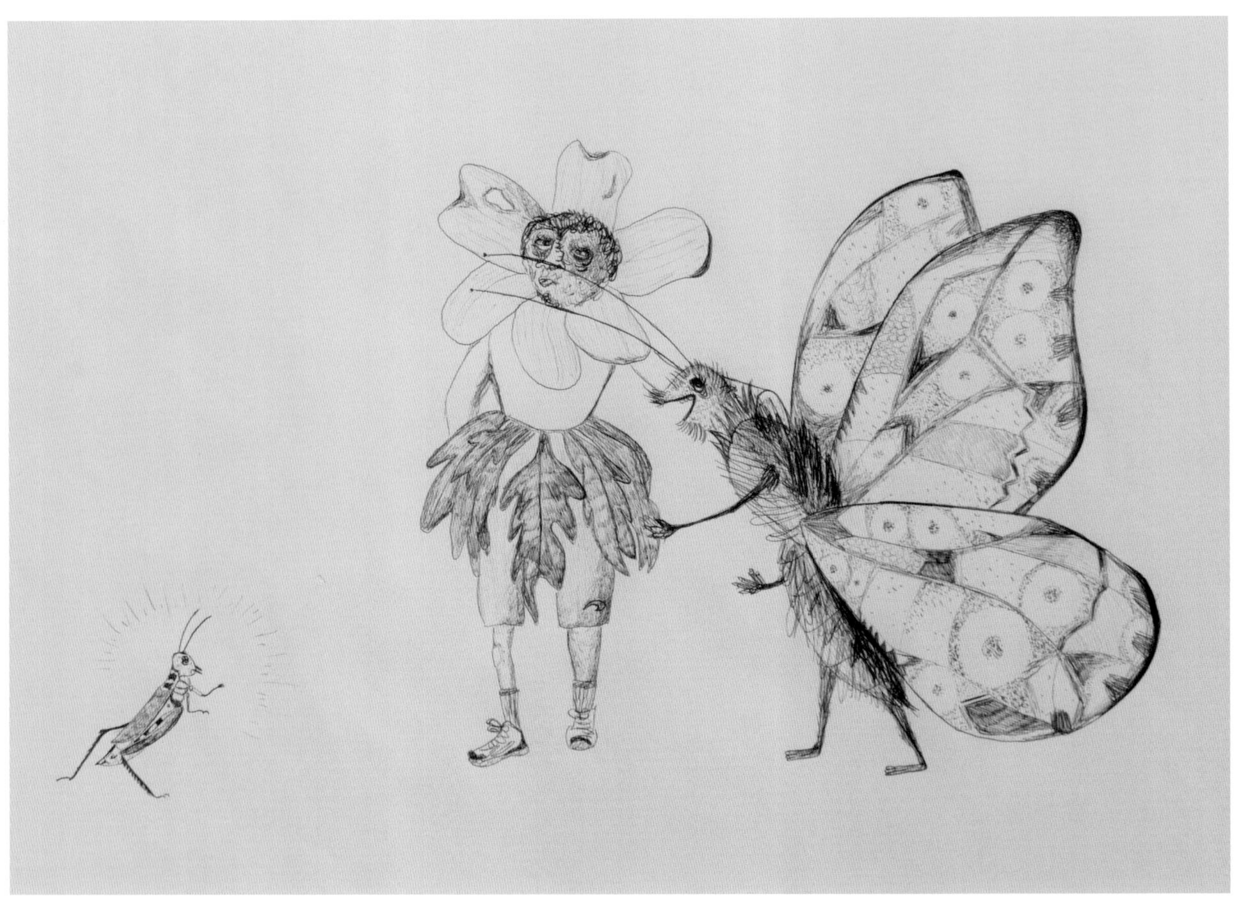

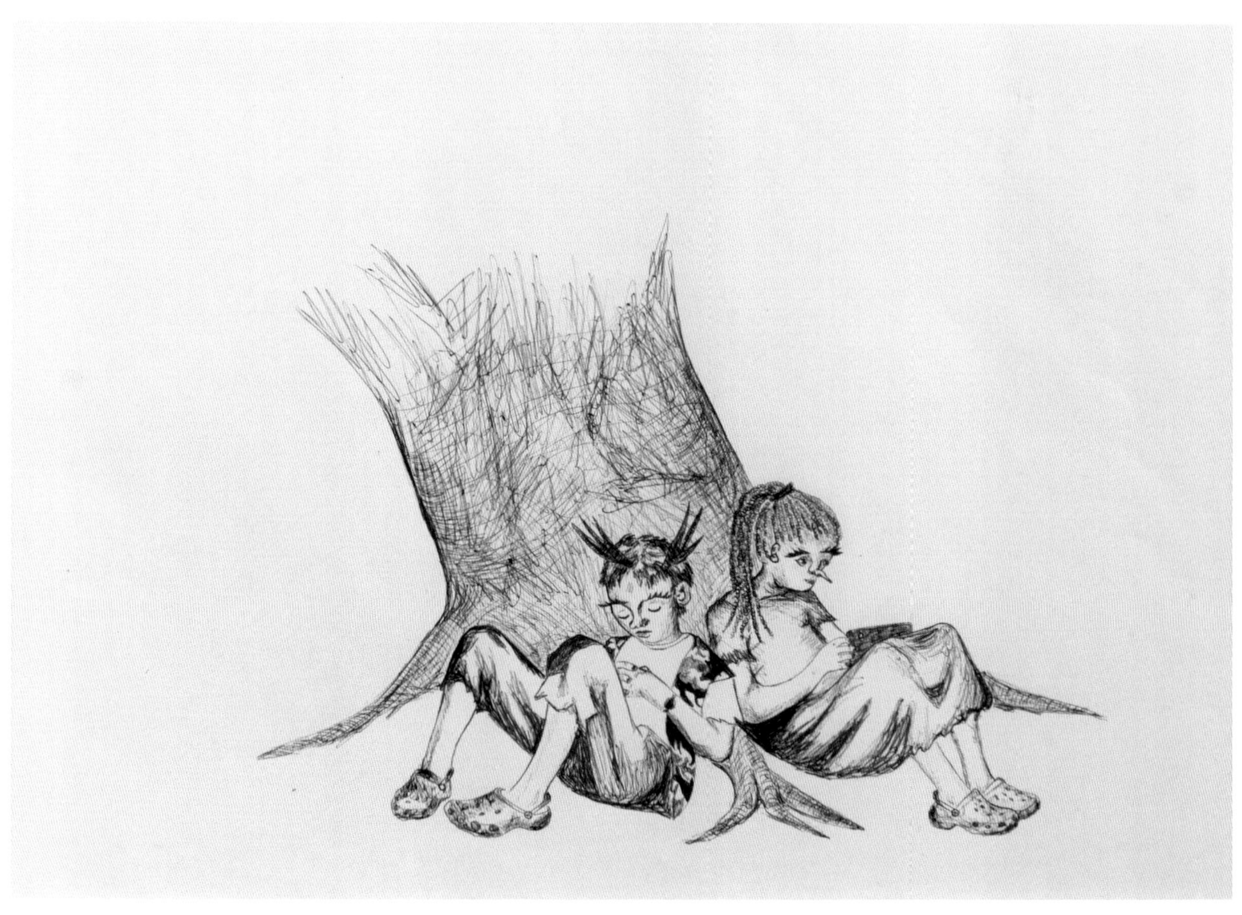

Untitled, 2021   29.7×42 cm

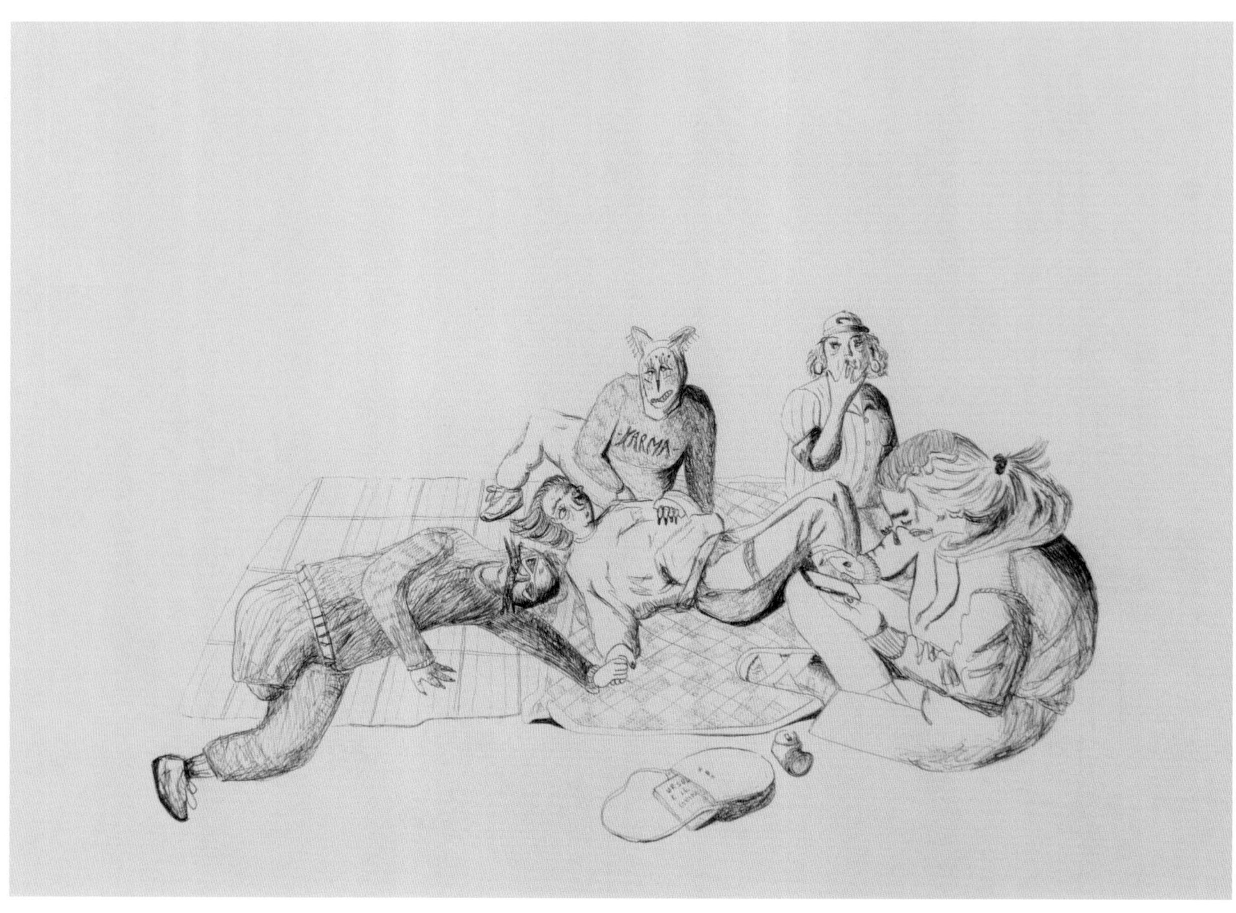

Colazione sull'erba, 2021   29.7×42 cm

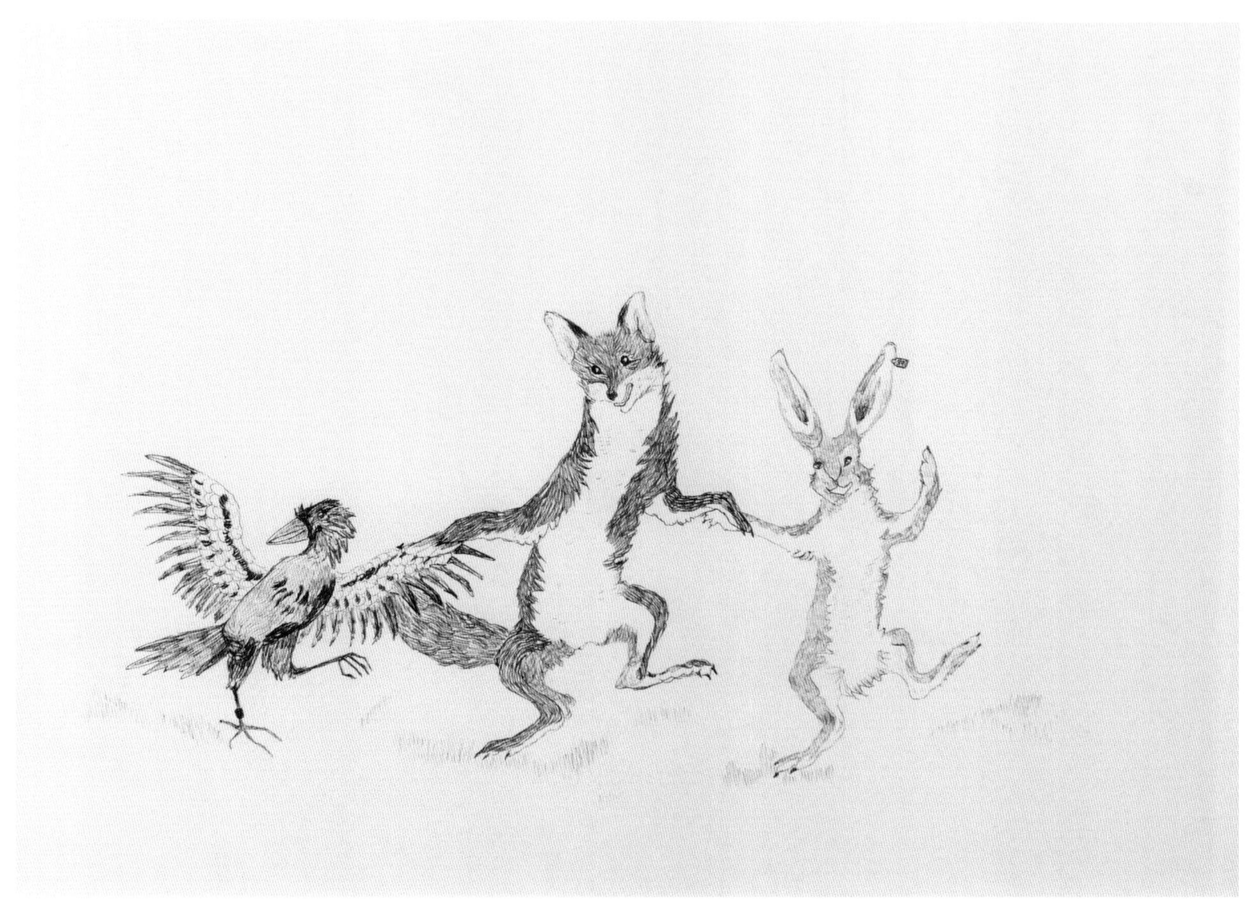

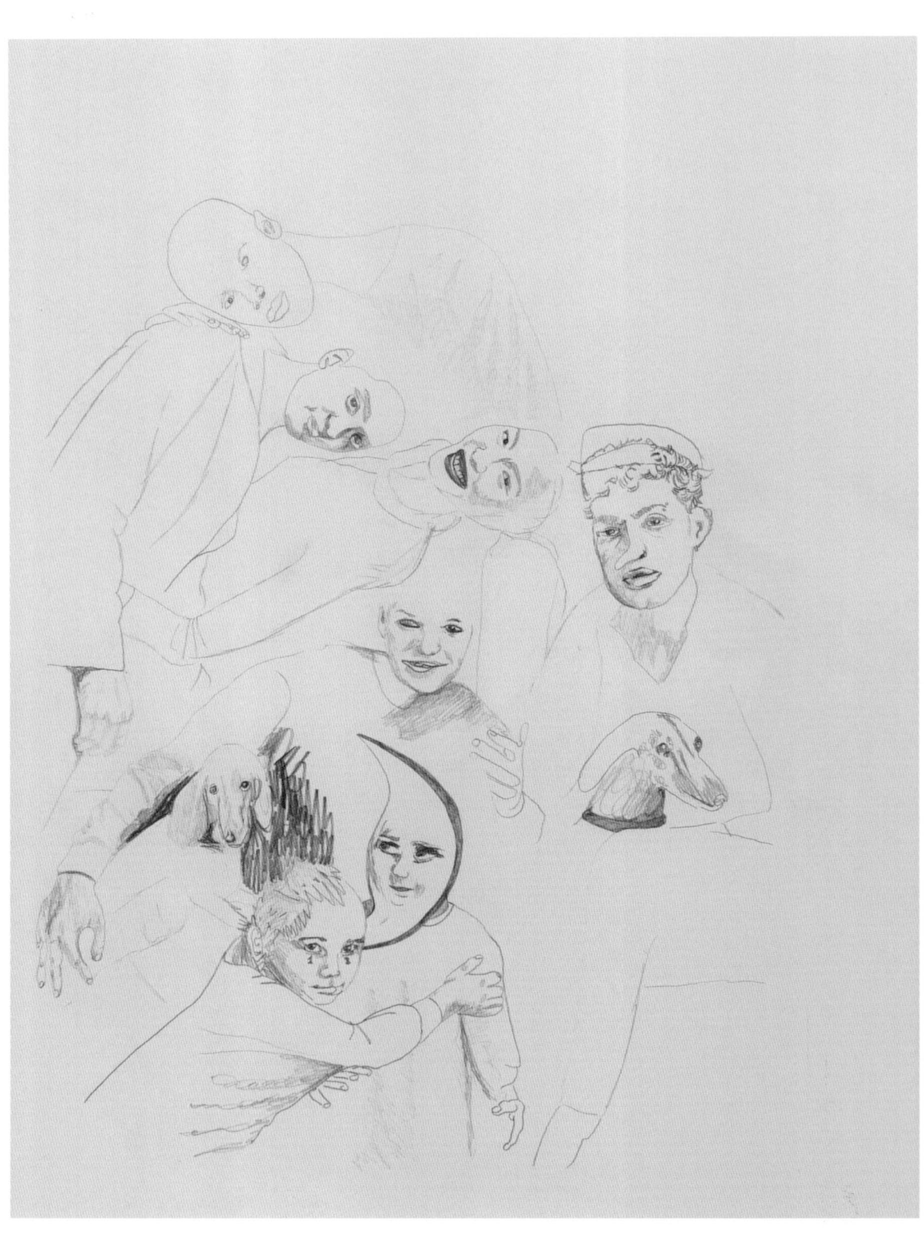

Family Photo, 2022   42×29.7 cm

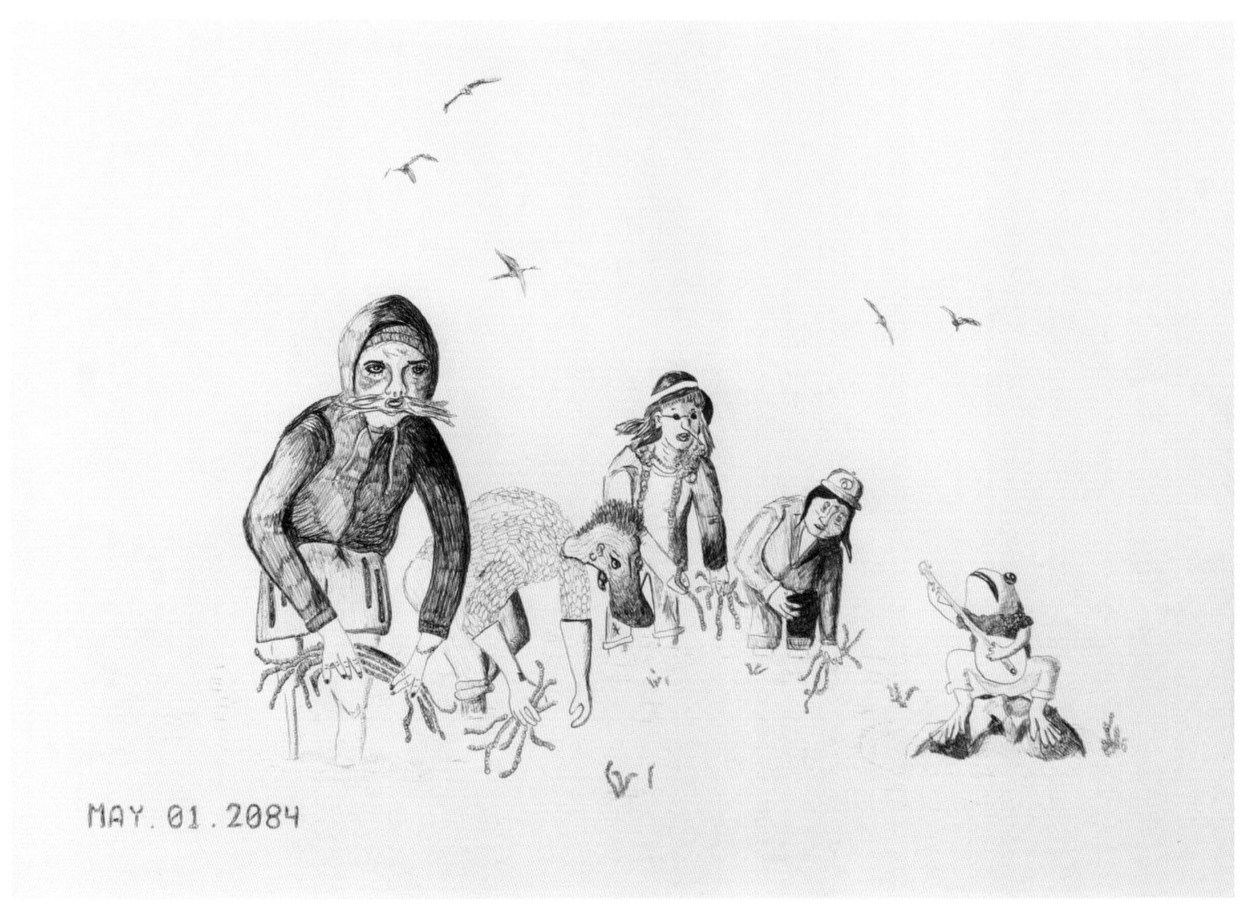

Omaggio alle Mondine, 2020   29.7×42 cm

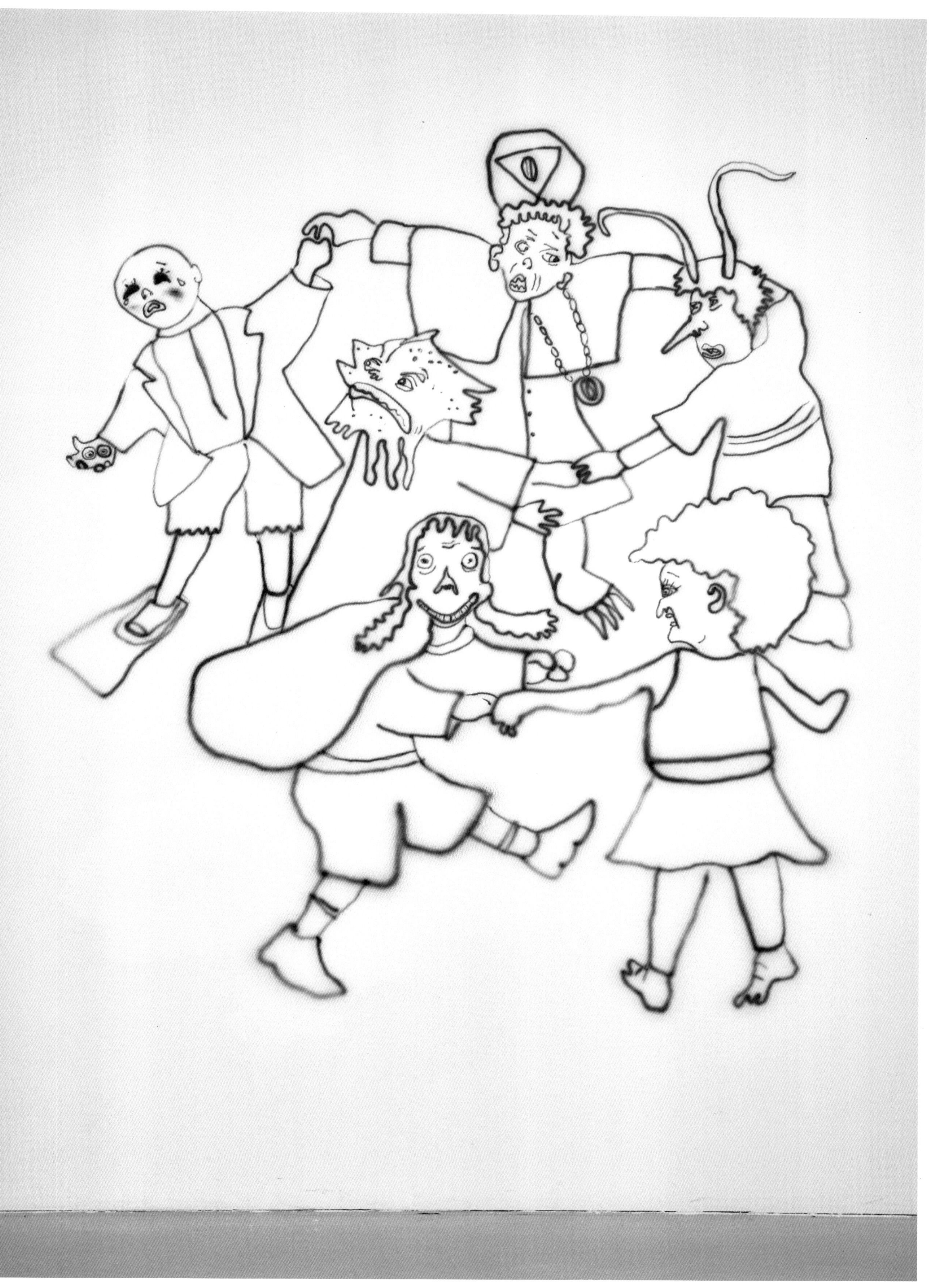

Giro giro tondo, 2019   220 × 220 cm

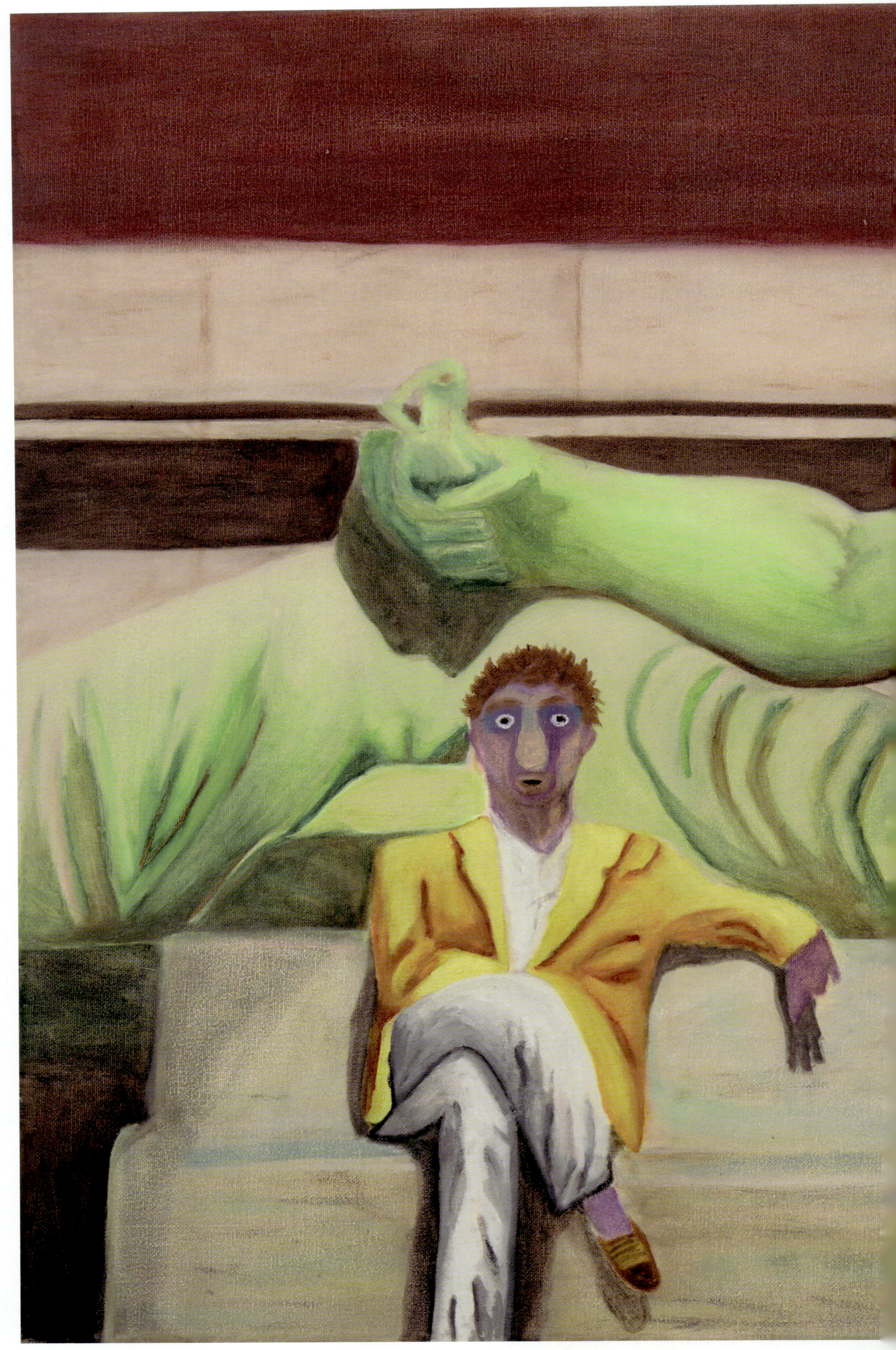

Untitled, 2017   60×80 cm

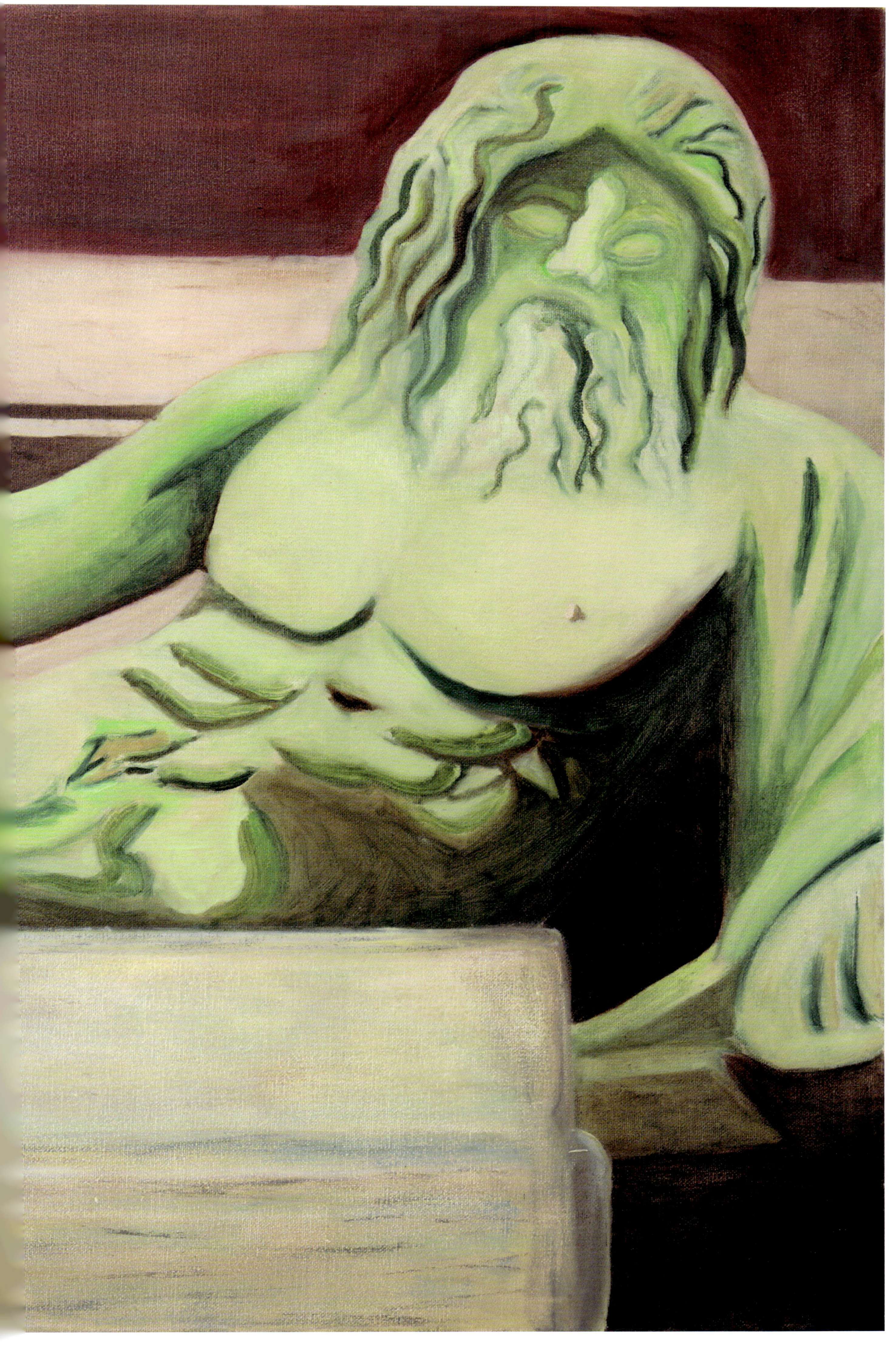

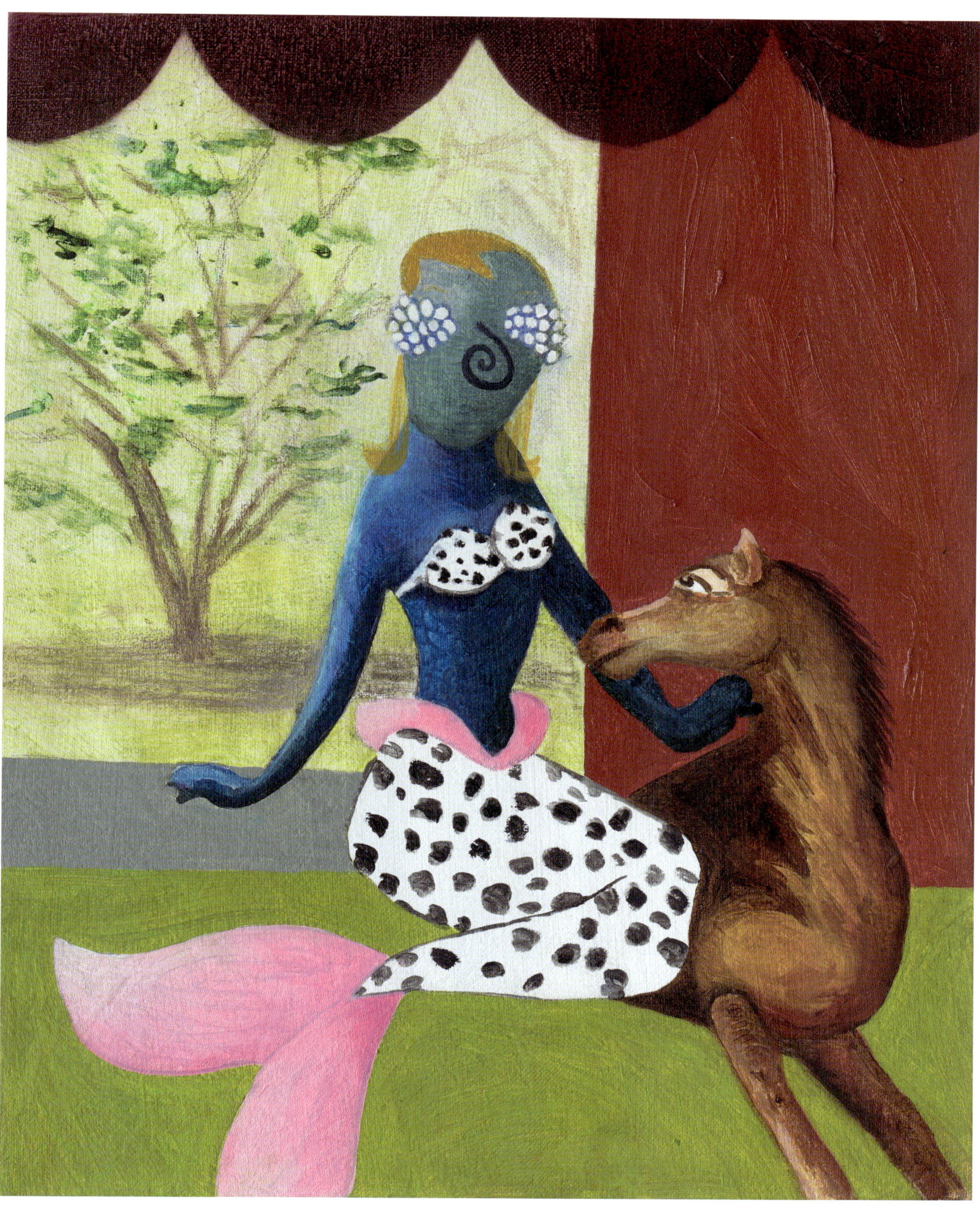

Untitled, 2021   41×33 cm

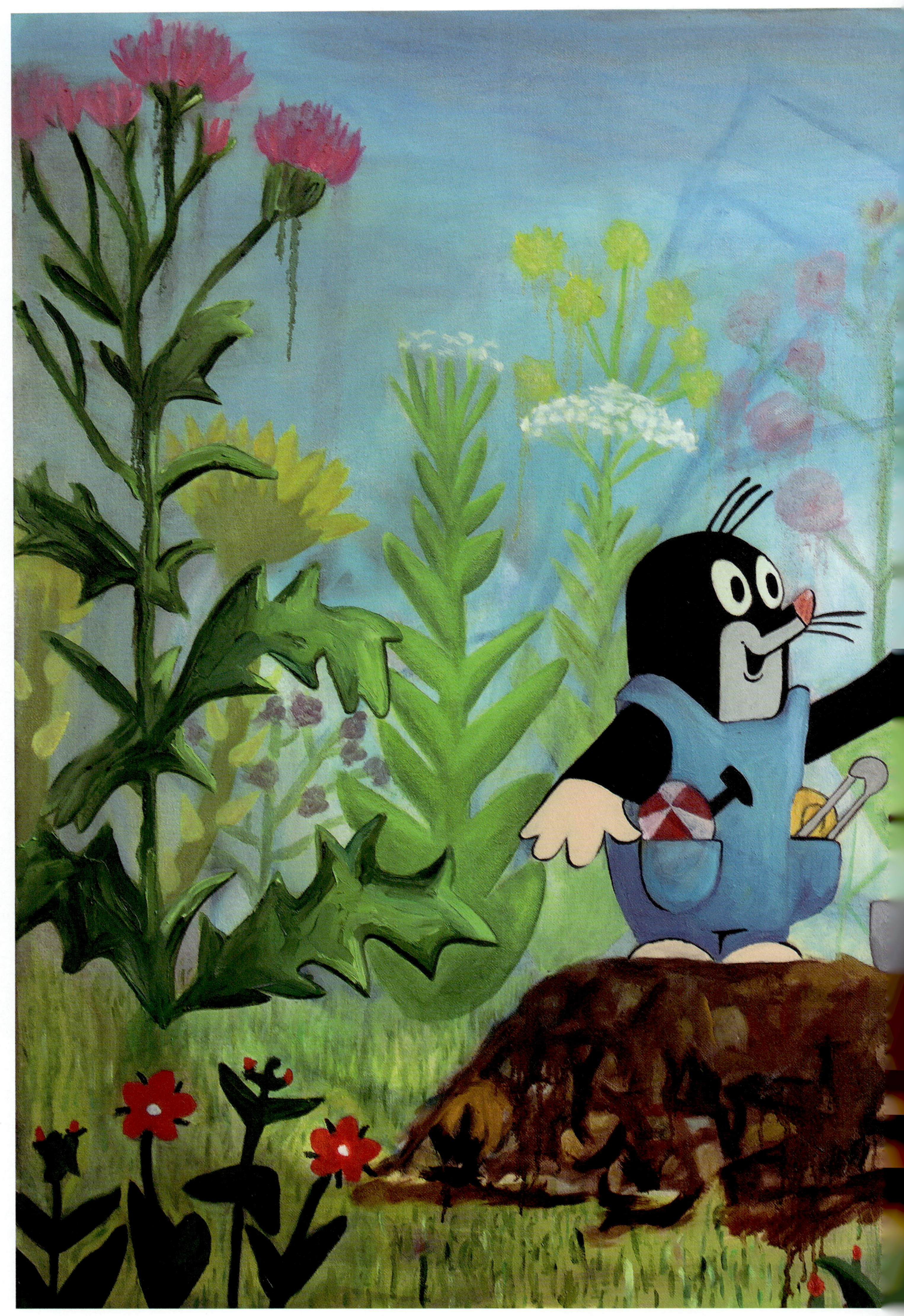

Pauli der Maulwurf, 2017   80×110 cm

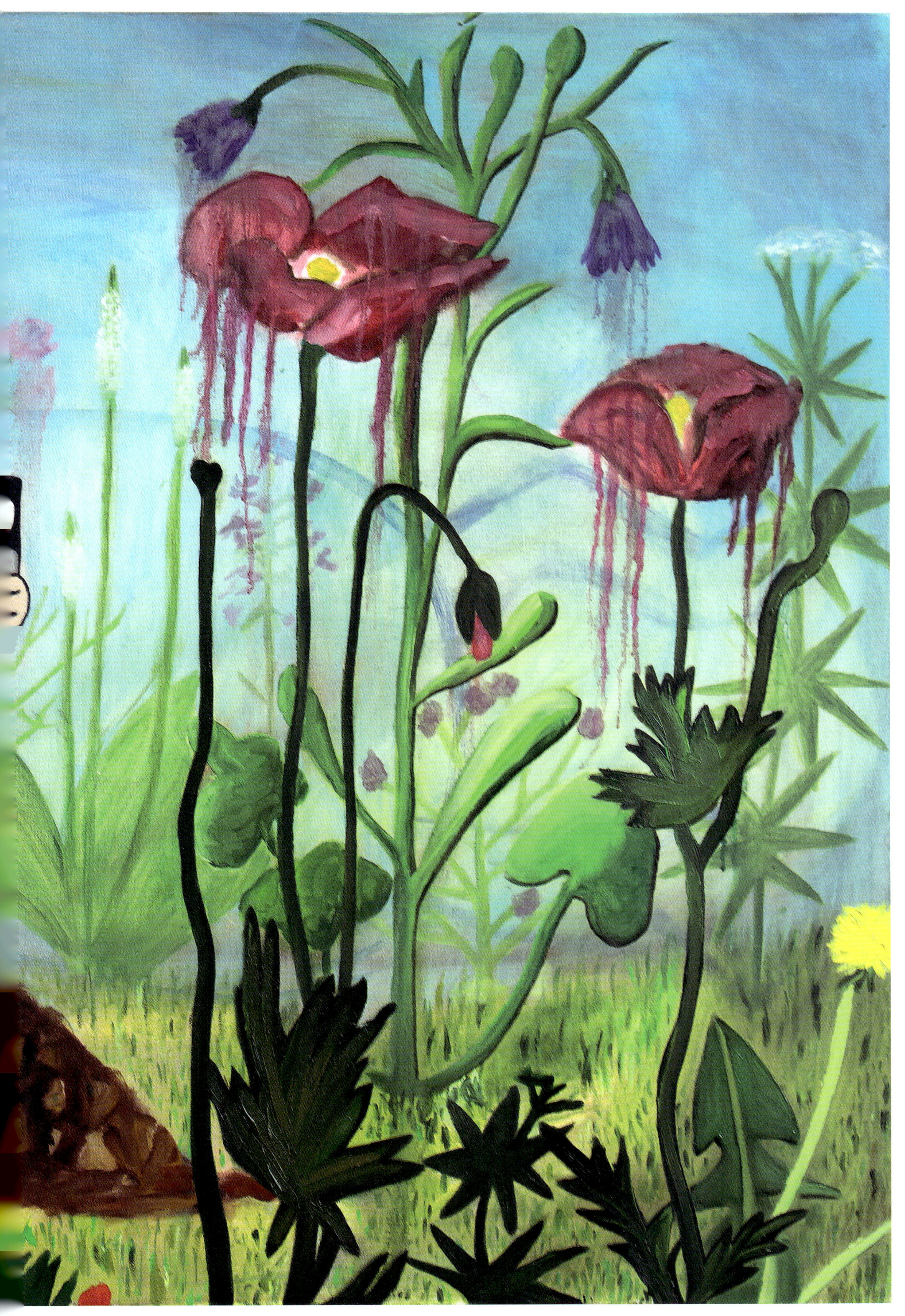

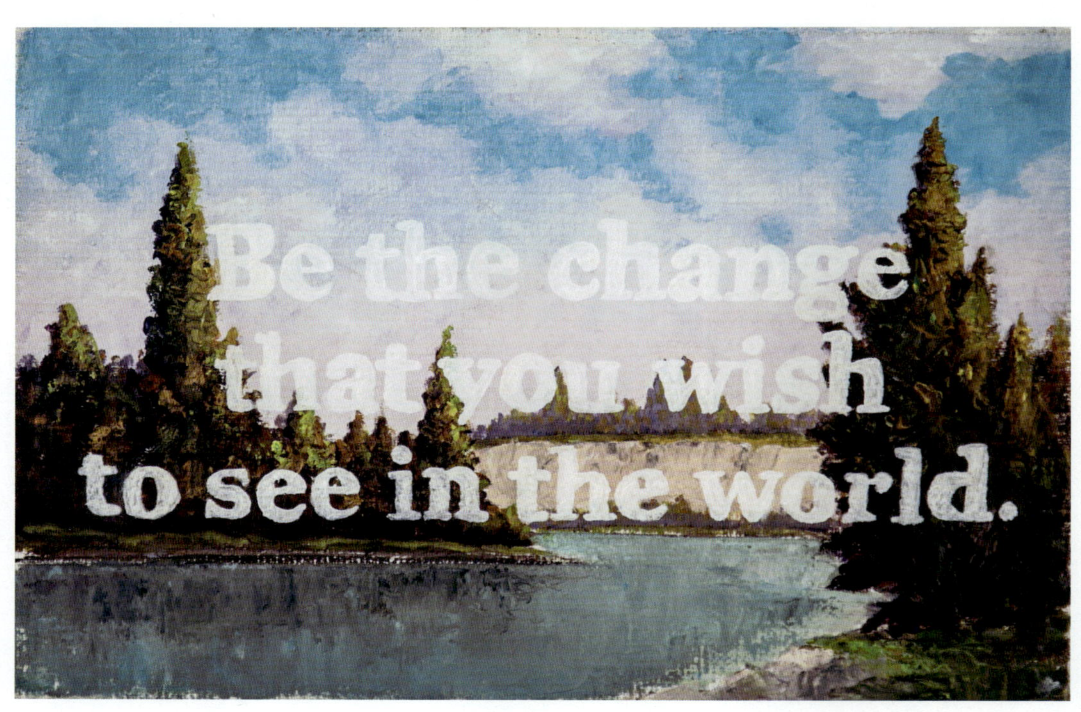

Be the Change That You Wish to See in the World, 2017
23×33 cm

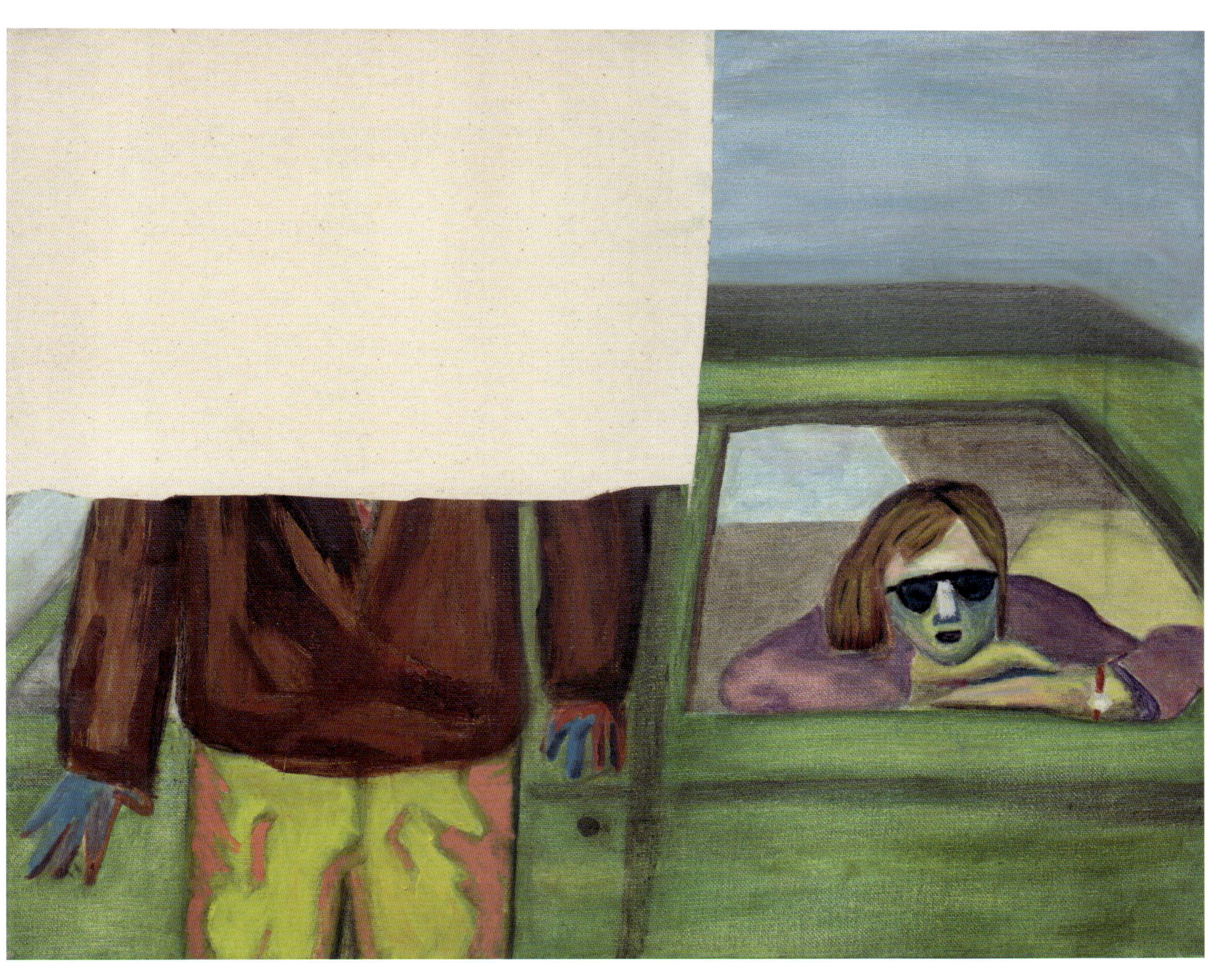

Lovers, 2017   40×50 cm

List of Works

pp. 28, 32–33, 44–45, 89 (detail)
No Counterpart, 2024
Oil on canvas, wood frame
61×95 cm
Collection Kunstkredit Basel-Stadt

pp. 2–3, 49 (detail)
The Long Sit, 2025
Oil and acrylic on canvas
190×300 cm

pp. 4–5
Harvest Time, 2025
Oil on canvas
190×300 cm

p. 7
In Your Arms, 2025
Oil on canvas
190×140 cm

pp. 8–9
Untitled, 2025
Oil and acrylic on canvas
190×300 cm

p. 10
Meltdown, 2025
Oil and acrylic on canvas
190×140 cm

pp. 12–13, 53 (detail), 55 (detail)
Sleepover (Tinfoil Dreams), 2025
Oil on canvas
190×300 cm

pp. 17, 88
Formen in Aufruhr (After I.W.), 2023
Oil on canvas
125×90 cm

pp. 20–21, 40–41
Anonymous Artists, 2024
Oil on canvas
195×306 cm

pp. 22–23
Ragazzi di vita, 2024
Oil on canvas, wood frame
63×97 cm
Collection Kunstkredit Basel-Stadt

pp. 24–25
Great Things End, Small Things Endure,
2024
Oil on canvas, wood frame
120×160 cm

p. 26
Art Basel Odyssey, 2024
Color print on flag fabric
160×240 cm
Courtesy of the artist and MÂT,
Neuchâtel

pp. 28–29, 32, 80
Untitled, 2024
Pillows with Swiss Army
blanket pillowcase
10×80×120 cm

pp. 28–29, 33, 38–39
Emma Kunz' Grotte, 2024
Oil on canvas, wood frame
90.5×125 cm

pp. 29, 43
Painting in the Age of Social Media, 2024
Oil on canvas, wood frame
18×24 cm

pp. 29, 42
Merde d'Artiste, 2024
Oil on canvas, wood frame
20×20 cm

pp. 29, 46
Hi, Here I Am, 2024
Oil on canvas, wood frame
18×24 cm
Private collection

pp. 31, 34–35
Città ideale, 2024
Oil and acrylic on canvas, wood frame
90.5×125 cm

p. 37
Till the Morning Rises, 2024
Oil on canvas, wood frame
60.3×80.2 cm
Reuter Müller Collection

pp. 48, 60, 62, 64–65, 88
Wo stehst du mit deiner Kunst Kolleg?,*
2023
Oil on canvas
18×24 cm

pp. 48, 51 (detail), 61, 113
All That Glitters Is Not Gold, 2021
Acrylic, oil, marker, pencil on canvas
63×51 cm

pp. 57, 109, 113
Omaggio a Marguerite Burnat-Provins,
2021
Oil and pencil on canvas
63×51 cm

pp. 58–59, 120–21
Blue, 2022
Oil and acrylic on canvas
150×320 cm

pp. 62, 81, 91 (detail), 98–99
Happily Aging & Dying, 2022
Oil and acrylic on canvas
210×310 cm

pp. 62–63, 70–71, 130–31
Border Sunset, 2022
Oil and acrylic on canvas
195×306 cm

pp. 63, 74–75
Crashing Sky, 2023
Oil on canvas
195×306 cm

pp. 66–67, 97 (detail), 100–01
Guerra e pace (After M.O.), 2023
Oil and acrylic on canvas
195×306 cm

p. 68
Too Late, Too Soon, 2023
Pencil on paper
42×29.7 cm

pp. 68–69
Nostalghia, 2023
Pencil on paper
29.7×42 cm

p. 69
Untitled, 2023
Pencil on paper
42×29.7 cm

p. 72
Untitled, 2024
Ballpoint pen on paper
29.7×42 cm

p. 72
Untitled, 2024
Ballpoint pen on paper
29.7×42 cm

pp. 73, 138
L'Annunciazione, 2021
Ballpoint pen on paper
29.7×42 cm

pp. 73, 139
Untitled, 2021
Ballpoint pen on paper
29.7×42 cm

pp. 82–83, 86–87, 95 (detail)
Speaking Rest, 2023
Oil on canvas
195×306 cm

pp. 84, 122–23
Untitled, 2022
Oil and acrylic on canvas
110×180 cm

pp. 85, 125
Omaggio a Sophie Taeuber-Arp, 2022
Oil on canvas
63×51 cm

pp. 93 (detail), 136–37
Colazione sull'erba, 2021
Oil, acrylic, marker, pencil on stitched
pieces of canvas
210×333 cm
MASI Lugano Collection

pp. 103, 142
Family Photo, 2022
Pencil on paper
42×29.7 cm

p. 104
On n'est pas sérieux, quand on a dix-sept
ans, 2023
Pencil on paper
29.7×42 cm
Private collection

pp. 106–07, 112
Eternal Return, 2022
Oil and acrylic on canvas
190×190 cm

pp. 110, 112
Die Malerin, 2018
Oil and ballpoint pen on canvas
59×50 cm
Reuter Müller Collection

pp. 112, 114–15
Pumuckl, 2022
Oil and marker on canvas
18×24 cm
Private collection

p. 126
Spleen, 2022
Oil on canvas
18×24 cm
Private collection

p. 128
*You Are So Brave and Quiet That
I Forget You Are Suffering,* 2022
Oil on canvas
63×51 cm
Kurt Aeschbacher Collection

p. 133
Everyone Needs a Friend, 2021
Oil on canvas
63×51 cm

p. 134
Untitled, 2021
Oil, acrylic, marker, pencil, and feather
on canvas
63×51 cm
Oskar Weiss Collection

p. 140
Colazione sull'erba, 2021
Ballpoint pen on paper
29.7×42 cm
Private collection

p. 141
Le ali della libertà, 2021
Ballpoint pen on paper
29.7×42 cm
Collection Kunstkredit Basel-Landschaft

p. 143
Omaggio alle Mondine, 2020
Ballpoint pen on paper
29.7×42 cm

p. 145
Giro giro tondo, 2019
Airbrush on wall
220×220 cm

pp. 146–47
Untitled, 2017
Oil on canvas
60×80 cm

p. 149
Untitled, 2021
Oil and acrylic on canvas
41×33 cm
Collection Kunstkredit Basel-Landschaft

pp. 150–51
Pauli der Maulwurf, 2017
Oil on canvas
80×110 cm
Private collection

p. 152
*Be the Change That You Wish to See
in the World,* 2017
Oil and acrylic on canvas
23×33 cm
Melanie Akeret Collection

p. 155
Lovers, 2017
Oil on canvas
40×50 cm

Unless otherwise stated, the works
are the property of the artist.

Noemi Pfister (b. 1991) grew up in Locarno, Switzerland, and she has been based in Basel since 2018. She completed her bachelor of fine arts with a focus on painting at the Haute école d'art et de design (HEAD) in Geneva in 2017. After completing one year in the program Work.Master in Geneva, she decided to move to Basel, where she received a master of fine arts at the Institute Art Gender Nature at the University of Applied Sciences and Arts in 2019. That same year, Pfister cofounded Palazzina, an exhibition space and artist house, which was awarded the Kulturpreis von Baselland in 2024.

Pfister has participated in numerous group exhibitions in Switzerland and abroad since 2018, including exhibitions at institutions, off-spaces, and galleries such as Kunsthalle Basel, Kunsthaus Baselland, Bark Berlin Gallery, Bündner Kunstmuseum Chur, Kunstverein Freiburg im Breisgau, Galerie Meyer Riegger in Karlsruhe, Kunsthaus Langenthal, Kunsthalle Palazzo in Liestal, and Sonnenstube in Lugano. She has had solo exhibitions at Espace 3353 in Geneva, Kunstraum Tunnel Tunnel in Lausanne, and unanimous consent in Zurich.

Pfister received a grant from Kunstkredit Basel-Stadt in 2021, she was artist in residence at the Cité Internationale des Arts in Paris in 2022, and she was nominated for the Swiss Art Award in 2023. Her paintings and drawings are included in various collections, including MASI—Museo d'arte della Svizzera italiana in Lugano, Collection Kunstkredit Basel-Stadt and Collection Kunstkredit Basel-Landschaft.

Noemi Pfister received the Manor Kunstpreis Graubünden in 2025. This prize consists of a solo exhibition at the Bündner Kunstmuseum Chur and the publication of this catalog, *Noemi Pfister: Heart on Sleeve.*

Noemi Pfister (geb. 1991) ist in Locarno aufgewachsen. Seit 2018 lebt und arbeitet die Künstlerin in Basel. Im Jahr 2017 absolvierte sie ihren Bachelor in bildender Kunst mit Schwerpunkt Malerei an der Haute école d'art et de design (HEAD) in Genf. Ein Jahr nach Beginn des dortigen Studiengangs Work.Master entschied sie, nach Basel zu ziehen, wo sie am Institut Art Gender Natur der Hochschule für Gestaltung und Kunst 2019 ihren Master in Fine Arts erhielt. Im selben Jahr gründete Noemi Pfister Palazzina mit, einen Ausstellungsraum und ein Künstler:innenhaus, das 2024 den Kulturpreis von Baselland erhielt.

Seit 2018 ist Pfister in zahlreichen Gruppenausstellung im In- und Ausland vertreten. Sie stellte in Institutionen, Offspaces und Galerien wie der Kunsthalle Basel, dem Kunsthaus Baselland, der Bark Berlin Gallery, dem Bündner Kunstmuseum Chur, dem Kunstverein Freiburg im Breisgau, der Galerie Meyer Riegger in Karlsruhe sowie dem Kunsthaus Langenthal, der Kunsthalle Palazzo in Liestal und in der Sonnenstube in Lugano aus. Einzelausstellungen realisierte Noemi Pfister im Espace 3353 in Genf, im Kunstraum Tunnel Tunnel in Lausanne und bei unanimous consent in Zürich.

Im Jahr 2021 erhielt Pfister vom Kunstkredit Basel-Stadt einen Förderentscheid für einen Werkbeitrag, 2022 war sie Artist in Residence in der Cité Internationale des Arts Paris und 2023 für den Swiss Art Award nominiert. Ihre Gemälde und Zeichnungen sind in verschiedenen Sammlungen vertreten, darunter das MASI – Museo d'arte della Svizzera italiana in Lugano, die Sammlung Kunstkredit Basel-Stadt und die Sammlung Kunstkredit Baselland.

Noemi Pfister ist Preisträgerin des Manor Kunstpreises Graubünden 2025. Der Preis umfasst neben einer Einzelpräsentation im Bündner Kunstmuseum Chur auch die Veröffentlichung des vorliegenden Katalogs *Noemi Pfister. Heart on Sleeve.*

Raphael Gygax (b. 1980) is a Locarno-based curator, art historian, and author. He has been an independent curator and curator-at-large at the Kunsthaus Zürich since fall 2023. He studied art history, film, and drama studies at the Universities of Bern and Zurich. His dissertation *Extra Bodies: Über den Einsatz des "anderen Körpers" in der zeitgenössischen Kunst* (published by Ringier Kunstverlag in 2017) explores the use of instrumentalized bodies in contemporary art. He was curator and head of publications at the Migros Museum für Gegenwartskunst in Zurich, where he curated numerous exhibitions, from 2003 to 2019. He has also curated exhibitions in places such as Paris, London, Locarno, and New York. He was deputy director of the Department of Fine Arts and director of the bachelor of fine arts program at Zurich University of the Arts from 2019 to 2023.

Damian Jurt (b. 1978) has worked at the Bündner Kunstmuseum since 2019; he has organized numerous exhibitions and publications as curator. He has collaborated with artists such as Yuri Ancarani, Denise Bertschi, Julius von Bismarck, Ludovica Carbotta, Andriu Deplazes, Susan Hiller, Olaf Holzapfel, Sofia Hultén, Annette Kelm, Wolfgang Laib, Bruce Nauman, Zenib Sedira, and Augustas Serapinas. Between 2014 and 2019 he worked at the Kunsthaus Pasquart in Biel/Bienne, where he curated exhibitions with artists including Céline Condorelli, Delphine Reist, Michael Sailstorfer, and Kemang Wa Lehulere. From 2008 to 2014 he was a research associate at the Art Institute of Basel Academy of Art and Design and mounted exhibitions at the Kunstmuseum Luzern and the Stadtgalerie Bern as an independent curator.

Valerie Keller (b. 1989) has been a lecturer and researcher at the Department of Social Anthropology and Cultural Studies (ISEK) at the University of Zurich since 2021, and she has codirected the exhibition space For in Basel and the eponymous magazine with Matthias Liechti since 2022. She studied pop culture, film studies, and Chinese (BA, 2012) and empirical cultural studies and film studies at the University of Zurich (MA, 2017). From 2015 to 2020 Keller was codirector of the exhibition space Milieu in Bern. She worked under Prof. Harm-Peer Zimmermann in an interdisciplinary research project between 2018 and 2021. Her dissertation, *Selbstsorge im Leben mit Demenz. Potenziale einer relationalen Praxis* (published by Transcript Verlag in 2022) examines ways of living with dementia.

Raphael Gygax (geb. 1980) ist Kurator, Kunsthistoriker und Autor in Locarno. Seit Herbst 2023 ist er als unabhängiger Kurator und Curator-at-Large am Kunsthaus Zürich tätig. Er studierte Kunstgeschichte, Film- und Theaterwissenschaften an den Universitäten Bern und Zürich. In seiner Dissertation *Extra Bodies. Über den Einsatz des «anderen Körpers» in der zeitgenössischen Kunst* (2017 im Ringier Kunstverlag erschienen) beschäftigte er sich mit dem Einsatz von instrumentalisierten Körpern in der zeitgenössischen Kunst. Von 2003 bis 2019 war Gygax Kurator und Leiter der Publikationsabteilung am Migros Museum für Gegenwartskunst in Zürich, wo er zahlreiche Ausstellungen kuratierte. Er organisierte auch Ausstellungen unter anderem in Paris, London, Locarno und New York. In den Jahren 2019 bis 2023 war er stellvertretender Direktor der Abteilung Bildende Kunst und Leiter des Studiengangs Bachelor of Fine Arts an der Zürcher Hochschule der Künste.

Damian Jurt (geb. 1978) ist seit 2019 am Bündner Kunstmuseum tätig und verantwortete in seiner Funktion als Kurator diverse Ausstellungen und Publikationen. Er arbeitete mit Kunstschaffenden wie Yuri Ancarani, Denise Bertschi, Julius von Bismarck, Ludovica Carbotta, Andriu Deplazes, Susan Hiller, Olaf Holzapfel, Sofia Hultén, Annette Kelm, Wolfgang Laib, Bruce Nauman, Zenib Sedira und Augustas Serapinas. In den Jahren 2014 bis 2019 war Jurt am Kunsthaus Pasquart in Biel/Bienne und kuratierte Ausstellungen mit Céline Condorelli, Delphine Reist, Michael Sailstorfer und Kemang Wa Lehulere. Von 2008 bis 2014 war er wissenschaftlicher Mitarbeiter am Institut Kunst der Hochschule für Gestaltung und Kunst Basel und realisierte als freier Kurator Ausstellungen im Kunstmuseum Luzern und der Stadtgalerie Bern.

Valerie Keller (geb. 1989) lehrt und forscht seit 2021 am Institut für Sozialanthropologie und Empirische Kulturwissenschaft (ISEK) an der Universität Zürich und leitet seit 2022 zusammen mit Matthias Liechti den Ausstellungsraum For in Basel und die gleichnamige Magazinreihe. Sie studierte Populäre Kulturen, Filmwissenschaft und Chinesisch (BA 2012) sowie Empirische Kulturwissenschaft und Filmwissenschaft an der Universität Zürich (MA 2017). Von 2015 bis 2020 war Keller Ko-Leiterin des Ausstellungsraums Milieu in Bern. In den Jahren 2018 bis 2021 arbeitete sie bei Prof. Harm-Peer Zimmermann in einem interdisziplinären Forschungsprojekt. Hier entstand ihre Dissertationsschrift *Selbstsorge im Leben mit Demenz. Potenziale einer relationalen Praxis* (2022 im Transcript Verlag erschienen).

This catalog is published in conjunction with the 2025 Manor Kunstpreis Graubünden and on the occasion of the exhibition *Noemi Pfister: Heart on Sleeve* at the Bündner Kunstmuseum Chur from September 6 to November 23, 2025.

Editor:
Damian Jurt, Bündner Kunstmuseum Chur

Texts:
Raphael Gygax, Damian Jurt, Valerie Keller

Copyediting:
Clemens von Lucius (German)
Tas Skorupa (English)

English translations:
Tas Skorupa

Graphic design:
Studio Marie Lusa
(Marie Lusa, Alberto Malossi)

Typeface:
UN-11 ST

Paper:
Magno Gloss, Maxi Offset

Color separations:
Musumeci S.p.a.

Printing and binding:
Musumeci S.p.a.

Edition:
700

Image credits:
Mattia Angelini (pp. 93, 103, 136–37, 138, 139, 140, 141, 142, 143);
Zoé Aubry (pp. 126–27);
Gina Folly (pp. 20–21, 22–23, 24–25, 48, 57, 58–59, 60–61, 80–81);
Julien Gremaud (pp. 28–29, 31, 32–33, 37, 40–41);
Kunstkredit Basel-Landschaft (p. 149);
MÂT, Neuchâtel (p. 26);
Cedric Mussano (pp. 70–71, 72–73, 74–75);
Noemi Pfister (pp. 51, 106–07, 109, 110, 112–13, 114–15, 133, 134, 145, 150–51, 152);
Nicolás Sarmiento (pp. 2–3, 4–5, 7, 8–9, 10, 12–13, 17, 34–35, 38–39, 42, 43, 44–45, 46, 49, 53, 55, 88, 89, 91, 95, 97, 98–99, 100–01, 120–21, 122–23, 128, 130–31, 146–47, 155, front and back cover);
Jennifer Merlyn Scherler (pp. 82–83, 84–85, 86–87, 125);
Philip Ullrich (pp. 62–63, 64–65, 66–67, 68–69, 104)

© 2025 Bündner Kunstmuseum Chur, Mousse Publishing, Noemi Pfister, and authors

Published and distributed by

Mousse Publishing
Contrappunto s.r.l.
Via Pier Candido Decembrio 28
20137 Milan
Italy

First edition: 2025

Available through Mousse Publishing, Milan
moussemagazine.it

Printed in Italy

CHF 35 / EUR 35 / USD 40

All rights reserved. No part of this publication may be reproduced in any form or by any electronic means without prior written permission from the copyright holders.

The publisher would like to thank all those who have kindly given their permission for the reproduction of material for this book. Every effort has been made to obtain permission to reproduce the images and texts in this book. However, as is standard editorial policy, the publisher is at the disposal of copyright holders and undertakes to correct any omissions or errors in future editions.

ISBN 978-88-6749-687-7

The artist would like to especially thank Raphael Gygax, Victoria Holdt, Damian Jurt, Valerie Keller, Stephan Kunz, Marie Lusa, Claudia and Julia Müller, Palazzina, Erica and Marcus Pfister, her siblings and her entire family, Nicolás Sarmiento, Camyl Vigneault, and all the friends and colleagues who have offered support over the past years.

A special thank-you is due to Manor AG for awarding the 2025 Manor Kunstpreis Graubünden and for their generous support of the exhibition and catalog.

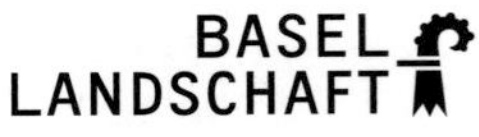

With kind support from

C. und A. Kupper-Stiftung

Charlotte und Nelly Dornacher Stiftung

Stiftung Dr. Valentin Malamoud

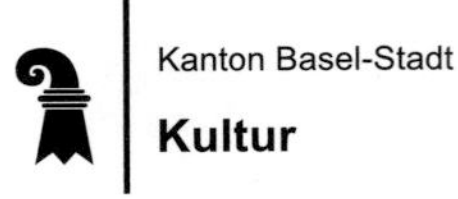

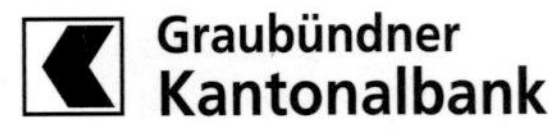

Partner

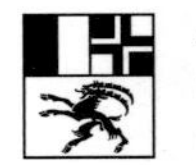

Front cover: *No Counterpart* (detail), 2024 (pp. 44–45)

Back cover: *La Danse* (detail), 2025